DICTION

of

BRITISH ARTISTS

Working 1900–1950

VOL. II

by

GRANT M. WATERS

Published & Available from

EASTBOURNE FINE ART PUBLICATIONS

47 SOUTH STREET

EASTBOURNE, SUSSEX

ENGLAND

© Copyright

ISBN 902010 06 9

To my wife Sue

Introduction

The biographical section contains details of more than 1100 artists, and is designed to complement the entries in Volume I of the Dictionary. Some entries have been brought up to date and where an artist also appears in the earlier volume, the fact is denoted by an asterisk.

I am grateful to the many artists who have replied to my enquiries for information and to the collectors and art dealers who have let me know of artists suitable for inclusion. This has been a great help. My thanks are also due to Mr. J. L. Naimaster for the notes he has passed to me.

The work of very nearly 400 artists is illustrated and the plates have been selected to provide a wide variety of subject which has not always been easy. Although I have concentrated on including examples of oils and water-colours, there are also sections devoted to prints and sculpture. As will be seen, a number of the plates illustrate examples by artists working during both the latter part of the nineteenth century and the early years of this century, and it is interesting to note from these the continuity of the tradition of painting developed in the Victorian era. Some of these paintings were executed as late as the 1920s. Of course, the art of the twentieth century is very much more than a mere extension of the methods and styles associated with the nineteenth century, and I hope the plates help to underline the extent of artistic achievement during this period.

The co-operation I have received from both individuals and galleries has been invaluable. I would especially like to thank the following for their assistance:

Thos. Agnew and Sons Ltd.; Bourne Gallery, Reigate; Cambridge Fine Art; P. & D. Colnaghi & Co. Ltd.; Deben Gallery, Woodbridge; Eastbourne Fine Art; Fine Art Society Ltd.; Gallery 33, Billingshurst; Richard Green (Fine Paintings); The Leger Galleries Ltd.; Andrew Leslie, Leva Art; Manchester City Art Gallery; Marlborough Fine Art (London) Ltd.; The Moorland Gallery Ltd.; Sir Alfred Munnings Art Museum; Anthony d'Offay Gallery; Michael Parkin Fine Art Ltd.; Phillips & Son, Marlow; The Reynolds Gallery, Plymouth; Southgate Gallery, Wolverhampton; E. Stacy-Marks Ltd., Eastbourne; Tate Gallery; Towner Art Gallery, Eastbourne; The Tryon Gallery Ltd.; Mrs. W. F. Wilson, Uckfield; Yoxford Gallery, Yoxford.

GRANT WATERS

A

* An asterisk denotes that an entry may also be found for the artist in volume I of this dictionary.

*ABELSON, Mrs. Evelyn, R.B.A., N.S., S.W.A. (1886–1967). Died on 7th March 1967.

ABLETT, William A. (died 1936).

Portrait painter. Exhibited at the New Gallery. Lived in London, and later in Paris. Died on 25th April 1936 aged 58.

*ACKLAND, Judith (1892–1971).

Painter in water-colour of landscapes and portraits, and model maker. Born at Bideford on 29th March 1892. Studied at Bideford Art School, and then at the Regent Street Polytechnic, where she met Mary Stella Edwards, who was to become her life-long friend. Exhibited at the R.A., R.I., R.B.A., N.E.A.C., S.W.A., and in the provinces. Held a series of two-man shows in London with Mary Stella Edwards. They painted together in various parts of the country, and lived at their Devon cottage, the Cabin at Bucks Mills, and in Staines. In 1945 she devised and gradually perfected a unique method of model making, at first single figures and groups, and then large companies of figures for historical dioramas. This work went on side by side with her outdoor painting. Represented in the Victoria and Albert Museum, the Museum of London, and also provincial museums. She died on 6th June 1971 and memorial exhibitions were held at Beaford Centre, Bideford, Exeter, South Molton, Windsor and Staines.

ADAMS, Beale (died 1939).

Marine and landscape painter. Exhibited at the R.B.A., R.O.I., and at galleries in the provinces. He was a West Countryman, and lived for many years at St. Ives in Cornwall. Died on 3rd March 1939.

ADAMS, John Quincy (died 1933).

Portrait painter. He exhibited for a time in Austria, and died in April 1933 aged 57.

ADAMS, W. Douglas (died 1920).

Landscape painter. Little known, he died at the age of 67 in June 1920.

ADDISON, Mrs. Eileen (born 1906).

Painter in water-colour of landscapes, architectural subjects and flowers. Born on 24th June 1906 in Leeds, née Hargreave. Studied at Leeds College of Art 1923–30 under Harold Holden and Douglas S. Andrews. In 1932 she married Joseph Addison, F.R.I.B.A., who was Head of Architecture at Leeds College of Art and later Head of the School of Architecture, Building and Surveying, at the Regent Street Polytechnic. She taught Interior and Colour Design at Regent Street 1942–51. Exhibited at the R.I., R.W.S. and R.B.A. Galleries, S.G.A., S.W.A., and in several provincial municipal art galleries. In 1956 she became Hon. Secretary and Treasurer of the Association of Sussex Artists, and has held similar positions in the Society of Sussex Painters since 1967. Represented in public collections at Chichester, Hove and Worthing, and has held several one-man shows. Lives at Angmering-on-Sea in West Sussex.

*AFFLECK, Andrew F. (born 1874).

Architectural etchings. Works include *Toledo Cathedral, Verona,* and *Hotel de Ville, Bruges.* Exhibited at the R.A. in 1915 and 1917.

ALEXANDER, Robert G. D. (died 1945).

Painter in oil of landscapes, river subjects and coastal scenes. Exhibited at the R.A. Lived at Brentwood in Essex, and worked in the Eastern Counties. Died on 12th September 1945.

ALLAN, Alexander, R.S.W. (1914–1972).

Painter in oil, water-colour, gouache and pastel of landscapes, portraits and still life. Born at Dundee on 26th October 1914. Studied at Dundee College of Art under J. McIntosh Patrick, also at Hospitalfield and the Westminster School of Art. Exhibited chiefly in Scotland, and also at the R.A. from 1939. He was a member of the Glasgow Group, and elected R.S.W. 1965. In 1968 he received a Scottish Arts Council Travel Award to paint and study in Italy. Held a number of one-man shows and is represented in several public collections. Lectured at Dundee College of Art, and lived at Newport-on-Tay, Fifeshire.

ALLAN, Henry, R.H.A. (1865–1912).

Painter of genre, portraits and landscapes. Born on 18th June 1865 at Dundalk in Eire. Studied art in Belfast and Dublin, later in Antwerp. Exhibited at the R.H.A., and was elected A.R.H.A. 1895, R.H.A. 1901. Died at Rathmines on 2nd September 1912.

*ALLEN, Charles John, F.R.B.S. (1862–1956).

Sculptor of portraits and figure subjects in bronze and marble. Died in January 1956.

ALLEN, Frederick E. (*fl. c.* 1920–1935).

Etcher of landscapes, especially subjects in the North of England. Exhibited at the R.A. first in 1923, also at the R.Cam.A. and at the Walker Art Gallery, Liverpool. Some of his etchings were published by Colnaghi's, the London art dealers. Lived at Birkenhead in Cheshire.

ALLEYNE, Miss Mabel (1896–1961).

Painter of flowers in tempera; wood engraver. Born in Southampton on 31st March 1896. Studied at Goldsmiths' College School of Art, and at the R.A. Schools. Exhibited at the R.A., R.H.A., S.W.A., and was a member of the Society of Mural Painters. Lived in London for many years.

ALMENT, Mary Martha (1834–1908).

Painter of landscapes and portraits. Born on 9th April 1834 at Londonderry. Studied in Dublin at the Metropolitan School of Art. Exhibited at the R.H.A. Died on 11th April 1908.

*ALSTON, Edward Constable (died 1939).

Painter of portraits and figure subjects. Died in February 1939.

ALTSON, Abbey, R.B.A. (born 1864).

Painter of portraits and landscapes. Born in Middlesbrough, brother of the artist Meyer Daniel Altson.

Settled in Australia 1882, and studied art at the Melbourne National Gallery School 1884–90. He returned to Europe 1890, and studied in Paris at Colarossi's until 1893. Then worked in London, and exhibited at the R.A., R.B.A., G.I. He painted on occasions in India during the years 1895–1936, and in 1937 settled in the U.S.A.

*ALTSON, Meyer Daniel (1881–1965).

Portrait painter. Brother of the artist Abbey Altson. Although he spent some years in Australia, he lived in Europe from 1902, and died in London.

ANDERSON, E. E., R.B.A. (*fl. c.* 1895–1910).

Oil painter. Exhibited at the R.A., R.B.A., R.O.I., and in the provinces. Lived in London and later at Whitby.

ANDERSON, G. G. (*fl. c.* 1895–1925).

Painter in oil of portraits, landscapes and marines. Exhibited at the R.S.A., G.I., in the North of England, and at the "Modern Scottish Artists" exhibition held at Brighton Art Gallery 1906. Lived in Glasgow.

ANDERSON, Martin "Cynicus" (1854–1932).

Scottish caricaturist. Born at Leuchars in Fifeshire. Studied at Glasgow School of Art. Published *The Satires of Cynicus* 1890, *The Humours of Cynicus* 1891, and other works. Lived at Leuchars, and died on 14th April 1932 aged 78.

ANDERSON, Percy (died 1928).

Portrait and figure painter, stage artist and costume designer. Exhibited at the R.I. in 1886. Lived in London, and died on 30th October 1928 aged 78.

ANDREAE, Conrad Rudolf (1871–1956).

Died in Brighton on 9th December 1956.

ANDREWS, Michael (born 1928).

Painter in oil and acrylic of landscapes and figure subjects. Born at Norwich on 30th October 1928. Studied at Norwich Art School and at the Slade School 1949–53. Received the Rome Scholarship 1953. He has held several one-man shows in London, and is represented in the Tate Gallery.

ANDREWS, Miss Sybil (*fl. c.* 1920–1940).

Painter, etcher and engraver. She was Secretary of the Grosvenor School of Art during the time Iain Macnab was Principal. Lived at Bury St. Edmunds in Suffolk.

ANGEL, John, N.A., F.R.B.S. (born 1881).

Sculptor of portraits and figure subjects. Born on 1st November 1881 at Newton Abbot. Studied at Exeter College of Art, Lambeth Art School, and at the R.A. Schools, where he won the Landseer Scholarship and several medals. Then to Rome and Athens 1912. He assisted Sir George Frampton for four years, and exhibited at the R.A. 1912–27. Worked in marble, stone and wood, and produced some statues and war memorials. Settled in the U.S.A. 1925, and elected A.N.A. 1944, N.A. 1948. Lived at Sandy Hook, Connecticut.

ANGEL, Robert J. (died 1944).

Painter of landscapes and town scenes. Lived in London and exhibited a work at the R.A. in 1914. Died on 14th March 1944.

*ANSON, Peter Frederick, S.M.A. (1889–1975).

Although better known as an artist, he was also an author of books on such subjects as fishing, travel and religion. He was a Cistercian monk, living at Caldy Abbey in Wales and later at Nunraw Abbey at Haddington in Scotland. Died in Edinburgh on 10th July 1975.

ARDEN, Edward (died 1909).

Landscape painter in water-colour. Exhibited from 1881 at the R.I., R.H.A., Grosvenor Gallery, and in the provinces. A founder member of the Lake Artists Society, he attended the first meeting at the home of David Gould on 12th October 1904. It is said that his real name was in fact Edward Tucker, and that he exhibited under the name of Arden. He was certainly connected with Arthur Tucker and Hubert Coutts Tucker (known professionally as Hubert Coutts) in the formation of the Lake Artists Society. They all lived at Windermere. Died in March 1909 aged 63.

ARMSTRONG, Elizabeth Caroline (1860–1930).

Painter of landscapes and figures in oil and water-colour. Born in South Australia. Studied art in London at the R.C.A. At the age of 33 she was appointed Art Instructor at the School of Design, Adelaide. Later in life returned to England.

ARNOLD, William Arthur, A.W.G. (born 1909).

Landscape and marine painter in water-colour. Born at Leytonstone on 4th December 1909. Studied at Leyton School of Art. Exhibited at the R.A., Britain in Water-colours, and held a one-man show at the Towner Art Gallery, Eastbourne 1947. A member of the Armed Forces Society 1947 and the Buckinghamshire Art Society 1969. Represented in Karachi Art Gallery. Lives at Chalfont St. Giles in Buckinghamshire.

ASHFORD, Colin James (born 1919).

Landscape and marine painter. Born on 3rd March 1919 at Ackworth in Yorkshire. Studied at Wakefield College of Art for four years, where he received a drawing diploma and three prizes, and then spent two years at Glasgow College of Art. Before the war he showed water-colours at the exhibitions of the West Riding Artists held in Wakefield. During the war he served as an artist in various branches of the Royal Engineers, and at the Allied Forces H.Q. at Caserta in Italy. He specialises in painting all kinds of historic transport by air, land and sea in both water-colour and oil. Exhibited at the R.S.M.A., the Guild of Aviation Artists, the Mall Galleries and Guildhall Art Gallery, also at many provincial art galleries, especially in Lancashire and Yorkshire. He is an associate of the Glasgow College of Art, and a founder member of the Guild of Aviation Artists. Represented in the Ashmolean Museum at Oxford, the Royal Air Force Museum at Hendon, the National Maritime Museum at Greenwich, and at the Maritime Museum at Long Island, U.S.A. Lives in London.

ASHMORE, Charles (died 1925).

Genre and landscape painter. Founded the Heeley Art Club at Sheffield, and died September 1925.

ASHTON, George Rossi (born 1857).

Landscape and portrait painter. Born in Penzance, Cornwall, brother of Julian R. Ashton. Studied art at South Kensington. Exhibited in London from 1874, and contributed illustrations to *The Graphic*. Settled in Melbourne 1879. Member of Australian Artists' Association. Returned to England 1901.

ASHTON, Miss Gertrude Annie (died 1918).

Glasgow painter, wife of the artist Charles James Lauder. Exhibited at the R.S.W., G.I., and at the Walker Art Gallery, Liverpool. Died in Lanarkshire on 8th August 1918.

ASHTON, Julian Rossi (1851–1942).

Painter in oil and water-colour of portraits, figure subjects and landscapes. Born at Penzance in Cornwall on 27th January 1851. Studied art in London and Paris. Settled in Australia 1878. He established the Académie Julian in Sydney, and trained many noted Australian artists. Represented in numerous public collections, he was President of the Royal Art Society 1886–92. His paintings were exhibited in England at the R.A.. R.B.A.

ASTON, Miss Evelin Winifred (died 1975).

Oil painter and sculptor in wood. Studied at Birmingham College of Art. Exhibited at the R.S.A., and the Paris Salon. Lived for many years at Erdington, Birmingham and died on 7th February 1975.

ATHERTON, Mrs. Olive E. D. (1905–1970).

Landscape and marine painter in oil. Exhibited at the R.A. Lived at Frensham, near Farnham in Surrey.

ATKINSON, Lawrence (1873–1931).

Vorticist painter. Exhibited at the London Salon and the Dore Gallery. Lived in London, and is represented in the Tate Gallery.

ATKINSON, W. E., A.R.Canadian A. (born 1862).

Landscape painter. Born in Toronto, Canada. Studied at Ontario School of Art, Pennsylvania Academy of Fine Arts under Thomas Eakins, and in Paris at the Académie Julian. Exhibited at the Paris Salon 1890–91. Painted in Holland and Belgium 1897, Devonshire 1898–1901, and returned to Canada 1902. He is represented in several Canadian public collections, and was a member of the New Society of Canadian Artists. Lived in Toronto for many years.

*AUSTEN, Miss Winifred Marie Louise, R.I., R.E. (1876–1964).

Married 1917. A Fellow of the Zoological Society.

AUSTIN-CARTER, Miss Mathilde, R.M.S. (born 1840).

Painter of flowers in water-colour, and miniatures on ivory. Born in Bristol. Received her art training from her mother, both her parents being artists. Exhibited at the R.I. from 1884, also at the R.M.S., S.M. Lived in London and later at Torquay.

*AYLING, George, S.M.A. (1887–1960).

Died on 25th May 1960.

*AYRTON, Michael, R.B.A. (1921–1975).

Died on 17th November 1975.

B

BABBAGE, Herbert Ivan (died 1916).

Landscape and genre painter. Exhibited at the R.A. firstly in 1908, and also at the R.W.A. He lived at St. Ives in Cornwall, and during the war served in the Cornish Light Infantry, being killed on active service on 14th December 1916 aged 41.

*BACHELOR, Philip H. Wilson, S.G.A. (died 1944).

Painter and etcher of landscapes. Exhibited at the R.A. from 1921, and died on 8th December 1944.

BACK, Robert (born 1922).

Marine painter in oil. Born in Australia of a Norwich family. Studied at Edinburgh College of Art. Served in the Royal Navy in World War II and later in the Merchant Navy. Exhibited at the R.S.A., R.S.M.A. Lives at Seaford in Sussex.

BAGSHAWE, Joseph Richard, R.B.A. (1870–1909).

Landscape and marine painter. Exhibited at the R.A., R.O.I., and at Liverpool. Lived in Kensington, and later at Whitby in Yorkshire.

BAILEY, John William (1831–1914).

Miniature painter. Born in London on 27th April 1831. Studied art under William Essex. Exhibited at the leading London galleries from 1859, including the R.A. and R.B.A. He painted enamels of portraits and animals, and lived in London. Died on 20th May 1914.

*BAKER, Miss Blanche (1844–1929).

Landscape painter.

BAKER, Bryant, F.R.B.S. (1881–1970).

Portrait sculptor in marble and bronze. Born in London on 8th July 1881. Studied art at the R.A. Schools. Exhibited at the R.A. from 1909, also at the Paris Salon and in America. He settled in the U.S.A.

in 1916 and lived in New York. Elected a Fellow of the National Sculpture Society. Died on 29th March 1970.

BAKER-CLACK, Arthur, L.G. (died 1955).

Landscape painter in oil and water-colour. Born at Boolaroo in South Australia. Came to Europe, and studied art in Paris under J. P. Laurens. Exhibited at the R.A., L.G., and at the Paris Salon. In 1925 a number of his works were included in the "Australian Artists" exhibition held at Brighton Art Gallery. Lived in France for many years.

*BALDWIN, J. Brake (1885–1915).

Painter in oil of portraits and figure subjects. Born at Lee, then in Kent but now part of Greater London. Studied art at Heatherley's School. Exhibited at the R.A., I.S., and at the Baillie Gallery. During the war he joined the Voluntary Aid Detachment of the Red Cross, and after a short illness brought on by immensely hard work died in July 1915. Lived in Kensington.

BALFOUR, J. Lawson (born 1870).

Painter in oil and water-colour of landscapes and portraits. Born at Melbourne, Australia. Studied art at the Académies Julian and Cormon. Exhibited at the leading London galleries from 1892. Represented in several public collections in Australia.

BALFOUR-BROWNE, Vincent R. (1880–1963).

Painter in water-colour of animal subjects. Born in London on 30th May 1880. Specialised in painting deer. Lived in London and in Scotland.

BANNERMAN, Mrs. Frances M., A.R.Canadian A. (1855–1940).

Painter in oil of genre and interiors. Born at Halifax

in Canada, *née* Jones. Elected A.R.Canadian A. 1882. Settled in England following his marriage and exhibited at the leading galleries from 1882, including the R.A., R.B.A., also showed at the Paris Salon. Produced some work for illustration.

BARKAS, Henry Dawson, A.R.C.A.(Lond.) (1858–1924).
Painter in water-colour of landscapes and coastal scenes. Exhibited at the R.A. and R.I. Lived in Reading, and found many of his subjects in East Anglia, Yorkshire and along the South Coast. Died in August 1924.

BARNARD, Mrs. Catherine (*fl. c.* 1895–1935).
Painter of landscapes in water-colour. Born in Edinburgh, *née* Locking. Exhibited at the R.A., R.I. and at the Walker Art Gallery, Liverpool. She was married to the artist J. Langton Barnard, living for a time at West Drayton in Middlesex and later in London.

BARNARD, Miss Marjorie B. (*fl. c.* 1890–1910).
Painter of landscapes and genre in water-colour. Exhibited at the R.A., R.S.A. and New Gallery. Lived in London and later in Glasgow.

BARNARD, Walter Saunders (1851–1930).
Painter of portrait miniatures. Exhibited at the R.A. from 1876. He was killed in a motor accident near his home in Islington, London.

BARNES, Walter Mayhew, A.R.C.A.(Lond.) (1871–1950).
Painter and art teacher. Born on 10th January 1871. Studied art at the R.C.A. He was appointed Design Master at Blackburn School of Art 1895–1918, Headmaster of Loughborough School of Art 1918–20, and Headmaster of West Ham School of Art 1920–32. Lived for a time at Debenham in Suffolk, and died on 31st December 1950.

*BARNETT, Dame Henrietta Octavia (1851–1936).
In 1924 she was created D.B.E. in recognition of her many years service on behalf of the community, especially children. Died in June 1936.

BARNS-GRAHAM, Miss Wilhelmina (Born 1912).
Abstract painter. Born in Scotland. Exhibited at the R.A., R.S.A. In 1940 she settled in Cornwall, at St. Ives, and in 1949 was a founder member of the Penwith Society of Artists. Visited France, Spain, Italy and Switzerland. Represented in the Tate Gallery.

BARRETT, Thomas, A.R.E. (*fl. c.* 1880–1910).
Landscape and genre painter and etcher. Exhibited at the leading London galleries from 1883, chiefly at the R.A. Elected A.R.E. 1887, his membership ceased on 17th February 1910. Lived in Nottingham.

BARRINGTON-BROWNE, W. E. (Born 1908).
Painter of fishing and sporting subjects. Son of the artist H. Nedeham Browne, he was educated at Repton School and Pembroke College, Cambridge. Studied art in Venice and at the Académie Julian in Paris. For ten years he was Art Master at Cheltenham College and during that time illustrated many books. A keen fisherman and sportsman, his knowledge being reflected in the accuracy of his paintings. He has exhibited at the Tryon Gallery, London.

BARTLETT, Paul W., N.P.S. (*fl. c.* 1910–15).
Portrait painter. Exhibited at the G.I., and spent some time in Paris before the outbreak of World War I.

BARTON SMITH, Mrs. Kathleen Kavanagh (1878–1970).
Painter of landscapes and miniatures. Born on 5th September 1878, *née* Haynes. She lived near Harrogate in Yorkshire.

BARWELL, Frederick Bacon (*fl. c.* 1855–1905).
Genre painter. Exhibited at the leading London galleries from 1855, chiefly at the R.A. He was a member of the Norwich Art Circle, and showed his work with that group into the twentieth century.

BASKETT, Charles Edward, A.R.E. (1845–1929).
Still life painter and etcher. Born in Colchester, Essex on 5th November 1845. Began as a plumber, and later studied art under Herkomer. Exhibited at the leading London galleries from 1872, including the R.A., R.B.A. Elected A.R.E. 1892. Lived at Colchester and died on 29th July 1929.

BATES, Leo F. (Died 1957).
Portrait painter. Exhibited at the R.A., and lived in London.

*BATESON, Miss Edith (died 1938).
Portrait sculptor. Lived for a time at Robin Hood's Bay in Yorkshire.

*BATLEY, Walter Daniel (1850–1936).
Member of Ipswich Art Club. Died March 1936.

BATT, Arthur (1846–1911).
Genre and animal painter in oil. Exhibited at the leading London galleries from 1879, chiefly at the R.A., R.B.A., and Grosvenor Gallery. Lived at Romsey in Hampshire.

BAYFIELD, Henry (died 1929).
Little known Buckinghamshire artist, who lived at High Wycombe. Died on 16th September 1929.

BAYNES, Philip (died 1916).
Member of the Chelsea Arts Club. Served in the London Rifle Brigade in the war, and was killed in action.

BEACON, Charles, F.R.B.S. (*fl. c.* 1895–1930).
Sculptor of portrait and figure subjects. Exhibited at the R.A., R.O.I., G.I., New Gallery, and at the Walker Art Gallery in Liverpool. Lived in London and later at Bushey in Hertfordshire.

BEAUMONT, A. (*fl. c.* 1910–15).
Painter in oil of coastal subjects. Lived at St. Ives in Cornwall and worked locally.

BEAUVAIS, Arnold Victor (born 1886).
Oil painter of landscapes, portraits, figures and still life, poster designer, illustrator and cartoonist; noted opera singer. Born at Catford 13th April 1886, son of the French painter Charles Henri Beauvais (1864–1911). Studied at the Bolt Court Art School, London, and later in Paris. Worked in Marseille for some years, returning to London 1913. Produced posters and general publicity for the cinema, and contributed caricatures of the stars to *Film Weekly*. In 1956 he reduced his commercial art commitments and devoted more time to painting. Elected a member of the London Sketch Club 1929, President 1936. An important retrospective exhibition of his work was held at Phillips and Son, Marlow 1975.

BEAVER, Robert Atwood (1906–1975).
Oil painter and distinguished doctor of medicine. Born at Poole in Dorset on 5th December 1906. Studied

art in Brussels. Exhibited at the R.A., R.I., R.O.I., N.E.A.C., N.S., and in the provinces. He died at his home at Cowes, Isle of Wight, on 22nd June 1975.

*BEDFORD, Miss Celia Frances, N.E.A.C., P.S., W.I.A.C. (1904–1959).
London artist who died 23rd February 1959.

BEDFORD, Francis Donkin (1864–1954).
Painter of figures, landscapes and architectural subjects; book illustrator. Born in London on 21st May 1864. Studied at the R.C.A., and the R.A. School of Architecture. Exhibited at the R.A. from 1892. Illustrated several books including *A Book of Nursery Rhymes* 1897, *A Book of Verses for Children* 1907, *A Christmas Carol* 1931. Member of the Art Workers Guild and the Mural Decorators and Painters in Tempera. Lived at Northwood, then in Wimbledon and later in London.

*BEDFORD, Mrs. Helen Catherine, P.S. (1874–1949).
Wife of the artist Francis Donkin Bedford. Died in London.

BEDFORD, Herbert (died 1945).
Painter of portrait and figure subjects. Exhibited at the R.A. in 1908 and 1912. Lived in London.

BEECROFT, Herbert (born 1865).
Painter in oil of portraits and religious subjects. Born in Reading. Worked there and in London for fourteen years as a lithographic artist. In 1905 he visited Australia, and decided to remain, painting a number of portraits.

*BEESON, Charles Richard (1909–1975).
Died at Christchurch in Hampshire on 3rd July 1975.

BEHENNA, Mrs. K. A., R.M.S. (*fl. c.* 1900–1925).
Miniature painter. Lived at Etaples, Pas de Calais, France and later in London.

BELDAM, George W. (died 1937).
Marine painter. Exhibited at the R.A. Lived at Ealing and died on 23rd November 1937.

BELL, George Henry Frederick (1878–1966).
Painter in oil of landscapes, portraits and figure subjects. Born at Kew, Victoria, Australia on 1st December 1878. Studied at the National Gallery School, Melbourne under Bernard Hall and Frederick McCubbin. Came to Europe for further study 1905, and exhibited at the R.A. Served as a war artist with the A.I.F. during World War I and returned to Australia 1920. In 1934 he was back in England again, and also worked in France and Spain. Died on 22nd October 1966.

BELL, Henry Jobson (*fl. c.* 1905–20).
Scottish landscape painter. Exhibited at the R.A., S.S.A. Lived in Edinburgh.

BELL, Miss Lucy Hilda, R.M.S. (*fl. c.* 1885–1920).
Painter of miniatures, specialising in flower subjects. Exhibited at the leading London galleries from 1889, including the R.A., R.I., R.B.A., R.M.S., also at the Walker Art Gallery, Liverpool. Lived in Hampstead.

BELL-SMITH, Frederic Marlett, R.Canadian A. (1846–1923).
Painter of landscapes, street scenes and figure subjects. Born in London on 26th September 1846 and studied drawing at the South Kensington Schools. In 1867 he settled in Canada and every year visited the Rocky Mountains. Exhibited widely in Canada, and

also at the R.A. Lived at Toronto and was President of the Ontario Society of Artists. Died on 23rd June 1923.

*BELLIS, Alan Waddington, A.R.C.A.(Lond.) (1883–1960).
Member of Ipswich Art Club. Died on 12th December 1960.

BELT, Richard C. (died 1920).
Portrait and figure sculptor. Studied art at the R.A. Schools. Exhibited at the leading London galleries from 1873, including the R.A. and Grosvenor Gallery. Lived in London for many years and executed portrait busts of a number of leading figures.

BENETT, Newton (died 1914).
Painter of landscapes and architectural subjects. Exhibited at the leading London galleries from 1875, chiefly the R.A., R.B.A., R.I., New Gallery and Grosvenor Gallery. Lived at Lyndhurst in Hampshire and later at Dorchester-on-Thames in Oxfordshire. Died on 24th November 1914.

BENGER, William Edmund (died 1915).
Landscape painter in oil and water-colour. Exhibited at the R.A., R.I., R.B.A., and in the provinces. Lived at Llandudno and later at Crowborough in East Sussex. Died May 1915 aged 74.

*BENNER, William Roger (1884–1964).
Died at Blythburgh in Suffolk.

BENNETT, Miss Florence E., R.M.S. (*fl. c.* 1895–1937).
Miniature painter, especially of portraits. Exhibited at the R.A., R.M.S., Walker Art Gallery in Liverpool, and at Birmingham. Lived in Wimbledon and later at Holmbury St. Mary in Surrey.

BENNETT, Joseph Arthur (1853–1929).
Painter of figure subjects in water-colour. Born at Ashton-under-Lyne. Studied art in Manchester and in France under Bonnat. Exhibited at the R.A. 1882. Settled in Australia 1886, and became a member of the Australian Watercolor Institute.

*BENOIS, Miss Nadia, N.E.A.C. (1896–1975).
Died on 8th February 1975 at her home in Gloucestershire.

BERLIN, Sven Paul (born 1911).
Figure and animal sculptor in stone and bronze; painter of landscapes, portraits and still life. Born on 14th September 1911 at Sydenham in South London, son of a Swedish paper merchant. Studied philosophy, comparative religion, psychology, and oriental art and literature at Exeter University. Received his art training at the Camborne and Redruth Schools of Art, and at Beckenham in Kent under Henry Carr. Settled in Cornwall, and with Peter Lanyon and John Wells founded the Crypt Group in St. Ives 1946, also was involved in the formation of the Penwith Society of Artists. In 1948 he published an authoritative biography *Alfred Wallis, Primitive,* and subsequently *I am Lazarus* 1961, *Dark Monarch* 1963, *Jonah's Dream* 1964, *Dromengro* 1971, *Pride of the Peacock* 1972. He has produced drawings and dust jackets for several books, and from 1958–70 cast his own bronzes. A member of the Bladon Society of Arts, he has held more than twenty one-man shows in Britain and the U.S.A. Lived in the New Forest for a time, and now in the Isle of Wight.

*BIDDLE, Miss Winifred Percy, S.W.A. (1878–1968).

Painter of portraits and flowers. Exhibited at the R.A. Lived at Kingston Hill and died on 6th May 1968.

BIEGEL, Peter (born 1913).

Painter of sporting subjects. Born on 22nd April 1913 at Croxley Green. Educated at Downside, after which he spent five years in the city. He determined to make art his career, and studied at the Lucy Kemp-Welch School of Animal Painting, Bushey, until the outbreak of war. After the war he studied figures for a year at Bournemouth School of Art, and then worked with Lionel Edwards. He has exhibited many times in London and has also received wide recognition in America.

BILLINGS, Mrs. Kathleen Wyatt (born 1911).

Painter in oil, water-colour, acrylic, collage. Born on 25th April 1911, *née* White, at Christchurch in New Zealand. Studied at Canterbury College School of Art 1928–31, and in 1930 received an Advanced Art Scholarship. Exhibited at the R.I., S.M., and in New Zealand. Painted in the Cook Islands 1964–66. Designed stamps for Niue and the Cook Islands. Lives at Waikanae, New Zealand.

BINNEY, Hibbert C., R.B.A. (*fl.* 1893–1921).

Sculptor of portraits and figure subjects. Exhibited at the R.A. from 1893, also at the R.B.A. and in Manchester. Lived in London.

BINNS, Mrs. Lorna, A.R.W.S., A.R.C.A.(Lond.) (born 1914).

Landscape painter in water-colour. Born at Wadsley Bridge, Sheffield on 23rd October 1914, *née* Harrison. Studied at Sheffield College of Art 1930–35 and the R.C.A. 1935–39. Exhibited at the R.A., and elected A.R.W.S. 1973. Lives at Kingston-on-Thames.

BIRD, Charles, A.R.E. (*fl.* 1892–1902).

Little known etcher. Elected A.R.E. 1892.

*BIRD, George Frederick (1883–1948).

Died on 9th April 1948.

BISHOP, Ethel Alicia (1892–1958).

Oil painter. Born in Bath. Studied art in South Australia under James Ashton 1906–11, and then at the National Gallery School in Melbourne. Settled again in England 1918. Represented in Adelaide Art Gallery.

BLAKE, John Henry (born 1924).

Aviation and marine painter in oil, water-colour and acrylic. Born at Penarth in South Wales on 13th November 1924. Studied at Glasgow School of Art and Stonyhurst College. Exhibited at the Kronfeld Club, Qantas Gallery and at Biggin Hill. Represented in the R.A.F. Museum at Hendon. Member of the Guild of Aviation Artists and Kronfeld Aviation Art Society. Lives at Dover.

BLAKER, Hugh, R.B.A. (died 1936).

Painter and museum curator. Studied art in Antwerp and Paris. Exhibited at the R.A., R.B.A., N.E.A.C., I.S. He was Curator of Holbourne Museum at Bath and later lived at Isleworth in Middlesex. Died October 1936.

*BLATHERWICK, Miss Lily, R.S.W. (1854–1934).

During her early years she lived at Rhu in Dumbartonshire. In 1896 she married the artist A. S. Hartrick. Her father, Dr. Charles Blatherwick, was an amateur water-colour painter, a founder of the R.S.W. and President of Glasgow Art Club, and made his second marriage to Hartrick's widowed mother.

BLOCK, Louis (died 1909).

Still life painter. Exhibited at the leading London galleries from 1879, including the R.I. and Dudley Gallery. Lived at Streatham and died June 1909.

*BLUNDELL, Alfred Richard (1883–1968).

Died on 18th December 1968.

BLUNT, Arthur Cadogan (died 1934).

Illustrator. Exhibited at the leading London galleries from 1890, including the R.I. Died in May 1934 aged 73.

BODDINGTON, Henry (*fl. c.* 1900–1910).

Water-colour painter of town scenes and landscapes. He took up art late in life after a business career. Painted some subjects in France.

BODDY, William J. (died 1911).

Painter of architectural subjects in water-colour. Exhibited at the leading London galleries from 1860, including the R.A., R.I., R.B.A. Lived in York and died in May 1911 aged 80.

*BOLTON, John Nunn (1869–1909).

Painter in oil and water-colour of landscapes, marines and portraits. Born in Dublin on 25th July 1869, son of Henry E. Bolton, an amateur landscape painter. Studied in Dublin at the Metropolitan School of Art and at the R.H.A. Schools, where he received the Taylor Scholarship. Exhibited at the R.A., R.H.A., and at Birmingham. Lived in Warwick for some years, and died there on 11th February 1909.

BONHAM-CARTER, Lady Gabrielle Madge Jeannette (*née* Fisher) (died 1962).

Sculptor of portraits and figure subjects. Exhibited at the R.A. from 1927. Married General Sir Charles Bonham-Carter 1911. Lived in London and at Shrivenham in Berkshire. Died on 29th December 1962.

BONNER, George Gilbert (born 1924).

Painter in oil and acrylic. Born in Toronto, Canada. Educated in Essex, and was mainly self-taught in art, although he did receive some instruction under Haydon Mackay. Settled in Sussex 1954, becoming a member of the Eastbourne Group 1960. Exhibited at the R.A., in the provinces and abroad. Represented in several public collections in Britain, Europe and North America. He became known in 1960 for his sombre large abstract collage and assemblage, and for his use of texture. Since 1973 his work has moved towards far brighter colour harmonies. Lives at St. Leonards-on-Sea, Sussex.

BORDASS, Mrs. Dorothy Trotman, A.R.E., W.I.A.C. (born 1905).

Painter of landscapes and architectural subjects; printmaker. Born in London on 19th November 1905. Studied as an illuminator under Alberto Sangorski 1923–25, then at Harrow Art School, in Paris at the Académie Julian 1926, in Florence, and at Heatherley's in London under Macnab 1927. Exhibited at the R.A., R.S.A., R.B.A., R.E., L.G., W.I.A.C. and abroad. She has held many one-man shows from 1958 in Britain, U.S.A. and Malaysia. Represented in several public collections. Fellow of the Free Painters and Sculptors, member of the St. Ives Society of Artists and the Penwith Society. Lives in Cambridge.

BOSE, Fanindra Nath, A.R.S.A. (died 1926).

Sculptor of figure subjects. Exhibited at the R.A., R.S.A. Lived in Edinburgh and died on 1st August 1926.

BOSSANYI, Ervin (1891–1975).

Artist in oil, tempera, water-colour, pastel, chinese ink, perspex, clay, plywood and glass of scenes with figures and animals. Born on 3rd March 1891 at Rigyica, at that time in Hungary but now a small village in Yugoslavia. Studied at the Royal College of Arts and Crafts in Budapest, at the Académie Julian in Paris under J. P. Laurens, and in London at the Camden School of Art. First one-man show held in Hamburg 1921, first in Britain 1935. Exhibited at the R.A., at the Bloomsbury and Beaux Arts Galleries in London, also in Germany and France. Member of the Imperial Art League and a Fellow of the Royal Society of Master Glass Painters. Represented in several public collections in Britain and on the continent. Lived at Pinner in Middlesex and died on 11th July 1975.

BOSSCHÈRE, Jean De (1881–1953).

Book illustrator, etcher and word engraver. Born in Belgium. Came to England in 1915, and returned on a number of occasions. Illustrated several books including *The History of Don Quixote* 1922 and *The Decameron* 1930.

*BOSTON, Eric James (1899–1975).

Died on 20th August 1975 near Charlbury in Oxfordshire.

*BOSWELL, James E., A.R.C.A.(Lond.) (1906–1971).

Painter of landscapes, town scenes and figures. Died on 15th March 1971.

*BOTCHERBY, Harold Llewellyn, R.B.A. (1907–1943).

Painter of portraits and still life. Lived at Danbury in Essex, and was killed on 20th October 1943.

*BOURDILLON, Francis William (1852–1921).

Painter in oil of landscapes and coastal scenes. Born on 22nd March 1852. Educated at Haileybury and Worcester College, Oxford, obtaining his M.A. degree. From 1876–79 he was resident tutor to the two sons of Prince Christian at Cumberland Lodge, and later took private pupils at Eastbourne. Published several works including *Among the Flowers and Other Poems* 1878, *A Lost God* 1891, *Through the Gateway* 1902. During the 1890's he painted scenes at Newlyn in Cornwall. In later life he lived at Midhurst in Sussex and died on 13th January 1921.

BOURDON, Eugene (died 1916).

Member of Glasgow Art Club, killed in action on 1st July 1916.

BOWELL, Alfred John (1868–1941).

Landscape painter, represented in the Victoria and Albert Museum.

BOWEN, Stella Esther (1893–1947).

Painter of portraits, landscapes and still life in oil and water-colour. Born at Adelaide in Australia. At the age of twenty-one she came to England and studied at the London School of Art also at Westminster School of Art under Sickert. Worked in England for some years, also in Spain and Italy, and was never to return to Australia.

BOWKER, Alfred (died 1944).

Sculptor in bronze and marble of portraits and figure subjects. Exhibited at the R.A. from 1926, also at the Walker Art Gallery in Liverpool. Lived at Shawford in Hampshire, and died on 18th March 1944.

BOXER, Percy Noel (born c. 1886).

Painter of street scenes, figures and river subjects. Studied at Blackheath School of Art and Goldsmiths College School of Art. Exhibited at the R.A. from 1911. Lived at Lee in south-east London, and worked in and around Greenwich.

BOYD, Mrs. Janet A., R.M.S. (*fl. c.* 1900–1910).

Miniature painter. Lived in County Durham.

BOYD, Stuart (died 1916).

Painter of figure subjects and landscapes. Son of the artist A. S. Boyd. Exhibited at the R.A. from 1909, also at the R.O.I., N.E.A.C., G.I., and Walker Art Gallery in Liverpool. Lived in St. John's Wood, and was killed in action on 7th October 1916 aged 29.

BOYD, Theodore Penleigh (1890–1923).

Landscape painter in oil and water-colour. Studied art at the Art Gallery Schools in Melbourne, Australia. Visited Europe 1911, and exhibited at the R.A. Served with the A.I.F. in World War I but was gassed at Ypres 1917. Represented in several Australian public art collections. Killed in a motor accident 28th November 1923.

*BOYES, Sidney, F.R.B.S. (*fl. c.* 1907–1931).

Sculptor in bronze and marble of portraits and figure subjects. Exhibited at the R.A. from 1910. Lived at Blackheath and later at Lee.

BOYLE, Hon. Mrs. Eleanor Vere (*née* Gordon) (1825–1916).

Figure painter and book illustrator. Exhibited at the leading London galleries from 1878, including the Grosvenor Gallery. Illustrated *A Dream Book* 1870, *Hans Andersen's Fairy Tales* 1872. Lived at Maidenhead.

BRADSHAW, Harold C. (1893–1943).

Architect. Born in Liverpool on 15th February 1893. Studied art in Liverpool, London and Rome. Exhibited at the R.A. from 1920, also at the Paris Salon. He was Secretary of the Royal Fine Art Commission and the first Rome Scholar in Architecture, British School at Rome 1913. Lived in London, and died on 15th October 1943.

BRADSHAW, Mrs. Kathleen Marion (born 1904).

Painter in oil, water-colour and tempera of portraits, figures and flowers. Born on 25th November 1904 at Barberton, Transvaal, South Africa, *née* Slatter. Studied at St. Ives School of Art 1920–26 under Charles and Ruth Simpson. Married the artist George Bradshaw. Exhibited at the R.A., Paris Salon, and St. Ives Society of Artists. Lives at St. Ives in Cornwall.

BRAINE, Miss Alice, R.M.S. (*fl. c.* 1900–1920).

Miniature painter, especially of portraits. Exhibited at the R.A., R.M.S., Walker Art Gallery in Liverpool, and in Manchester. Lived in London.

BRAMLEY-MOORE, Millicent, A.R.E. (*fl. c.* 1899–1904).

Little known etcher. Elected A.R.E. in 1899, her membership ceased on 14th April 1904.

*BRENAN, James, R.H.A. (1837–1907).

Painter in oil of figure subjects. In 1857 he went as an assistant to Birmingham School of Art, and the following year took up a similar position at South Kensington. From 1889–1904 he was Head of the Metropolitan School of Art in Dublin. Died at Rathmines aged 70.

*BREWER, Henry Charles, R.I. (1866–1950).

Exhibited widely in New Zealand and Australia, also at Venice in 1932. Died on 21st October 1950.

BRIDGMAN, Leonard (born 1895).

Painter in oil and water-colour of aviation subjects; journalist. Born on 15th February 1895. His first published drawing appeared in the programme for the Hendon Air Meeting 1913. After serving in the R.A.F. he joined *The Aeroplane* as artist and draughtsman 1919. Illustrated several air historical books including *The Clouds Remember* 1936, and for twenty years edited *Jane's All the World's Aircraft*. Founder member and Hon. Treasurer of the Society of Aviation Artists, he is now an Associate Member of the Guild of Aviation Artists and lives at East Finchley.

BRIDGMAN, Miss May, R.M.S. (*fl. c.* 1904–1914).

Miniature painter, especially of portraits. Exhibited at the R.A., R.M.S. Lived in London.

BROADBENT, A., F.R.B.S. (died 1919).

Sculptor of figure subjects in bronze and marble. Exhibited at the R.A. Lived in London and died September 1919.

BROCKLEBANK, Rev. John W.R. (1869–1926).

Landscape painter. Lived at Warminster in Wiltshire, and exhibited at the Walker Art Gallery, Liverpool. Represented in the Victoria and Albert Museum.

BROOK, Arthur B. (born 1867).

Painter in oil and water-colour of portraits and landscapes; mezzotinter. Born at Scholes in Yorkshire. Studied at the Brighouse Mechanics Institute and at the age of eighteen won a national competition for landscape painting in water-colour. Exhibited at the R.A. Influenced by the mezzotint engraver Ellen Jowett. Lived at Hale in Cheshire.

BROOKMAN, Miss Vera E. (died 1964).

Painter of portraits and landscapes. Exhibited at the R.A. from 1932. Lived in London, and later at Knebworth in Hertfordshire.

BROUGIER, Adolf W., R.B.A. (*fl. c.* 1900–1920).

Painter of landscapes and town scenes. Exhibited at the R.A., R.B.A., Walker Art Gallery in Liverpool, and in Birmingham. Painted some subjects in the South of France. Lived in Hampstead for some time.

BROUN-MORISON, Guy E., R.O.I. (*fl. c.* 1900–1925).

Oil painter, Exhibited at the R.O.I. Lived in London, then in Paris, and later at Errol in Perthshire.

BROWN, Miss Catherine Madox (Mrs. Hueffer) (died 1927).

Painter of portraits, landscapes and figure subjects. Exhibited at the leading London galleries from 1869, including the R.A. Died on 3rd June 1927 aged 76.

BROWN, G. Taylor (*fl. c.* 1905–1930).

Landscape painter in oil and water-colour. Exhibited at the R.A., R.S.A., G.I. Painted widely in south-west Scotland, and lived at Stewarton in Ayrshire.

BROWN, Miss Helen Paxton (*fl. c.* 1900–1950).

Portrait painter; needleworker. Studied at Glasgow School of Art. Exhibited at the R.S.A., G.I. Lived in Glasgow for many years.

BROWN, Mrs. Mia Arnesby (*née* Edwards) (1866–1931).

Painter of portraits, figures, and garden subjects. Married the artist Arnesby Brown 1896. Studied art at Herkomer's School at Bushey, and exhibited at the R.A. from 1893. Lived at Abergavenny, later at Haddiscoe in Norfolk and in London.

BROWNE, Alfred J. Warne (died 1915).

Painter in oil and water-colour of marines and coastal subjects. Exhibited at the leading London galleries from 1884, including the R.A., R.I. Lived in Cornwall, later in London and Lower Shiplake in Oxfordshire. Died in August 1915.

*BROWNSWORD, Harold, F.R.B.S. (1885–1961).

Sculptor of portraits and figure subjects. Died August 1961.

BROWNSWORD, Harry A., R.B.A. (*fl. c.* 1889–1903).

Landscape painter. Exhibited at the leading London galleries from 1889, including the R.A., R.B.A. Lived at Nottingham.

BRUCE, Martin B., R.B.A. (*fl. c.* 1893–1902).

Landscape painter. Exhibited at the leading London galleries from 1893, chiefly the R.A., R.O.I., R.B.A., also at Birmingham. Lived in London.

BRUCKMAN, William L., I.S., P.S. (born 1866).

Painter in oil of landscapes and portraits. Born at The Hague in Holland. Studied at the Académie of Fine Arts in his native city. At first he was interested in architecture, but turned to painting. In 1897 he settled in England, and exhibited at R.A., R.I., R.H.A., R.W.A., G.I., I.S., Walker Art Gallery in Liverpool, also in Manchester. Lived in London, and later at Great Bardfield in Essex.

BUCHANAN, Bertram (*fl. c.* 1900–1925).

Landscape etcher and aquatinter. He was a soldier in the regular army and after serving throughout World War I retired as a Colonel. In 1900 he commenced etching, and in 1920 an exhibition of his work was held in London at Bromhead, Cutts and Company. Lived in Sussex.

BUCHEL, Charles A. (*fl. c.* 1915–40).

Portrait and figure painter in oil. Exhibited at the Walker Art Gallery, Liverpool. Lived in London.

BÜHRER, Conrad (died 1937).

Sculptor of portraits and figure subjects. Exhibited at the leading London galleries from 1882, including the R.A. and New Gallery. Lived in London and died on 4th March 1937.

BULL, René (died 1942).

Illustrator. Born in Ireland. He sent contributions as a war artist to magazines such as *Black and White*, and was present at the conflicts in South Africa, India, Sudan and Armenia. Illustrated several books including *The Arabian Nights* 1912, and *Gulliver's Travels* 1928. Lived at Blackwater in Hampshire and died on 14th March 1942.

BUNBURY, H. St. P. (died 1916).

Painter of historical subjects. Exhibited at the R.A.

in 1911. Lived in London and died on 25th August 1916.

BURGESS, Miss Ethel Kate (*fl. c.* 1897–1907).

Figure painter in water-colour. In 1897 she won a scholarship from London County Council, studied at Lambeth School of Art and in 1899 received the Gilbert Sketching Prize for figure composition. Influenced by Nico Jungman. Lived in London, and exhibited at the R.A.

BURGESS, Walter William, R.E. (*fl. c.* 1874–1908).

Etcher and architect. Exhibited at the leading London galleries from 1874, chiefly at the R.A. Elected R.E. 1883, his membership ceased 18th August 1908. Lived in London.

*BURGOYNE, Miss Lorna, R.M.S. (Mrs. Von Ritschl) (died 1961).

Miniature painter, especially of flower subjects. Exhibited at the R.A. Died April 1961.

BURKE, Tom (died 1945).

Painter of figure subjects in oil. Exhibited at the R.A. from 1938. Lived in London and died July 1945.

*BURLEIGH, Mrs. Averil M., A.R.W.S., R.I., S.W.A. (died 1949).

Painter of landscapes and figure subjects in water-colour, oil and tempera. Exhibited at the R.A., N.E.A.C., I.S., and at the Paris Salon. Elected R.I. 1936, A.R.W.S. 1939, and a Member of the Society of Mural Decorators and Painters in Tempera. Died on 18th March 1949, and a memorial exhibition was held later that year at Brighton Art Gallery.

*BURLEIGH, C. H. H., R.O.I. (died 1956).

Painter in oil of landscapes. Studied at Brighton Art School, and in Paris under J. P. Laurens and J. E. Blanche. Exhibited at the R.A. from 1898, and was elected R.O.I. 1913.

*BURN, Gerald Maurice (1862–1945).

Died on 3rd November 1945.

BUSSY, Simon, I.S., N.P.S. (1870–1954).

Portrait and landscape painter in oil and pastel. Exhibited at the N.E.A.C., I.S., N.P.S., and at the Walker Art Gallery in Liverpool. Lived in London for some years, and is represented in the Tate Gallery.

*BUTLER, George Edmund, R.W.A. (1872–1936).

Landscape and genre painter. Lived in Bristol for a time.

BUTLER, Herbert E. (*fl. c.* 1880–1920).

Painter in oil and water-colour of landscapes and coastal subjects. Exhibited at the leading London galleries from 1881, including the R.A., R.B.A. Painted scenes of Cornish life, and also in Normandy. He had a studio at Polperro in Cornwall and ran his own art classes. His work was similar to that of the Newlyn School.

BUTLER, Samuel (1835–1902).

Figure painter in oil. Exhibited at the leading London galleries from 1869, including the R.A. Represented in the Tate Gallery.

BUTTERWORTH, Mrs. Margaret, R.M.S. (*fl. c.* 1905–1915).

Miniature painter. Lived in Kensington.

BYLES, W. Hounson, R.B.A. (*fl. c.* 1895–1925).

Painter of landscapes and figure subjects. Exhibited at the R.A., R.B.A., New Gallery, and at the Walker Art Gallery in Liverpool. Lived in London and later at Westhampnett, near Chichester in Sussex.

*BYNG, Leonard H. R. (1920–1974).

Born on 27th October 1920. Died on 2nd September 1974.

C

*CACKETT, Leonard, S.M.A., S.G.A., B.W.S. (1896–1963).

Died on 29th April 1963.

*CADOGAN, Sidney Russell (died 1911).

Painter of landscapes in oil. Although born in England, he was especially fond of Scotland, and many of his subjects were of the Scottish countryside and coast. He had a great love of trees and animal life in the forest, this being reflected in some of his paintings. Early in life he visited Corsica and Algeria, and was known as a fine raconteur, detailing the time he spent abroad. Works exhibited at the R.A. include *On the Dart, The Dead Hind,* and *Through the Forest.* Lived at St. Andrews in Fifeshire, and at Sevenoaks in Kent.

*CAIN, Charles William, S.M.A. (1893–1962).

Died on 7th February 1962.

CALTHROP, Dion Clayton (1878–1937).

Illustrator and writer. Born on 2nd May 1878. Studied at the St. John's Wood School of Art, and in Paris at the Académies Julian and Colarossi. Exhibited at the R.A., R.I. Wrote and illustrated several books including *Guide to Fairyland* and *A Trap to Catch a Dream.* Lived at Dorchester in Dorset and died on 7th March 1937.

CAMERON, John Jackson (born 1872).

Landscape painter. Born on 1st February 1872. Studied art at the Académie Julian in Paris. In 1914 he joined the Army, served in France and Ireland, and retired 1920 with the rank of Lt. Colonel. Lived in London.

CAMPBELL, John Patrick (*fl. c.* 1900–1915).

Illustrator of ancient Celtic romantic stories; poster designer. At school he produced posters for school functions, but received no formal art training. Illustrated such works as *Four Irish Songs,* and *The Tain.* Lived in Belfast and signed his drawings "Seaghan Mac-Cathmhaoil".

CAMPBELL, Yvonne Marjorie (born 1918).

Painter of portraits and landscapes in oil and water-colour; printmaker and weaver. Studied at Liverpool and Edinburgh Colleges of Art. Exhibited at the R.A., Walker Art Gallery in Liverpool, and widely in Australia. Several one-man shows held in East Anglia, where she has lived for many years.

CANNEY, Michael Richard Ladd (born 1923).

Oil painter. Born at Falmouth in Cornwall on 16th July 1923. Studied at the Redruth, Penzance and St. Ives Schools of Art 1939–42, at Goldsmiths' College

School of Art 1947–51, and at Hospitalfield at Arbroath. Exhibited at the R.W.A., L.G., Artists International Association, and widely in Cornwall. Represented in Plymouth Art Gallery by *Cornish Painting* and *Cornish Coast*. Secretary of Newlyn Society of Artists 1956–64. Curator of Newlyn Art Gallery 1956–64, in 1966 appointed Director of the Art Gallery of the University of California, Santa Barbara. For some years he has been Senior Lecturer in Painting at Bristol Polytechnic Faculty of Art and Design, and lives at Clapton-in-Gordano, Bristol.

CANZIANI, Madame Louisa (*née* Starr) (died 1909).

Painter of portraits and genre. Studied art at the R.A. Schools, she was the first woman to receive a gold medal for historical painting 1867. Exhibited at the leading London galleries from 1863, including the R.A., R.B.A., Grosvenor Gallery. Mother of the artist Estella Canziani, she lived in Kensington. Died May 1909.

CAPEY, Reco, A.R.C.A. (Lond.) (1895–1961).

Craftsman, carver and painter. Born at Burslem in Staffordshire on 5th July 1895. Studied art at the R.C.A. 1919–22, also in France, Italy, Sweden 1923–25. Exhibited at the R.A., Paris Salon, and in America. Elected R.D.I. 1938. Lived in London and later at Alfriston in Sussex. Died on 11th May 1961.

CARO, Anthony (born 1924).

Sculptor in bronze and steel. Born in London on 8th March 1924. Studied art at the Regent Street Polytechnic 1946, and at the R.A. Schools 1947–52. Assisted Henry Moore 1951–53. Exhibited widely in Britain, on the continent, and in America. Represented at the Venice Biennale 1958, 1966. Lives in London.

CARR, Alwyn C.E., A.W.G. (died 1940).

Metalworker. Studied at Sheffield School of Art and at the R.C.A. Went to France, Italy, Germany and Spain. Exhibited at the R.A. Worked with Omar Ramsden, and lived in London. Died on 22nd April 1940.

CARR, Bernard James (*fl. c.* 1910–1940).

Painter in oil and water-colour of landscapes and marines; etcher. Studied at Sheffield College of Art and at the Académie Julian in Paris. Lived in Sheffield and was art critic of the *Sheffield Daily Telegraph* from 1910. Works include *Before the Days of Steam, Yachtsmen, Passing the Lighthouse.*

CARRICK, Edward—see CRAIG, Edward Anthony.

CARSE, A. Duncan (died 1938).

Painter of figure subjects in oil and tempera; mural decorator. Exhibited at the R.A. and at the Fine Art Society, including some fans. Lived at Knebworth in Hertfordshire and later at Crowthorne in Berkshire.

*CARSTAIRS, John Paddy (1916–1970).

Died on 12th December 1970.

CARTER, Albert Clarence, A.R.B.S. (1894–1958).

Sculptor of portraits and figure subjects in stone, marble and wood. Born in London on 19th June 1894. Studied at Lambeth School of Art, and the Central School of Arts and Crafts. Exhibited at the R.A., G.I., and elected A.R.B.S. 1927. Lived in London and later at Reading. Died on 28th February 1958.

CARTER, Norman St. Clair (1875–1963).

Portrait painter and designer of stained glass. Born on 30th June 1875 at Kew, near Melbourne in Australia. Studied painting at Melbourne National Gallery School under Bernard Hall and Frederick McCubbin. In 1903 he settled in Sydney where he lived for many years. Exhibited at the R.A. and at the Paris Salon. Died on 18th September 1963.

*CARTER, Richard Harry, R.I. (1839–1911).

Member of the Royal Institute of Water-colour Painters.

*CARTLEDGE, William, R.I., R.S.M.A. (1891–1976).

Died on 30th March 1976 aged 85.

CAST, Jesse Dale (died 1976).

Portrait painter. Exhibited at R.A., N.E.A.C. Lived in London, then at Kew Gardens, and later in Tunbridge Wells. Died on 9th February 1976 aged 75.

CHADBURN, George Haworthe, R.B.A., A.W.G. (1870–1950).

Oil painter. Born in Yorkshire. Studied at St. John's Wood School of Art, the R.A. Schools, Westminster School of Art, and at the Slade School. In Paris he worked under Tony Fleury and Lefèvre. Exhibited at the leading London galleries from 1891, including the R.A., R.B.A. also at the Paris Salon. Elected R.B.A. 1902. Lived at Budleigh Salterton in Devon.

*CHADWICK, Tom (1914–1942).

Wood engraver of figure subjects. Born in Yorkshire. Studied under Iain Macnab at the Grosvenor School of Art, and was perhaps his finest pupil. Exhibited at the S.W.E. from 1932, and in 1936 won a prize and medal at the Chicago International Exhibition for his print *The Introduction.* Taught at Westminster School of Art. Killed at the Battle of Alamein in North Africa in an attempt to recover the body of his dead brother.

CHALKER, Miss Cissie (Mrs. Fison), R.M.S. (*fl. c.* 1890–1910).

Miniature painter. Exhibited at the R.A. from 1890. Lived at Bath, and later at Thetford in Norfolk.

CHALKER, Jack Bridger, R.B.A. (*fl. c.* 1950).

Little known artist. Although a member of the R.B.A., he appears to have exhibited little.

CHALLENER, Frederick Sproston, R.Canadian A. (1869–1959).

Genre painter in oil and water-colour. An Englishman, he was born at Whetstone. In 1883 he emigrated to Canada. Studied at Ontario School of Art, and in Toronto with G. A. Reid. He also spent some time working in England, Italy, Egypt and Syria. Exhibited widely in North America, and elected an Associate R. Canadian A. 1891 and a full member 1899. Works include *Workers of the Fields, When the Lights are Low, The Evening Breeze.* A member of the Canadian Society of Painters in Water-colour, he taught for fifty years at Ontario College of Art. Lived in Toronto.

CHALMERS, Hector (died 1943).

Landscape painter. Exhibited at the R.S.A., G.I. Member of the Scottish Arts Club, he lived in Edinburgh. Died on 1st April 1943 aged 94.

CHANCE, Miss Jane Linnell (died 1941).

Painter of portraits and figure subjects. Exhibited at the leading London galleries from 1888. Lived in London, and was a founder of Camden School of Art. Died on 26th April 1941 aged 84.

CHANDOR, Douglas (died 1953).

Portrait painter in oil. Born in England, he spent half of his life in this country. After meeting the art dealer Joseph Duveen he went at his suggestion to America, and settled in New York. Received many portrait commissions.

CHAPMAN, George, A.R.C.A.(Lond.) (born 1908).

Painter and etcher of portraits and landscapes; sculptor in bronze. Born on 1st October 1908. Studied at Gravesend School of Art, the Slade School, and at the R.C.A. Exhibited at the R.A., N.E.A.C., L.G., Leicester and Trafford Galleries, and at the Great Bardfield Festivals 1955, 1957, 1959. One-man shows held at Piccadilly Gallery, St. George's Gallery London, and Zwemmer Gallery. Represented in several public collections. Lives at Aberayron in Dyfed.

CHAPMAN, Mrs. Olive (*née* Simpson) (*fl. from c.* 1925).

Artist, writer and traveller. Studied art in London at Heatherleys School. Visited amongst other places Madagascar, America and the Arctic regions. Three one-man shows of her water-colours were held in Bond Street, London. Published *Across Iceland* 1930, *Across Cyprus* 1937, *Across Madagascar* 1947. Lived in London.

*CHARLTON, Edward William, R.E. (1859–1935).

Exhibited at the R.A., R.E., R.W.A.

CHARLTON, H. V. (died 1916).

London artist, who lived at the same address as the artist John Charlton indicating the probability of a family connection. Killed in action on 24th June 1916.

*CHASE, Miss Marian Emma, R.I. (1844–1905).

Elected A.R.I. 1875, R.I. 1879.

CHEATER, Mrs. Violet (*fl. c.* 1910–1930).

Painter in oil and water-colour; miniaturist. Daughter of the artist Sir James Dromgole Linton, P.R.I. Studied art at the R.C.A. Exhibited at the R.A., R.I., R.O.I., and at the Walker Art Gallery in Liverpool. Lived in London for many years.

CHEESWRIGHT, Miss Ethel S., R.M.S. (*fl. c.* 1905–1915).

Miniature painter. Lived in London, and later in Oxford.

CHENEY, Leo (died 1928).

Illustrator. Died on 29th March 1928 aged 50.

CHESSER, Mrs. Sheila, W.I.A.C. (born 1915).

Abstract painter in acrylic. Born in Cheshire on 21st February 1915 *née* Blayney-Jones. Received no formal art training. Exhibited in London at the Leicester, Redfern and Whitechapel Art Galleries, also at the R.S.A. and Paris Salon. Has held several one-man shows. Lives in London.

*CHESTERTON, Maurice, A.W.G. (1883–1962).

Architect and water-colour painter. Born in Kensington on 4th August 1883. Studied at St. John's Wood School of Art. Exhibited at the R.A., R.B.A., Paris Salon. Member of Ipswich Art Club.

CHILD, Charles Koe (died 1935).

Landscape painter. Studied at Westminister School of Art and at the Slade School. Lived in London for many years and taught at the Slade. Died on 2nd March 1935 aged 68.

CHRISTIANSEN, Nils H. (*fl. c.* 1890–1920).

Landscape painter in oil, especially of winter scenes. Norwegian by descent, much of his work is found in Britain, suggesting that he painted in this country.

CHRISTIE, Archibald H., R.B.A. (*fl. c.* 1888–1928).

Still life painter. Exhibited at the leading London galleries from 1888. Lived at Ewell in Surrey and later at East Runton in Norfolk.

CHRISTIE, Robert, R.B.A. (*fl. c.* 1890–1910).

Figure painter. Exhibited at the leading London galleries from 1891, including the R.A., R.B.A. Lived in London.

*CHURCHYARD, Miss Harriet (1836–1927).

Member of Ipswich Art Club.

CHUTE, Desmond (*fl. c.* 1915–1930).

Wood engraver. Follower of Iain Macnab. Exhibited at the S.W.E.

CLAPPERTON, Thomas John, F.R.B.S. (1879–1962).

Sculptor of figure subjects. Born on 14th September 1879 at Galashiels in Selkirkshire. Studied at Glasgow School of Art, and at the R.A. Schools, where he received a gold medal and travelling scholarship. Exhibited at the R.A., R.S.A., G.I. and the Walker Art Gallery in Liverpool. Elected A.R.B.S. 1913. Lived in London for many years, and died on 15th February 1962.

CLARK, Albert (*fl. c.* 1900–1910).

Animal painter in oil, especially of horses. Exhibited at the R.A. He obtained many commissions in Essex. Lived in London.

CLARKE, George Frederick (1823–1906).

Painter of portraits and figure subjects. Born on 13th April 1823 at Carrick-on-Suir. Exhibited at the R.H.A., later settling in London, where he exhibited at the R.A., R.B.A. Died on 8th March 1906.

*CLARKE, Harry Harvey (1869–1948).

Landscape painter in oil and water-colour; also many etchings, drypoints and aquatints. Chiefly inspired by the landscape of Leicestershire, Wales and Cornwall. Taught part time at Leicester College of Art and Market Harborough Grammar School, he was Chairman of Leicester Society of Artists for a number of years. Represented in Leicester, Nottingham and Northampton Art Galleries. Died in March 1948. His daughter, Joan Clarke, is a potter and lives at Ludham in Norfolk.

CLATWORTHY, Robert (born 1928).

Sculptor of figures and animal subjects. Born at Bridgwater in Somerset on 31st January 1928. Studied at the West of England College of Art 1944–46, Chelsea School of Art 1949–51, Slade School 1951–54. He taught at Chelsea and St. Martins Schools of Art.

*CLAUSEN, Miss Katharine Frances, A.R.W.S. (1886–1936).

Executed some etchings and aquatints including *The Way down from Ravello.*

CLAYTON, Miss Katharine M. (*fl. c.* 1925–1935).

Etcher. Exhibited at Colnaghi's in Bond Street, London, and the Walker Art Gallery, Liverpool. Lived at Hampstead.

CLEAVER, Thomas Reginald (died 1954).

Cartoonist. Contributed to *Punch* and was on the staff of *The Graphic.* Died on 15th December 1954.

CLEMENTS, William Charles (born 1903).

Painter in oil and water-colour of portraits and landscapes. Born in London on 9th November 1903. Studied art at Walthamstow and Bloomsbury. Exhibited at the R.B.A., U.A., and for some time was Chairman of Essex Art Club also President of the London Sketch Club. Lives at Chingford in Essex.

CLEVERLY, Charles F. M., R.B.A. (*fl. c.* 1890–1910).

Painter of figure subjects. Exhibited at the R.A. from 1893, also at the R.B.A., New Gallery, Walker Art Gallery in Liverpool. Lived in London and later at Ripley in Surrey.

CLOSE, Samuel P., A.R.H.A. (*fl. c.* 1885–1920).

Irish architect. Elected A.R.H.A. 1891. Lived in Belfast for some years.

CLOUSTON, Robert S. (died 1911).

Mezzotint engraver. Exhibited at the leading London galleries from 1887, chiefly at the R.A. Lived at Bushey and later in London. Died on 25th April 1911.

*CODRINGTON, Miss Isabel (1874–1943).

Painter in oil and water-colour of portraits and genre; miniaturist. Christened Isabel Codrington Pyke-Nott. Received a painting scholarship at age fifteen. Exhibited at the R.B.A. from 1893, and at the R.A. from the following year. Also showed her work at R.P., R.W.A., and Walker Art Gallery in Liverpool. For a time she exhibited under the name Pyke-Nott, but when she resumed painting about 1918 signed herself Isabel Codrington. Represented in several public collections at home and abroad. Married the art critic Paul G. Konody and later Gustave Mayer of Colnaghi's. Lived at Woldingham in Surrey.

COHEN, Harold (born 1928).

Abstract painter. Born in London on 1st May 1928, elder brother of the artist Bernard Cohen (born 1933). Studied art at the Slade School 1948–52, received the Abbey Travelling Scholarship 1952 and visited Italy. His first London one-man show held in 1954 at Gimpel Fils. In 1962 he joined the teaching staff of the Slade School. Represented in the Tate Gallery.

COHEN, Lewis (died 1915).

Anglo-American oil painter. Lived in London and exhibited at R.A., R.O.I. Died on 4th August 1915.

COKER, Peter Godfrey, R.A. (born 1926).

Landscape painter in oil. Studied at St. Martins School of Art and at the R.C.A. Exhibited at the R.A., in the provinces, and abroad. One-man shows held in London at the Grosvenor Gallery 1956, 1957, 1959, 1964, 1967 and Thackeray Gallery 1970, 1972, 1974, 1975. He finds his subjects in East Anglia, Yorkshire, Scotland and France.

*COLE, John Vicat, R.O.I., R.B.A., N.E.A.C. (1903–1975).

Elected a member of the Society of Sussex Painters 1963. Died on 5th September 1975.

COLLIER, Miss Ada L. (*fl. c.* 1915–1935).

Painter in oil and gouache; wood engraver. Studied under the printmaker William Giles. Lived at Fittleworth in Sussex and later at Crick, near Rugby.

COLLINS, Archibald (1853–1922).

Painter in oil of landscapes, portraits and figure subjects. Born at Worcester. Studied art at the R.A.

Schools. Exhibited at the R.A., R.B.A., and for some years was Professor of painting at the St. John's Wood Art School. Settled in Adelaide, Australia 1898, and is represented in Adelaide Art Gallery.

COLLINS, Joyce (born 1912).

Painter in oil and gouache of industrial scenes, docks and stations. Born at Brightlingsea in Essex. Studied at Colchester School of Art. Exhibited at the Alpine Gallery in London, and widely in the provinces. One-man show held in 1968 at the Trafford Gallery, London, and four exhibitions with her husband, Henry Collins, at The Minories in Colchester.

COLLINS, Patrick (born 1910).

Irish landscape and figure painter in oil.

*COLLISTER, Alfred James, R.B.A., A.W.G., A.R.C.A.(Lond.) (1869–1964).

He painted some landscapes and coastal scenes in water-colour.

*COLMORE, Mrs. Nina (1889–1973).

Painter of horses in oil. During World War II she drove ambulances in Birmingham, and later helped the war effort in Sicily and Italy. She took her painting lightheartedly, never had a studio, and would often sit on the floor with her canvas propped up on a chair. Died on 26th April 1973.

COMLEY, James Walter, A.R.C.A.(Lond.) (*fl. c.* 1900–1935).

Genre and landscape painter in oil and water-colour. Born in Coventry. Studied art at the R.C.A., receiving his diploma 1903. Exhibited his work in London and provincial galleries. Lived at Bridgwater in Somerset for many years.

CONDER, Miss H. Louise (*fl. c.* 1890–1925).

Painter of landscapes and miniatures. Exhibited at the leading London galleries from 1890, chiefly the R.A., R.B.A., R.I., R.M.S., also at the Walker Art Gallery in Liverpool. Lived in Hamstead for many years.

CONNOR, Jerome (1876–1943).

Irish sculptor.

CONSTANTINE, Harry Francis (born 1919).

Painter in oil and water-colour. Born in Sheffield on 11th February 1919. Studied at Sheffield and Southampton Colleges of Art. Exhibited at the R.A., also in Lancashire and Yorkshire. Director of Sheffield City Art Galleries.

*COOK, H. Moxon (1844–1929).

Exhibited at the leading London galleries from 1868.

COOKE, Stanley (born 1913).

Landscape and figure painter in oil, acrylic and water-colour. Born at Mansfield, Nottinghamshire, on 11th January 1913. Studied at Mansfield School of Art. Exhibited at the R.A., R.W.S., R.I., R.B.A., R.O.I., U.A., and in the provinces. One-man shows held at Mansfield Art Gallery and the Drian Galleries in London. Lives at Guildford in Surrey.

*COOPER, Alfred Heaton (1863–1929).

Landscape painter in water-colour and oil. Born at Swinton in Lancashire on 14th July 1863. At age 21 he relinquished his training as an accountant in Bolton Town Hall, and took up a scholarship at Westminster School of Art where he studied under Clausen. Influenced by Harpignies, the Maris brothers, and the

Impressionists. Visited Morocco and Gibraltar 1888, Norway 1891–92, and in 1894 married a Norwegian girl. After living in Bolton for three years they settled in the Lake District, where he found many subjects for his water-colours. In 1904 he received a commission to provide 75 illustrations for a book *The English Lakes*, published by A. and C. Black, and later illustrated *The Isle of Wight, The Isle of Man, The Norwegian Fjords* (the only book he also wrote), *Ireland, Wild Lakeland, Somerset, Dorset, Norfolk and Suffolk, Northumberland, Denmark and Sweden*. Died of cancer on 21st July 1929 and is buried at Ambleside.

*COOPER, Austin (1890–1964).
Represented in the Tate Gallery.

COPLAND, Patrick Forbes (died 1933).
Scottish artist, born in Aberdeen. Studied art under Henry Stacy Marks, R.A. Died in Montreal, Canada on 27th January 1933.

CORBET, Mrs. Edith (*fl. c.* 1890–1915).
Landscape and genre painter in oil. Exhibited at the R.A., New Gallery and the Walker Art Gallery in Liverpool. Married the artist Matthew Ridley Corbet and lived in St. John's Wood.

CORBOULD-ELLIS, Mrs. Eveline M., R.M.S., S.W.A. (*fl. c.* 1895–1935).
Miniature painter. Exhibited at the R.A., R.M.S., G.I., New Gallery, the Walker Art Gallery in Liverpool, and abroad. Lived in London and later at Goring-on-Thames in Oxfordshire.

*CORDEN, Victor Milton (1860–1939).
Established his own art school at Newbury, and exhibited at several provincial art galleries including Birmingham.

CORFIELD, Alfred James (born 1904).
Painter in oil, water-colour and pastel of landscapes, often without figures, and townscapes, especially views in Manchester. Born at Portsmouth on 17th September 1904. Largely a self-taught artist but did receive some private tuition. Member of Manchester Art Guild 1938, Stockport Art Guild 1938, Oldham Society of Art 1948, and has exhibited chiefly in Lancashire. He works mainly in the open, producing little in the studio, and lives in Manchester.

COTTERILL, Allan (born 1913).
Painter, and sculptor in wood. Born at Southport in Lancashire on 23rd March 1913. Studied at Liverpool College of Art, Central School of Arts and Crafts, and London University Institute of Education. Exhibited at the leading London and provincial galleries. Lives at Winchester.

COULSON, Gerald Davison (born 1926).
Painter of landscapes, coastal scenes, wildlife, aviation and motoring subjects. Born at Kenilworth, Warwickshire on 11th December 1926. Self-taught in art. Elected member of the Society of Aviation Artists 1955, Industrial Painters Group 1957, and Guild of Aviation Artists 1971. Represented in the R.A.F. Museum at Hendon and National Railway Museum at York. His work has been reproduced as fine art prints, and in recent years has exhibited widely in America. Lives at Cherry Hinton, Cambridge.

COUTTS, Gordon (1875–1943).
Painter in oil of landscapes, portraits and figure subjects. Born in Glasgow. Studied art at Glasgow, R.A. Schools, and at the Académie Julian in Paris. Exhibited at the R.A., R.P., and Paris Salon. He settled in Australia and taught art in Sydney. Represented in the "Australian Artists" exhibition held at Brighton Art Gallery 1925. Died in San Francisco.

COWLES, Miss Barbara (born 1898).
Oil painter. Born on 20th April 1898 at Melksham in Wiltshire. Exhibited at the R.A. Lived at Talybont in Cardiganshire and in London.

COWLES, W., R.H.A. (died 1917).
Irish artist killed near Ypres in October 1917.

COX, Arthur Leonard (born 1879).
Mezzotint engraver of more than 50 plates. Born in London on 23rd November 1879. Studied art in Paris. Exhibited at the R.A. Lived for a time at Bushey.

COX, Walter (died 1930).
Portrait painter. Born in England, he lived in America for some time. Died on 30th April 1930 aged 64.

CRAIG, Edward Anthony (born 1904).
Oil painter, wood engraver, etcher, designer and writer. Born in London on 3rd January 1904, son of Edward Gordon Craig. Studied art in Italy 1917–26. Exhibited at St. George's Gallery 1927, 1928, at the Redfern Gallery 1929, 1931, 1938, and with the Grubb Group 1928–38. His work has also been shown in North America, and he is represented in several public collections. Lives near Aylesbury in Buckinghamshire and works under the name of Edward Carrick.

CRAIG, Robertson H. (born 1916).
Irish landscape painter.

*CRAWFORD, Thomas Hamilton (died 1948).
Portrait mezzotinter and aquatinter. Born in Glasgow, son of John Crawford, a sculptor. Studied at Glasgow and Edinburgh Schools of Art, and later at the Herkomer School in Bushey. Lived at Berkhamstead.

*CRAWSHAW, Lionel Townsend, R.S.W., R.B.S.A. (1864–1949).
Exhibited at the G.I. Lived for a time in Doncaster, sending works from there to galleries chiefly in Scotland.

CRISP, F. E. F. (died 1915).
London artist, who exhibited at the R.A. Served in World War I as a 2nd Lieut. in the Grenadier Guards, and was killed in action January 1915.

CROMPTON, John (died 1927).
Landscape painter. Exhibited at the leading London galleries from 1872, chiefly the R.A., R.B.A. Principal of Heatherley's School of Art 1888–1908. Died on 5th February 1927 aged 72.

CROSSLEY, Bob (born 1912).
Painter in oil and gouache; printmaker. Born at Northwich in Cheshire on 30th August 1912. Chiefly a self-taught artist. Exhibited at R.I., L.G., S.G.A., Free Painters Group, in the provinces, and at the Paris Salon. One-man shows held Crane Kalman Gallery, Manchester 1959, Reid Gallery, London 1960, and Gallery Bique in Madrid 1965. Elected M.A.F.A. 1955, member of the Artists International Association 1963 and Penwith Society of Artists 1960. Represented in several

public collections. Lives at St. Ives in Cornwall, and commenced screen printing 1968.

CUMMING, William Skeoch (1864–1929).

Portrait painter. Exhibited at the R.A., R.S.A., and Walker Art Gallery in Liverpool. Lived in Edinburgh.

·CURSITER, Stanley, R.S.A., R.S.W. (1887–1976).

Erratum – born on 29th April 1887. Died April 1976, aged 88.

CURTIS, Vera F. (born 1916).

Painter in oil and water-colour of landscapes, portraits and still life. Studied at Chelsea School of Art and then worked for a period on posters. Exhibited at the R.A., R.I., R.O.I., S.W.A., in the provinces and abroad. Settled in Suffolk 1948.

CUTTER, Christiana (1893–1969).

Painter in oil of landscapes and figure subjects. Studied art at the Slade School. Influenced by Sickert, and was represented in the "Sickert Women and the Sickert Girls" exhibition held in London at Michael Parkin Fine Art 1974. Exhibited with the N.E.A.C.

D

DADD, Philip J. S. (died 1916).

Painter and illustrator. Exhibited at the R.A., R.I., and Walker Art Gallery in Liverpool. A nephew of Kate Greenaway, he was on the staff of *The Sphere* for some time. Killed in action in France in August 1916.

D'AGUILAR, Michael (born 1928).

Landscape and figure painter in oil; lithographer. Born in London, of part Spanish parentage, and spent much of his early life in Spain. Studied art at the R.A. Schools 1949–54, where he won the Armitage Prize, a silver medal and the Leverhulme Scholarship. Received gold, silver and bronze medals at the Royal Drawing Society. Exhibited at the R.A., R.B.A., N.E.A.C. and in Spain. One-man shows held at the Temple Gallery 1961, New Grafton Gallery 1971, and at the Southwell Brown Gallery 1974. Represented in Bradford City Art Gallery. Lives in London.

D'AGUILAR, Paul (born 1924).

Painter in oil and water-colour of landscapes, animals and figure subjects. Born in London on 9th September 1924, elder brother of Michael D'Aguilar. Studied painting and drawing at the R.A. Schools 1948–53. Exhibited at the R.A., R.B.A., N.E.A.C., L.G., N.S. and abroad. One-man shows held in London at Irving Gallery 1952, Temple Gallery 1960, Canaletto Gallery 1971, Langton Gallery 1973, and Southwell Brown Gallery 1974. Lives in London.

DALY, William Edward (1887–1962).

Landscape painter in oil; stained glass designer. Born in Manchester on 10th October 1887. Exhibited at the R.A., N.E.A.C. Appointed Headmaster of Llanelly School of Art 1915, and Head of Kidderminster School of Art 1925–45. Designed the stained glass windows in the Catholic Church of St. Ambrose, Kidderminster. Father of the artist J. E. Daly, he died in Worcester February 1962.

DANIELL, Frank Robinson (1868–1932).

Portrait painter. Exhibited at the R.A., R.P., and on the continent. Lived at Colchester in Essex.

·DARWIN, Sir Robin, R.A., R.S.A., P.R.W.A., N.E.A.C. (1910–1974).

Died on 30th January 1974.

·DAVIDSON, Miss Lilian (died 1953).

Irish portrait painter. Lived at Rathmines and later in Dublin.

·DAVIES, David, R.O.I. (1862–1939).

Australian landscape painter. Studied art in England and France, returning to Australia 1893. Worked in England 1897–1909, and then in France until 1930. Died in England.

DAVIES, John Alfred, R.S.M.A. (born 1901).

Painter in oil and water-colour of landscapes, seascapes, ships, aircraft and figure subjects; book illustrator and cartoonist. Born on 22nd April 1901 at Ware in Hertfordshire. Studied art at Heatherley's and privately under Jack Merriott. Exhibited at the R.A., R.I., R.S.M.A., and Paris Salon. Represented in the National Maritime Museum and Oregon Historical Society, U.S.A. Member of the Wapping Group, Guild of Aviation Artists, Hertford Art Society, Langham Sketch Club, and R.W.S. Art Club. Lives at Therfield, near Royston in Hertfordshire.

DAVIS, G. H., R.S.M.A. (*fl. c.* 1945–1960).

Painter of marine and aviation subjects. Founder member of the Society of Aviation Artists 1955.

DAVIS, Laurence (*fl. c.* 1905–1915).

Etcher of architectural subjects in France and Italy.

DAWNAY, Denis (born 1920).

Landscape and figure painter in oil. Studied art at the Euston Road School. Exhibited at the R.A. Lived at Binfield, near Bracknell in Berkshire.

DAWSON, Mrs. Edith Brearey (*née* Robinson) (*fl. c.* 1885–1920).

Painter and aquatinter of landscapes and coastal scenes. Exhibited at the leading London galleries from 1889, including the R.A., R.I., R.B.A. She worked on the east coast, and married the artist Nelson Dawson.

DEANE, Sir Thomas Manly, R.H.A. (1851–1933).

Irish architect. Born on 8th June 1851 at Ferney, County Cork. Studied architecture under William Burges and in France 1875. Received a Royal Academy Scholarship 1876, and studied in Italy 1878. On his return to Dublin he went into partnership and worked throughout Ireland. Elected A.R.H.A. 1898, R.H.A. 1910, and Knighted 1911. Lived in Dublin and died 3rd February 1933.

DE BRÉANSKI, Alfred Jnr. (born 1877).

Painter in oil of highland scenes. Born on 20th August 1877 at Lewisham, London. Studied at St. Martin's School of Art under Cecil Rea, and later in Paris under Whistler. Exhibited at the R.A., R.B.A., and in the provinces. Painted in Scotland, Wales, Lake District, Surrey, Sussex, Buckinghamshire and Italy. Lived in London.

DECKER, Elizabeth, A.R.E. (*fl. c.* 1895–1905).

Little known etcher, who was elected A.R.E. 1900. Her membership ceased four years later.

DE LISLE, Miss Edith Fortunée Tita (1866–1911).

Miniature painter. Exhibited at the R.A. from 1899, also at the New Gallery and in Birmingham. Lived at Chiswick.

DE ROSE, Gerard, R.B.A., A.R.C.A.(Lond.) (born 1918).

Portrait painter in oil. Born at Accrington in Lancashire. Studied at Accrington School of Art, and at the R.C.A., where he received his diploma 1949. Exhibited at the R.A., R.B.A. Elected R.B.A. 1964. Portrait commissions include Duke of Bedford, John Wayne, Rod Steiger, Sammy Davis Jnr. and Moshe Dayan. Lives in London.

*DERRICK, Thomas (1885–1954).

Married a daughter of the artist Sir George Clausen.

*DETMOLD, Edward Julius (1883–1957).

Books he illustrated include *Æsop's Fables, Birds and Beasts, Nature Pictures.* Exhibited at the Walker Art Gallery in Liverpool.

DE WET, Hugh Oloff (1912–1975).

Sculptor of portrait and figure subjects. Born in Jersey of South African descent. He fought for the Ethiopian Air Force in the war against Italy, and in 1936 joined the Republican Air Force in Spain during the Civil War. In July 1939 he and his wife were arrested in Vienna, and he was subsequently tortured by the Nazis as he was suspected of being a French agent. Tried in Berlin 1941 and sentenced to death but was not executed as Britain held a German agent as a hostage for his life. Escaped 1945, and later published a book— *The Valley of the Shadow*—describing his experiences. He was well known as a sculptor, and is represented in collections in many parts of the world. Died November 1975 aged 63.

*DEWHURST, Wynford (1864–1941).

Landscape painter. Born in Manchester. Studied art in Paris for five years at the École des Beaux Arts and at the Académies Julian and Colarossi. Exhibited at the Paris Salon 1896, also in Germany, Italy, America. One-man shows held in Germany 1910, Paris 1912, Walker Gallery in London 1923, and Fine Art Society 1925. Represented in several public collections, he lived in Hampstead.

DILLON, Gerard (born 1916).

Irish figure painter in oil.

DISMORR, Jessie (1885–1939).

Vorticist painter. Contributed illustrations to *Blast.* Represented in the Tate Gallery by an oil *Abstract Composition.*

DIX, Miss Eulalee, A.R.M.S. (*fl. c.* 1900–1915).

Miniature painter. Exhibited at the R.M.S., and Walker Art Gallery in Liverpool. Lived in London.

DODD, Charles Tattershall, A.R.C.A.(Lond.) (died 1949).

Kent painter. Studied art at the R.C.A. A founder of the Tunbridge Wells Art Club 1934, he also exhibited at the R.W.A. Lived in Tunbridge Wells.

DODSON, Miss Sarah Paxton Ball (1847–1906).

Painter of portraits and landscapes. Born in Philadelphia, U.S.A. on 22nd February 1847. Studied art in Philadelphia 1872, and in Paris for three years from 1873. Settled in England, and painted in Sussex, Kent, Surrey and Worcestershire. Lived in Brighton and died on 8th January 1906. A memorial exhibition was held at Brighton Art Gallery 1910.

*DOLLMAN, Miss Ruth (*fl. c.* 1900–1930).

Painter of water-colour landscapes. Exhibited at the R.I. and a show of her paintings of Sussex subjects was held at the Leicester Galleries 1909. Lived in London.

DONALD, David (*fl. c.* 1895–1925).

Painter of street scenes and figure subjects. Exhibited at the R.A., and in the provinces. Painted in Italy and Morocco. Lived at Streatham and later at Tilford in Surrey.

DONALDSON, Andrew B. (1840–1919).

Painter in oil and water-colour of historical subjects. Exhibited at the R.A., R.B.A., R.I., Grosvenor and New Galleries. Represented in the Tate Gallery.

DONNE, Walter J., R.O.I. (*fl. c.* 1885–1930).

Painter in oil and water-colour of landscapes and figure subjects. Exhibited at the leading London galleries from 1885, including the R.A., R.I., R.B.A., R.O.I., also at the G.I., I.S., and Walker Art Gallery in Liverpool. Principal of the Grosvenor Life School at Vauxhall Bridge, which he described in his advertising material as "a Parisian Studio". Lived in Scarborough, then in London, and later at Shoreham-by-Sea in Sussex.

DOUTON, Miss Isabel F., R.M.S. (*fl. c.* 1895–1925).

Miniature painter. Exhibited at the R.A., R.M.S. and Walker Art Gallery in Liverpool. Lived in London for many years.

DOVASTON, Miss Margaret, R.B.A., N.B.A. (born 1884).

Painter of portraits and figure subjects. Studied art under Thomas William Cole at Ealing Art School, under Arthur S. Cope at Kensington, and at the R.A. Schools, where she received three silver medals. Exhibited at the R.A. from 1908, and was elected R.B.A. 1910, N.B.A. 1911. Lived in London for many years.

DOWSON, Russell (*fl. c.* 1865–1905).

Landscape painter in oil and water-colour. Exhibited at the leading London galleries from 1867, chiefly the R.A., R.I., R.B.A., Grosvenor Gallery. Member of the Norwich Art Circle.

DREW, Sir Thomas, P.R.H.A. (1838–1910).

Irish architect. Born on 18th September 1838 in Belfast. Elected A.R.H.A. 1870, R.H.A. 1871, P.R.H.A. 1900, and knighted 1900. Exhibited at the R.A. 1892. Lived in Dublin and died on 13th March 1910.

DREY, Agnes (*fl. c.* 1920–1940).

Painter of portraits and figure subjects. Lived at St. Ives in Cornwall next door to the painter Alfred Wallis.

DRUMMOND, Miss V. H. (Mrs. Swetenham) (born 1911).

Painter of London scenes in water-colour; author and illustrator of children's books. Born in London on 30th July 1911. Studied at St. Martin's School of Art. One-man shows held at the Chenil Gallery and Upper Grosvenor Gallery. Received the Kate Greenaway Award for the best illustrated children's book of the year 1957. Lives in St. John's Wood.

DU CANE, Miss Ella (*fl. c.* 1890–1930).

Painter in water-colour of landscapes, figures and buildings. Exhibited at the R.I. from 1893. An exhibition of her water-colours was held at the Fine Art Society 1910. Illustrated books, including *Egypt.*

DUCKETT, R. (*fl. c.* 1910–1915).

Painter in water-colour of portraits and figure subjects. Represented in an exhibition "Camden Town Group and Others" held at Brighton Art Gallery 1913–14.

*DUFFY, Patrick Vincent, R.H.A. (1832–1909).

Landscape painter. Born in Dublin. Studied art at the Royal Dublin Society from 1847, and exhibited at the R.H.A. from 1851. Elected A.R.H.A. 1860 and a full member the same year. From 1870 to his death he was keeper of the R.H.A. Died on 22nd November 1909.

DUNCAN, George Bernard (born 1904).

Painter in oil and water-colour of landscapes and genre. Born on 7th January 1904 in Auckland, New Zealand. Went to Australia, where he studied at Julian Ashton's Art School, and then came to London. He painted for seven years, from the age of 29, in England, France, Germany and Spain, and exhibited at the R.A., R.O.I., R.W.A., Leicester Gallery. Returned to Sydney.

DUTHIE, A. Spottiswoode (*fl. c.* 1890–1930).

Painter of portraits and genre. Exhibited at the R.B.A. from 1892. Represented in Glasgow Art Gallery, and lived in Glasgow also in London.

DYRING, Moya (1908–1967).

Cubist painter in water-colour. Worked in Melbourne, and is represented in Sydney Art Gallery. Died in London on 4th January 1967.

DYSON, William Henry (1883–1938).

Etcher, illustrator and cartoonist. Born at Ballarat, Australia. Educated in Melbourne. Contributed drawings to *Sydney Bulletin* and *Melbourne Herald.* Married the artist Ruby Lindsay 1909, and settled in England. His work appeared in *The Daily Herald* and other journals. Died on 21st January 1938.

E

EAGLE, Edward (died 1910).

Irish landscape painter and etcher. Exhibited at the R.H.A. Died in Dublin on 28th March 1910 aged 60.

EASTMAN, Frank Samuel (born 1878).

Painter in oil of portraits and genre; miniaturist. Born on 27th April 1878. Studied at Croydon School of Art and at the R.A. Schools. Exhibited at the R.A., including *The Prophecies* 1949. Lived in London for some years. His wife was also an artist.

ECKHARDT, Oscar, R.B.A. (1872–1904).

Oil painter. Born in Sunderland. Exhibited at the R.O.I., R.B.A. Lived at Hurlingham, London.

EDWARDS, Mary Stella (born 1898).

Water-colourist, designer and painter of architectural settings for dioramas, book illustrator and poet. Born in Hampstead on 31st July 1898. Studied art at Battersea Polytechnic, then at the Regent Street Polytechnic where she met her life long friend Judith Ackland. Exhibited at the R.I., R.B.A., N.E.A.C., S.W.A., Britain in Water-colours, and in the provinces. Specialised in painting buildings and interiors although she has also executed mountain and beach scenes. She shared a home with Judith Ackland for many years and they worked together on the dioramas and in their mountain and other painting journeys. She has done much book illustration and jacket-designing. Her published poems include the collections *Time and Chance* and *A Truce with Time.* Represented in the London Museum. Lives at Staines in Middlesex.

EDWARDS, V. Ash (*fl. c.* 1910–1915).

Water-colour painter, works including *Shadow Strength* and *Majesty.* Lived in Brighton, and exhibited at provincial galleries along the South Coast.

ELIAS, Miss Annette (died 1921).

Landscape painter. Exhibited at the leading London galleries from 1881, chiefly the R.A., R.I., R.B.A., R.O.I., New Gallery, also in Birmingham and the Walker Art Gallery, Liverpool. Lived in Kensington, and later at Niton, Isle of Wight. Died on 21st January 1921.

ELLIOT, Miss Dorothy M., S.W.E. (*fl. c.* 1915–1930).

Wood engraver, influenced by Iain Macnab. Exhibited with the S.W.E. from 1920.

ELLIOT, Edward (*fl. c.* 1875–1910).

Landscape painter in oil and water-colour. Exhibited at the leading London galleries from 1879, including the R.A., R.B.A., R.I. Lived at Wymondham and exhibited with the Woodpecker Art Club, Norwich.

ELLIS, C. Wynne (died 1915).

Genre painter in oil and water-colour. Exhibited at the leading London galleries from 1880, chiefly the R.A., R.I., R.B.A., New Gallery. Lived at Bishop's Stortford in Hertfordshire, and later in London. Died in January 1915.

ELLIS, Ralph Gordon (1885–1963).

Painter, especially known for his signs for public houses. Member of the Society of Sussex Painters for many years. Lived at Arundel, and died on 6th May 1963.

*ELWES, Simon Edmund Vincent Paul, R.A., R.P., N.S. (1902–1975).

Died on 6th August 1975. His son Dominic, also a painter, died in London on 5th September 1975 aged 44.

EMANUEL, Walter Lewis (died 1915).

Illustrator, contributing to *Punch.* Died on 4th August 1915 aged 46.

EMSLIE, John Philip (1839–1914).

Genre painter in oil and water-colour. Exhibited at the leading London galleries from 1869, chiefly the R.A., R.B.A., R.I., Grosvenor Gallery. Lived in London, and found some of his subjects in the metropolis.

ENFIELD, Miss Mary P., R.M.S. (*fl. c.* 1890–1925).

Miniature painter. Exhibited at the R.A. from 1892, also at the R.M.S. and Walker Art Gallery in Liverpool. Lived in Nottingham for many years.

ENGLEFIELD, Arthur (born 1855).

Genre painter in oil and water-colour; miniaturist.

Born in London. Exhibited at the R.A. from 1891, also at R.I. and in the provinces. Lived in St. Albans, Gloucester, and London.

*ENNESS, Augustus W., R.B.A. (1876–1948).
Landscape painter in oil. Born at Bocking, Essex. Studied art at the Slade School and the Académie Julian in Paris. Represented in public art galleries in England and abroad.

ERTZ, Mrs. Ethel Margaret Horsfall, S.W.A., W.I.A.C. (1871–1919).
Landscape painter and miniaturist. Born on 19th January 1871. Married the artist Edward Ertz 1900. Exhibited at the R.A. from 1901. Lived at Polperro in Cornwall, then at Yealmpton in South Devon, and later at Pulborough in Sussex. One of the founder members of the W.I.A.C., she died suddenly in London on 4th February 1919.

ESTCOURT, Miss K. B., R.M.S. (*fl. c.* 1935–1955).
Miniature painter. Exhibited at the R.A., R.M.S. Lived at Northwood in Middlesex.

EVELEIGH, Fanny (*fl. c.* 1910–1915).
Oil painter of portraits, figures and town scenes. Represented in the "Camden Town Group and Others" exhibition held Brighton Art Gallery 1913–14.

EVETTS, Leonard Charles, A.R.C.A.(Lond.) (born 1909).
Stained glass designer and landscape painter in water-colour. Born at Newport in Gwent on 12th January 1909. Studied art at the R.C.A. 1930–33. Exhibited at the R.A., Roland Browse and Delbanco in London, and held a one-man show at the Stone Gallery, Newcastle upon Tyne 1973. Represented in the Laing Art Gallery, Newcastle. Author of *Roman Lettering* and numerous papers on medieval stained glass and armorial art. Lives in Newcastle.

F

FAED, James (1821–1911).
Landscape and genre painter in oil. Born on 4th April 1821 at Burley Mill in Kirkcudbrightshire. Exhibited chiefly in Scotland.

FAGAN, Louis Alexander (1846–1903).
Etcher of architectural subjects, portraits and genre. Exhibited at the leading London galleries from 1872, including the R.A. He is known for his series of views of Naples and surrounding areas entitled *Souvenir of Southern Italy* 1873.

FAITHFULL, Mrs. Leila (born 1898).
Portrait painter. Exhibited at the R.A., R.S.A., R.B.A., R.O.I., N.E.A.C. Lived at East Grinstead in Sussex.

FALKNER, Miss Anne Louise (1862–1933).
Landscape painter. Born at Dorchester in Dorset. Exhibited at the R.B.A. from 1893. Lived for a time in Bedford.

FARMER, Miss Emily, R.I. (died 1905).
Genre painter in water-colour. Exhibited at the leading London galleries from 1847, chiefly the R.I. but also the R.A. Elected R.I. 1854. Lived at Portchester in Hampshire and died 8th May 1905.

FARQUHAR, Sir Robert Townsend (1841–1924).
Landscape painter. Born at Goldings on 26th September 1841. Exhibited at the leading London galleries from 1873, including the R.B.A. and Dudley Gallery, also at R.S.A. and Walker Art Gallery in Liverpool. Lived for a time at Grasmere and later in Brighton. Died on 30th June 1924.

*FARRELL, Frederick Arthur (1882–1935).
Died on 22nd April 1935.

FEARON, Percy Hutton (1874–1948).
Cartoonist. Born on 6th September 1874 at Shanghai, China. Studied at the Art Students' League in New York, and at Herkomer's School at Bushey. Contributed to *Evening News* from 1913. Lived in London and died 5th November 1948.

*FERRIER, George Straton, R.I., R.S.W., R.E. (1852–1912).
Although elected R.E. 1881, his membership was short-lived, ceasing the following year. Exhibited at the R.A.

FFOULKES, Charles John (1868–1947).
Artist, metalworker and museum curator. Born in London on 26th June 1868. Studied art in Paris under Carolus Duran. Exhibited at R.A., R.B.A., and Paris Salon. Curator of Imperial War Museum 1917–33. Lived in London and later in Oxford. Died on 22nd April 1947.

FIELD, Walter, A.R.W.S. (1837–1901).
Landscape painter in water-colour. Born on 1st January 1837. Exhibited at the leading London galleries from 1856, including the R.A., R.W.S., R.B.A. Lived in London and died in Hampstead on 23rd December 1901.

FILDES, Denis Quintin (born 1889).
Portrait painter in oil and water-colour. Born in London on 30th May 1889, son of Sir Luke Fildes, R.A. Served in the Royal Navy for 18 years and retired 1922. Exhibited at the R.A. and Walker Art Gallery in Liverpool. He painted Queen Elizabeth II for the Grenadier Guards and received other important commissions.

FINBERG, Alexander Joseph (1866–1939).
Painter and art critic. Born in London. Studied art at Lambeth School of Art and in Paris. Exhibited at the R.I. 1888, also at the N.E.A.C. and Paris Salon. He was a well known writer on art subjects, and contributed illustrations to *The Graphic* and *Illustrated London News*. Lived in London and died 15th March 1939.

FINLAY, Miss Anne, A.S.W.A. (*fl. c.* 1935–1955).
Painter in oil of figure subjects. Exhibited at the R.A., R.S.A., N.E.A.C. Lived at Richmond in Surrey.

*FINN, Herbert John (1861–1942)
Some genre paintings.

*FINN, Leonard Richard (born 1891).
Erratum. Correct name as listed above.

FINN, Michael (born 1921).
Oil painter. Born in Surrey. Studied at Kingston-on-Thames School of Art, and at the R.C.A. Principal

of Falmouth School of Art, Cornwall from 1958. Represented in Plymouth Art Gallery by *Greek Landscape* 1962.

FISHER, Alexander, F.R.B.S. (*fl. c.* 1880–1925).

Craftsman and sculptor. Studied art at the R.C.A., winning a scholarship 1881, and went to Rome 1882, Paris 1884. Exhibited at the leading London galleries from 1886, including the R.A. Received a gold and silver medal at the Barcelona International Exhibition 1907. Represented in several public collections at home and abroad. Lived at Theydon Bois in Essex and in Kensington.

*FISHER, Stefani Melton, R.I., R.O.I., P.S. (1894–1963).

Painter of portraits in oil, pastel and water-colour.

FISHWICK, Mrs. Patricia (born 1929).

Oil painter. Studied at Liverpool College of Art 1946–49, and Exeter College of Art 1949–50. Exhibited at the R.W.A., in Liverpool and in Cornwall. Represented in Plymouth Art Gallery by *Almond Blossom.* Member of the Newlyn Society of Artists. Married the artist Clifford Fishwick.

FITCHEW, Edward H. (died 1934).

Water-colour painter. Lived in Bromley for some years. Died on 6th November 1934 aged 82.

FITTON, Mrs. Margaret Mary Elizabeth (*fl.* from *c.* 1920).

Oil painter, lithographer and sculptor. Born at Kilburn, London, *née* Cook. Studied painting and illustration at the Central School of Arts and Crafts, where she met her husband James Fitton, R.A. Exhibited at the R.A., N.E.A.C., L.G., and Senefelder Club. She has lived at Dulwich for many years.

FITZPATRICK, Thomas (1860–1912).

Illustrator. Born at Cork in Ireland on 27th March 1860. In Dublin he contributed to *The Weekly Freeman* and *The Weekly National Press,* and also illustrated books. He launched *The Leprechaun*—a cartoon monthly—in 1905. Died on 16th July 1912.

FLECHER, B. J., R.B.A. (*fl.* 1910–1930).

Leicester artist, who later lived at Edgbaston.

*FLETCHER, William Teulon Blandford (1858–1936).

Landscape and genre painter. Born in Hampstead, London on 8th November 1858. Studied art at the R.C.A. 1875–79, and until 1882 under Verlat in Antwerp. Painted in Brittany, where he met and was influenced by Bastien-Lepage. An early member of the Newlyn School, he was a lifelong friend of Stanhope Forbes. Represented in public collections in Ipswich, Worcester, Nottingham, and Brisbane.

FLINT, Savile Lumley William (*fl. c.* 1880–1910).

Landscape and genre painter. Exhibited at the leading London galleries from 1880, including the R.A., R.B.A., Grosvenor and New Galleries. Contributed works to the Woodpecker Art Club in Norwich, and Norwich Art Circle.

FOOT, Miss Rita (1886–1965).

Miniature painter. Born in Dublin on 8th October 1886. Lived in Dublin and exhibited at the R.H.A.

FORBES, John Colin, R.Canadian A. (1846–1925).

Portrait painter. Born on 3rd January 1846 in Toronto, Canada. Studied art at the R.A. Schools and at South Kensington. Member of Ontario Society of Artists 1872, and R.Canadian A. 1880. Painted portraits of King Edward VII, Queen Alexandra, and W. E. Gladstone. Lived in New York for a time, but died in Toronto in October 1925.

FORBES-ROBERTSON, Miss Frances (Mrs. Harrod) (1866–1956).

Painter and novelist. Born on 15th December 1866. Studied art at the Slade School and under Frank Brangwyn. Lived in London and died on 23rd May 1956.

FORD, William Bishop (1832–1922).

Miniature painter. Born in London on 3rd May 1832. Studied art under William Essex. Exhibited at the R.A., R.B.A. His works included a number of portraits.

FORSTER, F. L. M., N.E.A.C. (*fl. c.* 1895–1905).

London artist who exhibited with and became a member of the N.E.A.C.

*FOTHERGILL, George Algernon (1868–1945).

Exhibited at the Walker Art Gallery in Liverpool.

FOWLER, Walter, R.B.A. (*fl. c.* 1885–1915).

Landscape painter in oil and water-colour. Exhibited at the leading London galleries from 1887, including the R.A., R.B.A., R.I., R.O.I. Lived at Kew in Surrey.

FOX, Charles James (*fl. c.* 1880–1910).

Landscape and genre painter in oil and watercolour. Exhibited at the R.A., R.I., R.B.A.

*FRANCIS, Eric Carwardine, R.W.A. (1887–1976).

Died at West Monkton on 26th January 1976.

FRASER, Peter (Born 1888).

Illustrator. Born on 6th November 1888 in the Shetland Islands. Studied art in London at the Central School of Arts and Crafts. Contributed to *Punch, Tatler,* and other magazines.

FREEMAN, Miss M. Winefride (*fl. c.* 1885–1920).

Genre painter in water-colour. Exhibited at the leading London galleries from 1886, including the R.A., R.I., New Gallery, and also at Birmingham and the Walker Art Gallery in Liverpool. Lived at Bushey in Hertfordshire.

FRENCH, Miss Annie (1872–1965).

Illustrator. Exhibited at the R.A., R.I., R.W.A., G.I. Works include *The Picture Book, The Daisy Chain,* and *The Garland.* In 1914 she became the second wife of the artist George Woolliscroft Rhead. Lived in Glasgow and later in London.

FRENCH, Percy (1854–1920).

Landscape and genre painter; poet. Engaged in civil engineering for six years, he then edited a Dublin journal for two years. Took up art, and painted some scenes in Ireland. Exhibited at the Dudley Gallery, and lived in London for some years. Died on 24th January 1920.

FRIPP, Mrs. Susan Beatrice (died 1913).

London artist, who does not appear to have exhibited on many occasions. Died on 7th July 1913.

FRIPP, Thomas William (1864–1931).

Landscape painter. Born in London, son of artist George Arthur Fripp. Studied art under his father, then at St. John's Wood Schools of Art, R.A. Schools, also in France and Italy. Exhibited in London 1890–92, chiefly at the R.B.A. In 1893 he settled in British Columbia, Canada, and took up farming. Following an accident he returned to painting and became founder and first president of British Columbia Society of Fine Arts. Died in Vancouver.

FRY, Douglas (1872–1911).

Painter in oil of animal subjects. Born in Ipswich. Studied art in London and at the Académie Julian in Paris. At the age of 27 he settled in Australia, and is represented in Sydney Art Gallery.

FRY, Miss Edith M. (*fl.* 1920s).

Painter in oil and water-colour of still life and landscapes. Represented in the "Australian Artists" exhibition held at Brighton Art Gallery 1925. Lived in London for a time.

FRY, James William (born 1910).

Painter in oil, water-colour and pastel. Born in London on 23rd December 1910. Studied at Watford School of Art. Since 1955 he has had his own gallery at Corfe Castle, Dorset, where his work has been on show.

FUCHS, Emil, R.B.A. (1866–1929).

Sculptor of portraits and figure subjects; medallist. Born in Vienna. Studied at the Royal Academy of Berlin, receiving the German Travelling Scholarship for Sculpture 1891, and in Italy. Lived in London for some years, and designed postage stamps during the reign of King Edward VII. Died on 13th January 1929.

FULLARD, George, A.R.A., A.R.C.A.(Lond.) (1923–1973).

Sculptor of figure subjects. Born on 15th September 1923. Studied at Sheffield College of Art, and the R.C.A. Exhibited at the R.A., and in North America. Held several one-man shows, and is represented in a number of public collections. Lived in London, and

was Head of Department of Sculpture at Chelsea School of Art from 1963. Died on 25th December 1973.

FULLER, Miss Violet (born 1920).

Landscape painter in water-colour and oil. Born at Tottenham. North London on 26th July 1920. Studied at Hornsey School of Art under Russell Reeve 1937–40. Exhibited at the R.A., R.I., W.I.A.C. One-man shows held at the Woodstock Gallery (several from 1958), East London Gallery, Ditchling Gallery, Loggia Gallery and elsewhere. Founder member of the Free Painters and Sculptors 1953, elected a fellow 1959, also a member of the Hesketh Hubbard Art Society. Represented in the collections of the London Boroughs of Harringay and Enfield. She is especially interested in the landscape of Essex and Sussex, and lives in Tottenham.

FULLER-MAITLAND, Alexander (1851–1920).

Landscape painter in oil. Exhibited at the R.A., in the provinces and at the Paris Salon. Principal works include *The English Channel, Mountain Torrent, Among the Western Isles* and *Sand Dunes—Pas de Calais*. Painted in England, Wales, Scotland, France and Holland. Lived at Hove, and following his death a memorial exhibition was held at Brighton Art Gallery 1921.

*****FULLWOOD, Albert Henry** (1863–1930).

Died in Sydney, Australia on 1st October 1930.

FURSE, J. H. Monsell, F.R.B.S., I.S. (*fl. c.* 1890–1910).

Sculptor. Exhibited at the R.A. from 1891, also at I.S., New Gallery, G.I., and Walker Art Gallery in Liverpool. Lived in London and later near Salisbury.

*****FYFE, Miss Elizabeth** (1899–1933).

Died on 24th August 1933.

G

GAIR, Miss Frances, A.S.W.A. (*fl. c.* 1935–1960).

Landscape painter in tempera. Her childhood was spent travelling with her parents, who were well known for their Marionette Theatre. Studied art at Chelsea Polytechnic and in Budapest. Exhibited at the R.A., R.W.A., N.E.A.C., S.W.A. Lived for a time at Spaxton in Somerset.

GALSWORTHY, G. C. (*fl. c.* 1890–1925).

Landscape and genre painter in oil. Exhibited at the R.B.A. from 1893. Lived at Steyning in Sussex, and painted Downland subjects.

GALTON, Miss Ada (*fl. c.* 1900–1930).

Water-colour painter and etcher of architectual subjects and interiors. Studied art at the Slade School under Brown and Tonks. Learned etching from William Monk and was influenced by Alfred Rich in her water-colour painting. Lived in London.

GAMBIER-PARRY, Major Ernest (1853–1936).

Soldier and artist. Educated at Eton College. Became a soldier, served in the Sudan where he was seriously injured 1885. Exhibited his work at the R.A. and other leading galleries. Lived in Gloucester and died 15th April 1936.

GARDINER, Clive (1891–1960).

Oil painter. Exhibited at the R.A., R.P. Lived in London, and is represented in the Tate Gallery.

GARRIDO, Leandro Ramon, R.O.I. (1869–1909).

Oil painter of genre, landscapes and portraits. Born near Bayonne, France, his father a Spaniard and his mother English. His father, Fernando Garrido, was an artist and politician exiled from Spain. Studied art at South Kensington and the École des Beaux Arts in Paris. Exhibited at the R.O.I., G.I., and the Walker Art Gallery in Liverpool. Represented in Glasgow and Liverpool Art Galleries. He loved painting in France, and received many honours in that country. All his life he was dogged by ill health, and died at an early age at Grasse.

*****GARSTIN, Miss Alethea,** R.W.A. (born 1894).

Painter of figure subjects. Born at Penzance, Cornwall. She has held several one-man shows in London, and is represented in Plymouth Art Gallery by *Village Band*. Member of Penwith Society of Artists and Newlyn Society of Artists.

*****GARSTIN, Norman,** R.B.C. (1847–1926).

Genre painter. Born on 28th August 1847 in County Limerick, Ireland. He always wished to paint but this idea was not welcomed by his guardian who thought he should go into the church (like his grandfather) or into the army (like his father). Eventually he was sent to the engineering college in County Cork but could not cope with the mathematics. This also contributed to his subsequent failure in a London architect's office. He then went to the diamond fields of Kimberley, South Africa, where he met the Rhodes brothers. Later went to Cape Town, and wrote leading articles for the *Cape Times*. Returned to Ireland, and after losing an eye in a hunting accident took up art. Studied painting in Antwerp under Verlat, but soon went to Paris, where he studied under Carolus Duran for three years. Shortly after his marriage he settled at Newlyn, and it was in Cornwall that his three children were born; Crosbie in 1887, Denis in 1890, and Alethea in 1894. Denis was killed in Russia 1917, and Crosbie drowned whilst saving another's life c. 1930. Their mother died aged 93 in 1945. Garstin took painting classes abroad, one of the first artists to do so, and visited Brittany, Normandy and Holland. Before his marriage he had also painted extensively in Morocco. Alethea tells of an amusing encounter between her father and George Bernard Shaw—N.G. "Mr. Shaw, I think we have several things in common". G.B.S. (in a bored tone) "Oh, is that so?" N.G. "Yes, you see we are fellow countrymen, and we are both great admirers of Bernard Shaw". At this up went Shaw's beard, and with head back he roared with laughter. Garstin died at Penzance.

GATTER, F., F.R.B.S. (*fl. c.* 1910–1935).
London sculptor. Exhibited at the R.A. and Walker Art Gallery in Liverpool. Lived in Chelsea and later in Putney.

GAUDIER-BRZESKA, Henri, L.G. (1891–1915).
Sculptor and draughtsman of figure and animal subjects. Henri Gaudier was born on 4th October 1891 at Saint Jean de Braye, near Orléans in France. In 1906 he came to England on a scholarship, and three years later visited Holland, Belgium and Germany. Met Sophie Brzeska 1910, and the following year began to use the name of Gaudier-Brzeska. Settled in London, and took a job as a clerk in the city. Founder member of the London Group 1913, he was also associated with the Vorticists. Represented in the Tate Gallery. Joined the French Army and was killed at Neuville Saint Vaast on 5th June 1915.

*****GAWTHORN, Henry George,** S.G.A. (died 1941).
Designer of some railway posters. Died on 11th September 1941 aged 62.

GEDDES, Miss Wilhelmina Margaret (1888–1955).
Water-colour painter and stained glass designer. Born in Ireland, she studied art in Belfast and Dublin. Exhibited in London, Ireland, and on the continent. Lived in London for a time.

GEORGES, Charles E., R.B.A. (died 1971).
Genre painter. Exhibited at the R.A. from 1893. Lived at Worcester and later for many years at Weymouth. He was an early member of the R.B.A., and lived to a great age.

*****GERE, Miss Margaret,** N.E.A.C. (1878–1965).
Lived at Painswick in Gloucestershire for many years, and is represented in the Tate Gallery.

GERRARD, Prof. Alfred Horace (born 1899).
Sculptor. Born on 7th May 1899. Studied at Manchester School of Art and at the Slade School. He was Head of the Department of Sculpture at the Slade School 1925–48, and Professor of Sculpture there

1948–68. Served as a war artist 1944–45. Lives at Groombridge in Sussex.

GIARDELLI, Arthur (born 1911).
Painter in water-colour of landscapes and still life; maker of abstract relief constructions in wood, also utilising brass, silver, ivory, sacking and paper. Born in London on 11th April 1911. Educated at Hertford College, Oxford, received an M.A. degree, and studied art in that city at the Ruskin School. Exhibited in London at the Redfern, Gimpel Fils, Grosvenor and Qantas Galleries, also in Paris, Amsterdam and America. He has held several one-man shows, chiefly in Wales. Elected a member of the 56 Group Wales in 1956, and has been chairman since 1958. Lives at Pembroke in Dyfed.

*****GIBB, Stanley Watson** (1898–1973).
Died on 25th August 1973.

GIBSON, Jessie (*fl.* 1920s).
Oil painter of interiors and landscapes. Represented in the "Australian Artists" exhibition held at Brighton Art Gallery 1925.

GILBERT, Charles Web (1867–1925).
Sculptor of portraits and figure subjects. Born on 18th March 1867 near Talbot in Victoria, Australia. Studied art at the National Gallery School, Melbourne 1888. Settled in London 1914, and exhibited at the R.A. 1915–18. Returned to Australia 1920, and died at Melbourne on 30th October 1925.

GILBERT, Walter (1871–1946).
Sculptor and metalworker. Born at Rugby on 12th August 1871. Studied at Birmingham School of Art, at the R.C.A., and on the continent. Travelled widely abroad, and lived at Birmingham.

GILL, Harry Pelling, A.R.C.A.(Lond.) (1855–1916).
Landscape painter in water-colour. Born at Brighton. Studied at Brighton School of Art and the R.C.A. Settled in Adelaide, Australia 1881, where he was appointed first principal of the South Australian School of Arts. He occupied that position for 33 years and was also curator of the South Australia Art Gallery. In 1916 he embarked on a trip to Europe to buy works for the gallery, but died on board ship in the Mediterranean.

GILLBE, Edwin (1917–1974).
Painter in oil, gouache and water-colour. Born in London on 19th April 1917. Studied at St. Martin's School of Art and Camberwell School of Art. Exhibited at the R.A., R.W.S., R.B.A., R.O.I. Lived in London and died in April 1974.

GILLIGAN, Miss Barbara Helen (Mrs. Carr) (born 1913).
Oil painter of landscapes and portraits, Born in London on 3rd February 1913. Studied at the East Anglian School of Art, the Central School of Arts and Crafts, and at the Slade School. Held a one-man show in London at the Leicester Galleries 1948. She has worked in East Anglia for many years.

GIMSON, Ernest (1864–1919).
Architect, furniture designer and craftsman. Born in Leicester. In 1881 he was articled to a Leicester architect, stayed three years, and also studied at Leicester School of Art. Met William Morris 1884, and came under his influence. He learned the craft of chair making

and in partnership with several others, including W. R. Lethaby, founded the firm Kenton and Company. In 1924 a book, by Lethaby and others, *Ernest Gimson, His Life and Work,* was published. He died August 1919.

GLAZEBROOK, Miss Ellen L. (*fl. c.* 1900–1920).
Painter of figure subjects. Studied art for three years at the Slade School under Legros, and later under Norman Garstin. Exhibited at Walker's Gallery in London.

GLEADOWE, Richard Morier Yorke (1888–1944).
Painter, sculptor and craftsman. Born in London on 6th May 1888. Studied art at the Slade School 1912. He spent some years in the Civil Service, but in 1928 was appointed Slade Professor of Fine Art at Oxford, a post he held until 1933. Exhibited at the R.A., N.E.A.C., Paris International 1937, and at the World's Fair in New York 1939. Lived for a time in Cornwall and died on 9th October 1944.

GLEN, Graham (*fl. c.* 1900–1925).
Painter of portraits and genre. Exhibited chiefly in Scotland, and was chairman of the S.S.A. In the early 1920s he was recorded at a Chelsea address.

GLENDENING, Alfred Augustus (*fl.* 1861–1903).
Landscape painter in oil, often featuring cattle grazing beside a river. Began as a railway clerk, but then took up art, exhibiting at the R.A. from 1865. His paintings were often shown at the R.B.A. Worked extensively in Sussex, Scotland and Wales.

GLOVER, Mrs. Sybil Mullen, R.I., R.S.M.A., R.W.A. (*fl. from c.* 1940).
Water-colour painter of architectural subjects, especially those with some bearing on naval tradition. Born in Cheshire, *née* Jeffrey. Studied art privately and at St. Martin's School of Art. Exhibited at the R.A., R.S.A., R.I., R.O.I., R.S.W. and abroad. Elected R.I. 1962, R.S.M.A. 1964, R.W.A. 1971. Represented in several public collections, and received gold and silver medals at the Paris Salon. Lives at Stoke, near Plymouth.

GLYNN, John (*fl. c.* 1895–1930).
Landscape painter in water-colour. Exhibited at the R.I., and on many occasions at the Walker Art Gallery in Liverpool. His wife Maud was also a painter. Lived at Hoylake and Caldy in Cheshire, and later at Crowborough in Sussex.

*GODDEN, Charles Edward Victor R.W.A. (1901–1976).
Died at Bath on 10th March 1976.

*GODMAN, Mrs. Jessie, A.R.E. (*fl. c.* 1890–1940).
Born at Dowlais, South Wales. Influenced by Frank Short.

GODSON, John Barclay, A.R.C.A.(Lond.) (born 1882).
Oil painter and etcher. Born at Newcastle-on-Tyne. Studied at Leeds School of Art and at the R.C.A. Exhibited at the R.A. In 1911 he went to Auckland, New Zealand, and a few years later removed to Sydney. Founder member of the Australian Painter-Etchers' Society 1921.

GOMMON, David (born 1912).
Painter in oil of portraits and figure subjects. Represented in the "Wertheim Collection" exhibition held at Worthing Art Gallery 1958.

GOODCHILD, John Charles (born 1898).
Water-colourist, lithographer and etcher of landscapes, figures and architectural subjects. Born in London on 30th March 1898. Settled in Australia at age of 15, and studied at the South Australian School of Arts and Crafts. Removed to London, and served with the A.I.F. in World War I. Studied at the Central School of Arts and Crafts, and in 1921 returned to Adelaide. Visited Europe 1926–29, and exhibited at the R.A. He was Principal of the South Australian School of Arts 1941–45.

GOODMAN, Miss A. Maude (Mrs. Scanes) (died 1938).
Genre painter. Studied art at South Kensington. Exhibited at the leading London galleries from 1874, including the R.A., R.B.A., R.I. Lived in Kensington and in Southport. Died on 23rd March 1938.

GOODMAN, Robert Gwelo, P.S. (died 1939).
Landscape painter in oil, water-colour and pastel. Born in Cape Colony, South Africa. In 1896 he went to Paris and studied art at the Académie Julian. Settled in London 1898. Exhibited at the R.A. from 1899, also in the provinces and at the Paris Salon. Painted subjects in England, Italy, India and South Africa. Returned to South Africa later in life, and died on 11th March 1939.

GOODRICH, W. R. E. (born *c.* 1886).
Figure painter. Studied at Sheffield School of Art and in Italy. Lived at Crooksmoor, Sheffield.

GORDON, Alexander Esmé, R.S.A. (born 1910).
Architect and water-colour painter. Born in Edinburgh on 12th September 1910. Studied at Edinburgh College of Art 1928–34. Elected R.S.A. 1967, and lives in Edinburgh.

*GORDON-BELL, Miss Joan Ophelia (1915–1975).
Died in Kendal on 12th August 1975.

GRANT, Carleton, R.B.A. (*fl. c.* 1890–1902).
Landscape and genre painter in water-colour. Exhibited at the R.A. from 1892, also at the R.B.A. Lived at Shanklin, Isle of Wight.

GRAVENEY, William C. (born 1904).
Woodcarver and sculptor. Born in London on 29th January 1904. Studied art at the R.C.A. Exhibited at the R.A. from 1926, and is represented in the Tate Gallery.

GREEN, Mrs. Florence (*née* Page) (*fl. c.* 1915–1940).
Etcher of architectural subjects. Exhibited at the R.A. Works include *The Belfry, Dinan; Christchurch Gate, Canterbury* and *Alfriston, near Brighton.* Wife of the artist Reginald H. Green. Lived at Bassett, Southampton and West Byfleet, Surrey.

*GREENHAM, Robert Duckworth R.B.A., R.O.I. (1906–1976).
Died in Southampton on 13th March 1976.

*GREENUP, Joseph, R.I. (died *c.* 1946).
Studied art at the R.A. Schools *c.* 1913–16.

GREG, Margaret (*fl.* 1920s).
Wood engraver, influenced by Iain Macnab. Member of the English Wood Engraving Society.

GRESLEY, James Stephen (1829–1908).
Painter in oil and water-colour of landscapes and portraits. Born at Sandiacre in Derbyshire. Exhibited at the leading London galleries from 1866, including

the R.B.A., R.I. Father of the artist Frank Gresley. Died at Wakefield.

GREY, James, R.H.A. (died 1905).

Genre painter in oil. Exhibited at the R.A., R.H.A. Elected R.H.A. 1875. Lived in Dublin.

GRIBBLE, Mrs. Eleanor Mary, P.S. (1883–1960).

Painter and book illustrator. Born in London on 9th September 1883, *née* Woolmer. Studied at Ipswich School of Art and the R.C.A. Exhibited at the P.S., S.W.A. and abroad. Lived at Ipswich for many years, and was a member of Ipswich Art Club.

GRICE, Mrs. W. Sarah (born 1913).

Painter in oil and water-colour. Born at Bootle, near Millom in Cumberland. Studied art in France.

GRIER, Sir Edmund Wyly, P.R.Canadian A. (1862–1957).

Landscape, portrait, and genre painter. Born at Melbourne, Australia. Settled in Canada 1876. Studied art at the Slade School under Legros, and at the Académie Julian in Paris. Exhibited at the R.A. 1886–96, and the Paris Salon. Returned to Canada 1894. Elected A.R.Canadian A. 1893, full member 1894, and President 1930–39. Knighted 1935. Lived at Preston, Ontario and died 7th December 1957.

GRIFFITH, Frank (*fl. c.* 1908–1914).

Landscape painter in water-colour, chiefly of French subjects. Lived in Paris and exhibited at the London Salon.

GRIFFITHS, John (1838–1918).

Painter of figure subjects in oil and water-colour. Exhibited at the leading London galleries from 1869, chiefly the R.A. He painted Indian subjects and is represented in the Tate Gallery.

GRIMALDI, Miss Argenta Louisa (born 1884).

Miniature painter. Lived at Bournemouth and exhibited at the R.A. in the early years of the century.

GRINEAU, Bryan De (1883–1957).

Painter and etcher of motor racing and aeroplane subjects, landscapes, portraits and architecture. Born at Stroud Green, London, on 11th May 1883, son of Charles Grineau, a caricaturist. Although christened Charles William Grineau, he worked at first under the name John Bryan, his father being known as Alfred Bryan. In 1908 he married Florence Gertrude Ratcliff (1882–1975) who painted flower subjects in oil under the name Phyllis de Grineau. Joined the Royal Field Artillery in France 1916 as a 2nd Lieut. and sent home sketches of the war for publication by the *Illustrated London News* and *Illustrated War News*. After the war he travelled extensively in order to recover from shell shock, and studied art in London, Paris, Antwerp and New York under Joseph Pennell. Visited every country in Central and South America, Australia, and many countries in Europe and Asia. Exhibitions of his work were held in South America, and he became well known in that continent. He came to prominence in this country for his paintings of motor racing scenes and aeroplanes, many of which were reproduced. Contributed regularly to *The Sketch, The Motor,*

Bystander and *Illustrated London News.* In 1939 an exhibition of his work was held at Walker's Galleries, London, entitled "The Caribbean Islands". During World War II he acted as a special war artist and executed drawings of the war at sea, on the ground, and in the air. Died in London on 18th May 1957.

GRIXONI, Count M., P.S. (*fl. c.* 1915–1945).

Landscape and figure painter in water-colour and pastel. Exhibited at the R.I., R.P., P.S. Lived in London for some Years.

GRÖNE, Ferdinand E., R.B.A. (*c.* 1845–1920).

Landscape painter. Born at Minden in Germany. Trained as a teacher and matriculated at London University 1867, but instead took up art. Studied in Paris at the Académie Julian under Bouguereau and Tony Fleury. Exhibited at the R.A., R.I., R.B.A., and was a member of Ipswich Art Club. Lived at Colchester for many years.

GRÖNVOLD, Henrik (1850–1940).

Bird artist and naturalist. Born in Denmark, he came to London in 1892. He found employment at the British Museum (Natural History) and within a short time was engaged on plates for scientific journals. In 1895 he took part in an expedition to the Salvages Islands and on his return was in much demand as an illustrator of natural history books. His work was shown to great advantage in Eliot Howard's monograph *The British Warblers* published between 1907 and 1915.

GROOME, William H. C., R.B.A. (*fl. c.* 1880–1910).

Landscape painter. Exhibited at the leading London galleries from 1881, including the R.A., R.B.A., R.I. Lived at Ealing for some years.

GROSVENOR, Mrs. Stella Athalie (*fl.* from *c.* 1935).

Portrait sculptor in bronze, clay, wood and stone; oil painter. Born at Beaconsfield in Buckinghamshire, *née* Henderson. Studied art at the Slade School under Schwabe and received her diploma 1937. Exhibited at the R.A., R.B.A., and held a one-man show at Foyles Art Gallery 1968. Member of the Society of Portrait Sculptors. Lives in London.

GROVES, Robert E. (*fl. c.* 1885–1920).

Painter in water-colour of landscapes, coastal scenes and figure subjects. Exhibited at the leading London galleries from 1887, including the R.A., R.I., R.B.A., also at the G.I. Painted some scenes of Morocco. Lived at St. Albans for many years.

GUNNING, Robert Bell (*c.* 1830 – *d.* 1907).

Painter in oil of portraits and landscapes. Born at Dumfries. Painted subjects in Cumberland and taught art at Whitehaven for more than forty years. Died at Dumfries, but interred at Whitehaven.

GUNTHER, Miss Edith (*fl. c.* 1900–1920).

Portrait and figure painter in oil. Pupil of Orpen. Exhibited with the N.E.A.C. and at the Goupil Gallery.

GUNTHORPE, Henry, F.R.B.S. (*fl. c.* 1884–1912).

Sculptor. Exhibited at the R.A. from 1884, he was one of the early members of the R.B.S. Also exhibited at the Walker Art Gallery in Liverpool. Lived in London.

H

HAGREEN, Philip, S.W.E. (*fl. c.* 1915–1965).
Wood engraver of landscapes and figure subjects. Founder member of the S.W.E. 1920. Lived in Sussex.

HAIG, Miss E. Cotton, R.M.S. (*fl. c.* 1890–1920).
Genre and miniature painter. Exhibited at the R.A. from 1891, also at the R.S.A., R.M.S., G.I., and Walker Art Gallery in Liverpool. Lived in Edinburgh.

HAILSTONE, Harold William (born 1897).
Illustrator, cartoonist, landscape painter in water-colour and oil. Born in London on 14th July 1897. Studied at Goldsmiths College School of Art 1919–22. Visited the U.S.A. and Canada 1928, and on his return in 1931 contributed to *Punch, Illustrated London News,* and other periodicals. During World War II served as an official war artist, and travelled extensively in all theatres of the war. Later continued as an illustrator and press cartoonist for *The Daily Mirror.* Represented in the Imperial War Museum. Lives at Hadlow in Kent.

HALHED, Miss Harriet (died 1933).
Portrait and genre painter. Pupil of Deschamps. Exhibited at the leading London galleries from 1890, including the R.A., R.B.A., and also at the G.I. and Walker Art Gallery in Liverpool. Lived in London and later at Wokingham. Died on 5th February 1933.

HALL, Miss Jessie, W.I.A.C., S.W.A. (died 1915).
Landscape and genre painter. Exhibited at the leading London galleries from 1893, including the R.B.A., R.I. Died as a result of a cycle accident.

HALL, Kenneth (1913–1947).
Painter in oil of town scenes, including London and Paris. Represented in the "Wertheim Collection" exhibition held at Worthing Art Gallery 1958.

HALL, Miss Mildred M. (*fl. c.* 1900–1930).
Landscape painter. Exhibited at the M.A.F.A., and Walker Art Gallery in Liverpool. Lived at Newport in Shropshire.

*HAMILTON, Cuthbert (1885–1959).
Vorticist painter, represented in the Tate Gallery by *Reconstruction.* Much of his work from the period 1913–20 appears to have been lost.

*HAMILTON, Miss Letitia Marion, A.R.H.A. (1879–1964).
Sister of Eva H. Hamilton, an artist.

HAMILTON, Mrs. Olivia, R.M.S. (*fl. c.* 1904–1922).
Miniature painter. Exhibited at the R.M.S. and lived at St. John's Wood, London.

HAMILTON-WOOD, Sydney Ernest (born 1918).
Painter in oil and water-colour; sculptor in copper tube and wire. Born in Norwich on 26th September 1918. Studied at Norwich School of Art 1936–40 and the Central School of Art 1946–47. Exhibited in London and East Anglia. Lives in Norwich, and lectures and writes on art.

*HAMMOND, Miss Gertrude E. Demain, R.I. (1862–1952).
Received sketch club prizes at the R.A. Schools 1886, 1887, and for decorative design 1889.

*HANDLEY-READ, Edward Harry, R.B.A. (1869–1935).
Died in Salisbury.

*HANKEY, Mrs. Mabel, R.M.S. (died 1943).
Born at Bath, daughter of Henry Eddington Hobson, an artist, and undoubtedly related to Cecil James Hobson, R.I. Exhibited at the R.A. from 1889, also at the Walker Art Gallery, Liverpool. First wife of the artist William Lee-Hankey.

HANSON, Albert J., R.B.A. (1866–1914).
Landscape painter in oil and water-colour. Born in Sydney, Australia. Maintained an art school in Dunedin, New Zealand 1889, and in 1892 came to England. Exhibited at the R.A., R.B.A., R.I. Represented in several public collections in Australia and New Zealand.

HARDY, Miss Mary (1841–1915).
Dorset artist, sister of the poet and novelist Thomas Hardy (1840–1928), who also produced some water-colours.

HARGRAVE, John Gordon (born 1894).
Illustrator, cartoonist and writer. Illustrated *Gulliver's Travels* and *The Rose and the Ring* at the age of 15. When 17 he became the chief cartoonist to the *London Evening Times.* Publications include *Young Winkle* 1925, *The Imitation Man* 1931, and *Words Win Wars* 1940. Lives in Hampstead.

HARLAND, Miss Mary (born 1863).
Miniature painter. Exhibited at the R.A. Lived in London during the early years of this century.

HARMSWORTH, Lord Cecil Desmond Bernard (born 1903).
Painter of portraits and figure subjects. Educated at Eton College and Christ Church, Oxford. Studied art in Paris at the Académie Julian. Exhibited in London, Paris, and North America. Succeeded his father 1948, and lives at Egham in Surrey.

*HARPER, Edward Samuel, P.R.B.S.A. (1854–1941).
Exhibited at the R.A. from 1885. Presumably father of the artist Edward Steel Harper.

HARRIES, Leslie S.G. (*fl. c.* 1930–1960).
Painter of flower subjects and landscapes. Studied art at the St. Martin's School of Art. Exhibited at the R.I. Some of his works were reproduced as prints.

*HARRINGTON, Charles (1865–1943).
Although a Sussex artist, he painted extensively in the Midlands and the Eastern Counties.

*HARRIS, Edwin Lawson James, B.W.S. (1891–1961).
Painted many water-colours of Sussex subjects, some of which are regretably not standing the test of time as the quality of the paper employed was of an insufficient standard.

HARRISON, Charles (died 1943).
Cartoonist. Began as an actor, but turned to art, contributing drawings to *Pall Mall Gazette, Daily Mail, Evening News* and to *Punch* from 1895. Lived in London and died December 1943.

*HARRISON, Miss Sarah Cecilia (1863–1941).
Irish portrait painter.

HARVEY, George, A.R.Canadian A. (1846–1910).

Landscape painter. Born at Torquay. Settled in Halifax, Canada about 1882, and elected A.R.Canadian A. 1883. Principal of Victoria School of Art and Design 1887–94.

HARVEY, Mrs. Gertrude (*née* Bodinnar) (*fl. c.* 1900–1950).

Landscape painter. Exhibited at the Leicester Galleries, London, including such water-colours as *A Fishing Village* and *Spring*, and also at the R.A. Married the artist Harold Harvey, and lived at Newlyn in Cornwall.

HARVEY-BLOOM, J., R.B.A. (*fl. c.* 1930–1960).

Painter and wood engraver of landscapes and architectural subjects. Exhibited in London, and the provincial galleries.

HASTIE, Edward (1876–1947).

Architect and water-colour painter. Studied under Ernest Newton R.A. 1896. Lived in London and at Thames Ditton. Died on 23rd March 1947.

'HATCH, Miss Ethel C., S.W.A. (1870–1975).

A friend of Lewis Carroll. One-man show held in London at Walker's Galleries 1925. Painted in Italy for some years. Died on 3rd April 1975.

HAVELL, Alfred C. (died 1928).

Painter of figures and sporting subjects. Exhibited at the R.A. from 1878. Died on 13th March 1928 aged 73.

HAVERS, Val, R.O.I. (*fl. c.* 1895–1912).

Oil painter. Exhibited at the R.A., R.O.I., G.I., Walker Art Gallery in Liverpool, and in Manchester. Lived in London and at Gomshall in Surrey.

HAVILAND, Frank O. A., R.M.S. (died 1912).

Painter of miniatures, figure subjects and portraits. Exhibited at the R.A. from 1894. Lived in London, and died March 1912 aged 42.

HAWTHORNE, Elwin (born 1905).

Painter in oil of urban scenes, especially London. Born in London. Worked for three years in Sickert's studio. A member of the East London Group, he was influenced by John Cooper. Represented in several public collections. Lived in London at Bow.

HAY, George, R.S.A. (died 1912).

Edinburgh artist, who exhibited chiefly at the R.S.A. Died on 1st September 1912 aged 81.

HAYLETT, Malcolm John (born 1923).

Portrait painter in oil and pastel. Born on 25th September 1923 in Montreal, Canada. Studied at Southend College of Art and St. Martin's School of Art. Lives in Cornwall and has exhibited with St. Ives Society of Artists.

HEALY, Michael (1873–1941).

Painter in water-colour of figure subjects and town scenes; stained glass artist. Lived in Ireland.

HEATH, Miss Isobel Atterbury (Mrs. Prati) (born 1908).

Painter in water-colour and oil of portraits and landscapes; poet. Born on 29th December 1908 at Hull, Yorkshire. Studied art at the Académie Colarossi in Paris, Torquay Art School, Kingston-on-Thames Art School, and St. Ives School of Painting. Exhibited at the R.S.A., R.W.S., R.S.W., R.I., R.O.I., and in the provinces. War artist 1940–45. One-man shows held in London at the Woodstock Gallery 1950, and later

at Clarges Gallery. Member of St. Ives Society of Artists 1938, Penwith Society of Artists 1949, R.W.S. Art Club 1955. Organised and sponsored a show at the R.W.S. galleries 1962, entitled "The Cornish Experiment", featuring the work of unknown artists working in Cornwall. Lives at St. Ives.

HEATH, Lionel, R.M.S. (*fl. c.* 1890–1915).

Miniature painter. Exhibited at the R.A. from 1892, also at the R.M.S. and Walker Art Gallery in Liverpool. Lived in London.

HEATON, Clement (*fl. c.* 1890–1935).

Water-colour painter and stained glass designer. Exhibited at the R.A. from 1892. Wrote articles on the history of architectural decoration.

HECTOR, W. Cunningham (*fl. c.* 1900–1915).

Painter in oil of landscapes and genre. Lived in Glasgow and exhibited with the Glasgow Society of Artists.

HELCKÉ, Arthur, R.B.A. (*fl. c.* 1865–1907).

Painter in oil and water-colour of marines and coastal scenes. Exhibited at the leading London galleries from 1865, chiefly the R.A., R.B.A., R.I., Grosvenor and New Galleries, also in Liverpool and Birmingham. Lived in Guernsey and later at East Molesey in Surrey.

'HELPS, Francis A., R.B.A. (*fl. c.* 1907–1950).

Studied art at the Slade School, where he received a scholarship of £35 for a period of two years.

'HENDERSON, Miss Elsie M. (Baroness de Coudenhove) (1880–1967).

Exhibited at the Leicester Galleries 1924, and at that time lived in London.

HENDERSON, James (1871–1951).

Painter in oil of portraits and landscapes; lithographer. Born in Glasgow. Studied at Glasgow School of Art, visited the Canadian Prairies 1910, and settled at Saskatchewan 1916. Died in Canada at Regina.

'HENDERSON, John (1860–1924).

Born in Glasgow, son of Joseph Henderson, R.S.W. and brother of Joseph Morris Henderson, R.S.A. Studied art under Greenlees, he was later director of Glasgow School of Art. Died at Busby, near Glasgow.

HENDRY, George E. (died 1915).

London artist, who exhibited at the R.A. and at Birmingham. Served in the Rifle Brigade in World War I and was killed in Flanders.

HENGHES, Heinz (1906–1975).

Sculptor. Born in Germany. His *Madonna and Child* was on show in Battersea Park during the Festival of Britain 1951. Died in France on 20th December 1975 aged 69.

'HENRIQUES, Miss Ethel Quixano, W.I.A.C. (1868–1936).

Painted some scenes in Gloucestershire.

'HENRY, Mrs. Grace (died 1952).

Painter of landscapes, genre and portraits. Wife of Paul Henry, R.H.A.

'HEPWORTH, Dame Barbara (1903–1975).

Died tragically in a fire at her home at St. Ives on 20th May 1975.

HEREFORD, Edgar (*fl. c.* 1884–1930).

Water-colour painter of landscapes and figure subjects. Exhibited at the R.I. from 1884, also at the Dudley Gallery and the N.E.A.C. Lived in Kensington.

HERKOMER, Herman G., R.O.I., R.P. (*fl. c.* 1883–1920).

Portrait painter. Exhibited at the leading London galleries from 1883, including the R.A., R.B.A., R.O.I., also at the Walker Art Gallery in Liverpool and in Birmingham. Lived in London.

*HESS, Miss Florence W.I.A.C. (1891–1974).

Represented in an exhibition held in 1974 at Michael Parkin Fine Art Ltd, entitled 'Mark Senior of Leeds and Runswick Bay, and a few friends".

HETHERINGTON, Ivystan, R.B.A. (died 1917).

Landscape painter in oil. Studied at Heatherley's School of Art and at the R.A. Schools. Exhibited at the R.A. from 1877, also at R.B.A., Grosvenor and New Galleries. Works include *The Silent Marsh, The Manor Garden,* and *An Old Fashioned Summer.* Lived at St. John's Wood, London, and died 23rd December 1917.

*HEWARD, Howard Cornelius (1881–1973).

Represented in "A View of the Downs" exhibition at Worthing Art Gallery 1975.

HEWITT, Henry George, R.B.A. (*fl. c.* 1884–1908).

Landscape painter. Exhibited at the leading London galleries from 1884, including the R.A., R.B.A., R.I. Lived in London and later at Hereford.

HEYWOOD, Brookes (died 1926).

Lancashire artist, member of the M.A.F.A. Died July 1926.

*HEYWORTH, Alfred, R.W.S., R.B.A., N.E.A.C., A.R.C.A.(Lond.) (1926–1976).

Portrait and figure painter. Died January 1976.

HICKS, George Elgar (1824–1914).

Genre and portrait painter in oil. Studied art at the R.A. Schools. Exhibited at the leading London galleries from 1847, chiefly at the R.A., and at the Walker Art Gallery in Liverpool. Lived at Odiham in Hampshire.

HICKS, Jerry, R.W.A. (born 1927).

Painter of contemporary genre in oil and pastel. Born in London on 12th June 1927. Studied art at the Slade School under Coldstream and Freud. Exhibited at the R.A., and in the provinces. Elected R.W.A. 1965. Joint shows held with his wife Anne, who also trained at the Slade, at Bristol and Cardiff. Lives in Bristol.

HIDER, Frank (died 1933).

Landscape painter in oil and water-colour. Born at Dulwich, London. Studied at Heatherley's Art School. Travelled extensively in Britain, and in his early years painted in Italy and Belgium. Belonged to the Burnham School of Painters, a colony of artists who settled at Burnham Beeches in Buckinghamshire. Produced a great quantity of work, but exhibited infrequently. Died at age 72.

HILL, J. Alan (born 1903).

Preston artist. Exhibited at R.A., R.W.A.

HILL, J. Hollyer (died 1952).

Mezzotint engraver of plates after French painters of the 18th century. Exhibited at the R.A. Lived in Hertfordshire.

*HILL, Nathaniel, R.H.A. (*fl.* 1886–c. 1935).

Elected A.R.H.A. 1892, R.H.A. 1894.

*HILL, Rowland Henry (1873–1952).

Died on 6th September 1952.

HILL, Vincent, F.R.B.S. (*fl.* 1910–1915).

Sculptor. Lived in London and exhibited with the N.E.A.C.

*HILTON, Roger (1911–1975).

Died in Cornwall on 23rd February 1975.

HINCHLIFF, Woodbine K., A.R.E. (*fl. c.* 1890–1930).

Etcher. Elected A.R.E. 1895. Lived at Headley in Hampshire.

HINDLEY, Godfrey C., R.O.I. (*fl. c.* 1876–1914).

Painter in oil and water-colour, including some flower subjects. Exhibited at the leading London galleries from 1876, chiefly the R.A., R.B.A., R.O.I., R.I. Lived in London.

HISLOP, Walter B. (died 1915).

Landscape painter. Studied at Edinburgh College of Art. Exhibited at the S.S.A. and other galleries in Scotland. Served in World War I as a 2nd Lieut. in the 5th Battalion of Royal Scots and was killed at Gallipoli.

HODGSON, George B. (died 1921).

Nottingham artist, including some still life subjects. Exhibited at the R.A. from 1886, also at the Walker Art Gallery in Liverpool. Lived for a short time at Grange-over-Sands in Lancashire. Died November 1921.

*HOGARTH, Miss Mary Henrietta Uppleby (died 1935).

Died at the age of 73.

HOLDER, C. Vincent (died 1916).

London artist, who exhibited at the R.A. Served in World War I in the 2nd Batt. London Regiment and was killed at Delville Wood.

HOLFORD, Lord William Graham, R.A. (1907–1975).

Architect. Born in South Africa 22nd March 1907. Studied at the University of Liverpool, and in 1930 received the Rome Scholarship in Architecture. In 1933, the year of his marriage to Marjorie Brooks, a painter, he became senior lecturer at Liverpool and in 1936 was made Lever Professor of Civic Design. Professor of Town Planning, University College, London 1948–70, he was involved in many of London's public planning projects. Knighted 1953, and created life peer 1965. Received the Gold Medal of the Town Planning Institute 1961, and the Royal Gold Medal for Architecture 1963. President of the R.I.B.A. Died in London on 17th October 1975.

HOLGATE, T. W., R.B.A. (*fl. c.* 1895–1910).

London artist, who exhibited at the R.A., R.B.A., and Walker Art Gallery in Liverpool.

HOLLAND, Alwyn H. (born 1861).

Little known Sheffield artist.

HOLME, Charles Geoffrey, R.B.A. (1887–1954).

Illustrator, caricaturist, wood carver and maker of marionettes. Born at Hampstead on 20th April 1887, son of the founder of *The Studio*. Educated at Abbotsholme. Elected R.B.A. prior to the Great War, and at that time lived at Church Crookham, Fleet, Hampshire—the village has a war memorial designed by him. A close friend of the artist George Sheringham, he was also an admirer of Japanese works of art. Edited *The Studio* from 1919, and in 1932 sponsored the foundation of "The Studio Publications Inc"., New York. In 1930 he organised the British Section of the Exhibition of

Decorative and Industrial Art at Monza. Member of the first Government Committee of Industrial Design and of the Council of the Royal Society of Arts for several years. Died in Mexico on 12th December 1954.

HOLMES, Sir Richard Rivington (1835–1911).

Landscape painter. Born in London on 16th November 1835. Exhibited at the leading London galleries from 1872, including the R.A., Grosvenor and New Galleries. Died in London on 22nd March 1911.

HOLROYD, Newman, R.B.A. (*fl. c.* 1905–1915).

Isle of Wight artist, who exhibited at the R.A. and R.B.A. Lived at Ryde and later at Brading.

*HONE, Nathaniel, R.H.A. (1831–1917).

Landscape painter in oil and water-colour. Began as an engineer, and did not take up painting until the age of 22. Studied art in Paris under Yvon and Couture. Settled at Barbizon, and spent 20 years there, working with such artists as Millet and Harpignies. Returned to Ireland in the mid 1870s, and elected A.R.H.A. 1879, R.H.A. 1880. Appointed Professor of Painting at the R.H.A. 1894. Represented extensively in the National Gallery of Ireland.

HONEYMAN, John, R.S.A. (1831–1914).

Architect. Born in Glasgow on 11th August 1831. Exhibited at the R.A. from 1879. Elected A.R.S.A. 1892, R.S.A. 1895. Lived at Bridge of Allan, Stirlingshire and died 8th January 1914.

HOOPER, W. H. (died 1912).

Wood engraver. Died February 1912 aged 77.

HOPE-PINKER, Henry Richard, F.R.B.S. (*fl. c.* 1875–1925).

Sculptor. Exhibited at the R.A. from 1875, also at the Walker Art Gallery in Liverpool. Lived in Kensington for some years.

HOPKINS, Mrs. Frances Ann (*née* Beechey) (1838–1919).

Landscape and genre painter. Lived in Canada 1858–70 as the wife of the secretary to the Governor of Hudson's Bay Company, and painted subjects in that country. Exhibited at the R.A. from 1860, also at the R.B.A. and Walker Art Gallery in Liverpool. Resided in London during the early years of this century, and died on 5th March 1919.

HOPPÉ, Ernest O. (born 1878).

Photographer, water-colourist, poster designer and textile designer. Born in Munich, and studied art in that city, also in Vienna and Paris. Lived in London for many years, and exhibited both in this country and on the continent.

HORNIMAN, Emslie John (1863–1932).

Painter of landscapes, genre and portraits. Studied art at the Slade School and in Antwerp. Exhibited at the leading London galleries from 1889. Visited many countries, painting as he went, including China, Japan, America, Egypt and India. Lived in London and died 11th July 1932.

HORTON, Ronald, A.R.C.A.(Lond.) (born 1902).

Painter in oil and water-colour, mainly landscapes and still life, some marine and genre subjects. Born in Brighton on 31st October 1902, younger brother of the artist Percy Frederick Horton. Studied at Brighton School of Art under Louis Ginnett and Lawrence Preston 1919–23, at St. Martin's School of Art 1925–

26, and after winning a scholarship, at the R.C.A. under Rothenstein and Schwabe 1926–29. Worked in the studio of Rex Whistler and assisted him on large mural paintings in private houses in Mayfair 1929–31. Taught art at Parmiter's School, Bethnal Green, London 1932–45, and at Hackney School of Art 1932–39. Exhibited at the R.A., N.E.A.C., and in Sussex galleries. Lived in London from 1924, returning to Brighton when appointed to the staff of Brighton College of Art 1945–66.

HORTON, William T. (1864–1919).

Architect, writer and illustrator. Born in Brussels. Studied architecture in Brighton and at the R.A. Schools 1887. Exhibited at the R.A. from 1890. In his later years worked chiefly as an illustrator.

HOUCHEN, Harry, A.R.C.A.(Lond.) (died 1915).

Landscape painter and etcher; worker in wood, metal, enamel, leather, gesso, and jewellery. His father came from Norfolk, and his mother was a grand niece of John Constable, R.A. In 1903 he took up an appointment as an art teacher in County Cork, and in 1913 became Headmaster of Derry School of Art. Exhibited at the R.H.A. and elsewhere in Ireland.

HOUGHTON, Will (died 1916).

Member of the London Sketch Club. Killed in the Great War.

HOWE, Charles Kingsley (died 1916).

London artist. Exhibited with the I.S., and taught at Goldsmiths' College School of Art. Joined the Artists Rifles September 1914, and later served as a 2nd Lieut. in the Berkshire Regiment. Killed on 1st July 1916 aged 27.

HOWLETT, Miss Rosa (*fl. c.* 1895–1930).

Genre painter in oil. Exhibited at the Woodpecker Art Club, Norwich, and with Norwich Art Circle. Works include *Home from School, Etaples Peasant Girl,* and *Life of Toil.* During the 1920s lived at Bushey in Hertfordshire.

HOYLE, Walter, A.R.C.A.(Lond.) (born 1922).

Painter and printmaker. Born in Lancashire. Studied at Beckenham School of Art, and at the R.C.A., where he received his diploma 1946. Exhibited at the R.A., in the provinces, and abroad. One-man shows held in Paris 1952, Leicester Galleries in London 1952, and at the Kettle Yard Gallery, Cambridge University 1972. During the past few years he has not painted a great deal, as his main interest is in producing artists prints. Lives at Braintree in Essex.

HUDSON, Miss Anna Hope, L.G. (*fl. c.* 1910–1950).

Painter of urban scenes and figures in oil. Exhibited with the N.E.A.C., L.G., and was represented in the "Camden Town Group and Others" exhibition at Brighton Art Gallery 1913–14. Lived in London and in Hove.

HUDSON, Miss Gwynedd M. (*fl. c.* 1910–1935).

Painter of figure subjects in water-colour, illustrator and poster designer. Studied at Brighton School of Art. Lived in Hove and exhibited at the Arts and Crafts Society and Sussex Womens' Art Club.

HUDSON, Paul Grenville (1876–1960).

London born artist, who worked at Carlisle.

*HUGHES, Mrs. Eleanor, R.I. (1882–1959).

Wife of the artist Robert Morson Hughes. Represented in Newlyn Art Gallery.

*HUGHES, John, R.H.A. (*fl. c.* 1890–1945).
Elected A.R.H.A. 1895, R.H.A. 1900.

HUISH, Marcus Bourne (died 1921).
Water-colour painter. Exhibited at the R.A. Editor of the *Art Journal* and founder of *The Year's Art* 1880. Died on 4th May 1921.

HULK, Abraham, Jnr. (*fl. c.* 1876–1920).
Landscape painter in oil. Exhibited at the R.A., R.B.A. His father, known as Abraham Hulk, Senior also painted landscapes. Lived in Surrey.

HULK, F. W. L. (*fl. c.* 1895–1908).
Landscape and marine painter. Lived at Shere, near Guildford, in Surrey.

HUTCHESON, Walter (died 1910).
Scottish artist, who lived at Crosshill. Exhibited at the G.I., and at Manchester. Died on 23rd August 1910.

*HUTCHISON, George Jackson (1896–1918).
Son of the artist Robert Gemmell Hutchison. Exhibited at the R.S.A. Killed in the Great War.

HUTTON, John, S.M.P. (born 1906).
Mural painter; glass engraver. Born in New Zealand on 8th October 1906. Self-taught in art. Exhibited at the S.M.P., L.G., and in the provinces. One-man shows held at Stafford Gallery, London, 1937 and the Commonwealth Art Gallery, London 1969. Chairman of the S.M.P. 1966–68. Represented in the Victoria and Albert Museum and the Royal Museum of Scotland. Lives in London.

HYAMS, William (*fl. c.* 1930–1960).
Landscape painter. Born in Portsmouth, but spent his childhood in Guernsey. Studied at Brighton School of Art. Spent some years at sea which gave him the opportunity to paint marine subjects. Exhibited at the R.A., R.I., in the provinces, and abroad. Represented in Brighton and Hove Art Galleries. Painted many Sussex scenes, and was Chairman of Brighton Arts Club 1947.

HYDE, William (died 1925).
Painter and illustrator. Exhibited at the R.A. from 1889. Lived at Shere in Surrey, and died September 1925.

I

I'ANSON, Charles, R.O.I. (*fl. c.* 1875–1908).
Landscape painter in oil and water-colour. Exhibited at the leading London galleries from 1875, including the R.A., R.B.A., R.O.I., R.I., and in Manchester and the Walker Art Gallery in Liverpool. Lived in London.

*IHLEE, Rudolph, N.E.A.C. (*fl. c.* 1910–1955).
Studied art at the Slade School. In 1909 he received second prize in figure painting and first prize in figure drawing, and the following year won the Melvill Nettleship prize for figure composition.

ILLINGWORTH, Leslie Gilbert (born 1902).
Cartoonist. Born on 2nd September 1902 at Barry, Glamorgan. Studied art at the R.C.A., and the Slade School. He has contributed many illustrations to *Punch*, the first in 1927. Lives at Robertsbridge in East Sussex.

IMAGE, Selwyn, A.W.G. (1849–1930).
Stained glass designer. Studied art at the Slade School, Oxford, under Ruskin. Designed windows for a number of churches, and also for the Pavilion of the Prince of Wales at the Paris Exhibition. Elected Master of the A.W.G. 1900. Slade Professor of Fine Art at Oxford 1910–16. Lived in London and died 21st August 1930.

INCE, Miss A.C. (born 1868).
Flower painter. Born in Cardiff on 4th February 1868. Studied at Westminster School of Art under Fred Brown. She then spent some time at the Slade School, but gave up painting for nearly thirty years owing to very poor eyesight. Encouraged by Adrian Bury she took up art again seriously in 1933, and exhibited in London and the provinces.

INGALL, J. Spence (died 1936).
Painter, chiefly in water-colour, of landscapes and genre. Born in Barnsley. In his youth he produced designs, especially for fabrics, and then went to Paris to study painting at the Académie Julian. He undertook a considerable amount of decorative work for journal such as "Magazine of Art". Painted on the continent, and also spent some time in Tangiers around the turn of the century for he had a small house there which he used in the winters. During the summers he would tend to paint at Runswick Bay, Yorkshire, and was a founder member of the Staithes Group. He numbered among his friends the Ambassadors of many nations, arising from his stay in Tangiers. On one occasion he narrowly escaped being kidnapped at the same time as M. Perdicaris, the French Ambassador, who was held as a political hostage by Moorish brigands. Whilst in Morocco, he met Kaiser Wilhelm II, and was commissioned to paint scenes for him in Assam. In his early years he exhibited at the R.A., but later only submitted work on rare occasions. Died on 28th May 1936, aged 86.

INGLIS, J. Johnston, R.H.A. (*fl. c.* 1885–1912).
Irish landscape painter. Exhibited at the R.A. from 1890, and elected A.R.H.A. 1892, also a full member the same year. Ceased to be a member 1912. Lived at Donnybrook, Dublin.

INLANDER, Henry (born 1925).
Landscape painter. Born in Vienna on 14th January 1925. Settled in England 1938, becoming a British subject 1947. Studied at St. Martin's School of Art 1939–41, Camberwell School of Art 1945–46, and Slade School 1949–52. Exhibited at the R.A., L.G., in the provinces, also on the continent and in America. Represented in the Tate Gallery. Lives in London.

IRVINE, Miss Henrietta (died *c.* 1924).
Painter in oil of figure subjects. Worked in Australia and Europe. Represented posthumously in the "Australian Artists" exhibition held at Brighton Art Gallery 1925. Lived for some years at Malvern in the State of Victoria.

J

JACKSON, Alexander Young, R.Canadian A. (1882–1974).
Landscape painter in oil. Born on 3rd October 1882 at Montreal, Canada. Studied art in Montreal and later in Chicago. Visited Europe, and studied at the Académie Julian in Paris under Laurens 1907. Returned to Montreal 1910, and three years later settled in Toronto. Served as a private in France during the Great War and then as an official war artist. Elected R.Canadian A. 1919, and a member of the Group of Seven 1920. Author of *A Painter's Country* 1958. Died on 5th April 1974.

JACKSON, B. Leslie, A.R.C.A.(Lond.) (born 1866).
Painter and art teacher. Studied at Stoke and Halifax Schools of Art, and then at the R.C.A. Lived at Newark-on-Trent, and was Principal of Newark Science and Art School.

JACOBS, John E., R.B.A. (*c.* 1860–1925).
Landscape painter. Born in London. Exhibited at the leading London galleries from 1878, chiefly the R.B.A., and at the R.A. from 1884. Visited Australia 1887. Returned to London, and lived at Mill Hill for some years.

JAGGER, Miss Edith (*c.* 1890–1955).
Artist sister of David and Charles Sargeant Jagger. Lived in London and later in Sheffield.

JAMES, Gilbert (*fl. c.* 1910–1950).
Illustrator. Born in Liverpool. Settled in London and contributed to various magazines. Illustrated the *Rubaiyat of Omar Khayyam*, and was especially interested in Eastern subjects. Lived in London.

JAMIESON, Mrs. Biddy (*née* Macdonald) (*fl. c.* 1910–1950).
Oil painter of landscapes, genre and coastal scenes. Married the painter Alexander Jamieson, and lived at West Turville, near Aylesbury.

*JAMIESON, F. E. (born *c.* 1895).
Scots painter of lochs. He used to bring his work to Eastbourne for sale, and achieved some success. A short, thick set man, he often appeared in plus fours. His works are often inscribed with the title on the stretcher.

JARVIS, Hubert (born 1882).
Landscape painter in oil. Born in Devon. Studied art in London under George Sheringham. Settled in Australia 1915, he became a member of the Royal Queensland Art Society.

*JARVIS, William Howard, R.S.M.A. (1903–1964).
Founder member of the Society of Aviation Artists. Born on 6th February 1903. Painted marine and aviation subjects. Died at Rake in Hampshire on 28th June 1964.

JAY, Miss Cecil (Mrs. Hitchcock), R.M.S. (*fl. c.* 1900–1915).
Miniature painter. Exhibited at the R.A., R.M.S., and Walker Art Gallery in Liverpool. Lived at Bushey in Hertfordshire and later in Paris.

JEFFCOCK, Robert Salisbury, A.R.M.S. (*fl. c.* 1905–1915).
Miniature painter. Exhibited at the R.M.S. and Walker Art Gallery in Liverpool. Lived at Harpenden in Hertfordshire.

JELLETT, Miss Mainie (1896–1943).
Abstract painter. Studied art in Dublin, then in London under Sickert, and later in Paris under André L'Hôte. In 1921, in conjunction with Evie Hone, she studied cubism under Albert Gleizes, and returned to him for further training over a number of years. Exhibited at the R.H.A., and other galleries in Ireland. Assisted in the foundation of the Irish Exhibition of Living Art 1943. Lived in Dublin.

*JENKIN, Mrs. Margaret M. (*née* Giles), R.W.A. (1868–1949).
Sculptor in stone and marble of portraits and figure subjects. Studied art for eight years at the R.C.A. under Lanteri. Exhibited at the R.A., in the provinces, and the Paris Salon. Visited France, Italy, Greece and India. Lived in Bristol and died 31st March 1949.

JENNINGS, Walter Robin (born 1927).
Painter in oil of landscapes, portraits and horses. Born in Staffordshire on 11th March 1927. Chiefly self taught in art. Exhibited at the R.I., N.E.A.C., R.B.S.A., R.W.A., R.Cam.A., U.A., and in France, Germany, America. Lives near Kidderminster in Worcestershire.

JEWELLS, Mary (*fl. c.* 1915–1965).
Primitive painter in oil. Began painting in 1915 at the suggestion of Cedric Morris, and later received help from Christopher Wood, who had also encouraged Alfred Wallis. A Cornish artist, she is represented in Plymouth Art Gallery by *The Black Ship*.

JOHN, Alain (died 1943).
Sculptor and modeller. Received encouragement from Eric Gill, who had admired his *Christ in Blessing*. Served during World War II as a navigator sergeant and was killed in action on 23rd December 1943.

JOHN, C. R. d'Oyly (born 1906).
Landscape painter in oil, especially of mediterranean subjects. Born in South Africa. Visited India, Ceylon and Japan in the employ of the Asiatic Petroleum Company, and served in the Tanganyika Police Force 1930–34. Fought in World War II, substaining serious injuries, and took up painting during his convalescence. His works have often been reproduced as prints.

*JOHNS, Edwin Thomas (1862–1947).
Landscape painter; architect. Born at Ipswich. Studied at Ipswich School of Art. Exhibited at the R.A. Member of Ipswich Art Club from 1897.

JOHNSTONE, Miss Dorothy (born 1892).
Painter in oil of figure subjects. Daughter of George W. Johnstone, R.S.A. Studied art in Paris and Florence. In 1914 she began teaching at Edinburgh College of Art. Exhibited at the R.A., R.S.A., R.P., G.I. Married the artist D. M. Sutherland 1924. Lived in Edinburgh and later at Cults in Aberdeenshire.

JOHNSTONE, Henry James (1835–1907).

Painter in oil and water-colour of landscapes and genre. Born in Birmingham. Settled in Melbourne, Australia 1853, and founded a photographic business. Lived in America 1873–80, and then returned to London. Exhibited at the leading London galleries from 1884, chiefly the R.A., R.B.A. Died in London.

JONES, Miss Barbara (Mrs. Barry), A.R.C.A.(Lond.) (*fl.* from *c.* 1940).

Landscape painter in oil and water-colour; murals in oil, tempera, acrylic, mosaic. Born in London. Studied art at the R.C.A. Exhibited with the S.M.P., being Chairman of the Society at one time, and is represented in the Victoria and Albert Museum also several provincial galleries. Author of *Design for Death*

1963, *The Unsophisticated Arts* 1951, *Follies and Grottoes* 1974. Lives in London.

JONLEIGH, Leonie, R.B.A. (died 1974).

Landscape painter in oil. She received no art school training, but studied privately under Carel Weight. Exhibited at the R.A., R.S.A., R.B.A., L.G., and in the provinces. Elected R.B.A. 1957. She had her studio and an art gallery near Guildford in Surrey.

JOWETT, Ellen (born 1874).

Portrait mezzotint engraver. Born at Brighouse, Yorkshire in March 1874. Studied engraving under Joseph Pratt, and later at the Slade School and the R.C.A. under Frank Short. Exhibited at the R.A. Many of her engravings were after painters of the late 18th and early 19th centuries.

K

*KAPP, Edmond Xavier (born 1890).

Since 1960 his work has been exclusively abstract. Represented in the National Gallery Exhibition 1945, and a big retrospective held at Whitechapel Art Gallery 1961. Some 240 of his drawings were acquired by the Barber Institute of Fine Art, Birmingham 1969.

KAUFFER, Edward McKnight (died 1954).

Poster designer. Born at Great Falls, Montana, U.S.A. Studied art at night school, while working as a scene painter in a theatre. Then spent six months at the Art Institute of Chicago, a similar period in Munich, and two years training in Paris. Settled in London 1914. Exhibited with the L.G., and at the Ashmolean Museum, Oxford 1926. He illustrated several books. A retrospective exhibition of his posters was held at New York Museum of Modern Art 1937. Lived in London for many years and died on 22nd October 1954.

KAVANAGH, Joseph Malachy, R.H.A. (1856–1918).

Painter of landscapes, marines, and architectural subjects. Studied art in Antwerp. Exhibited at the R.A. from 1886. Elected A.R.H.A. 1889, R.H.A. 1892. Lived in Dublin.

KEATES, John Gareth, L.A.A. (born 1915).

Painter in oil and gouache. Born at Birkenhead on 18th January 1915. Studied at Liverpool College of Art 1933–38, and after the war at the Central School of Art. Exhibited in London, the provinces, and abroad. One-man shows held in Bolton and Southport. A member of the Free Painters and Sculptors, he is represented in several public collections. Lives at Birkdale in Lancashire.

KELLY, Mrs. Annie Elizabeth (died 1946).

Portrait painter. Born in New Zealand, *née* Abbott. Studied art in New Zealand at Canterbury College of Art. Exhibited at the R.A., R.S.A., R.P., R.W.A., R.O.I., R.Cam.A., and at the Paris Salon where she received a silver medal 1934. Lived at Christchurch, New Zealand, and is represented in several of that country's public collections. Died 4th October 1946.

KENDERDINE, Augustus (1870–1947).

Landscape and portrait painter. Born in Manchester. Studied at Manchester School of Art and in Paris at

the Académie Julian. Settled in Canada 1907, beginning as a rancher at Saskatchewan. Director of Fine Art, University of Saskatchewan from 1935. Died at Saskatoon.

*KENNEDY, Cedric John (1898–1968).

Died on 11th March 1968.

KERSHAW, J. Franklin, A.R.C.A.(Lond.) (died 1917).

Member of Oldham Society of Artists, and student of the R.C.A. Killed in action on 14th October 1917.

KEULEMANS, John Gerard (1842–1912).

Painter and illustrator of bird subjects. Born in Rotterdam. At age 18 he found employment at the Leyden Museum, where he worked for two years, and subsequently visited Africa and many European countries. In 1869 he settled in England, painting for the Zoological Society of London and the *Ibis*. His paintings are to be found in the London Zoo Library and the Natural History Museum. Lived at Southend-on-Sea.

KINGSTON, Miss Gertrude Angela Mary (Mrs. Silver) (died 1937).

Mural painter; actress. Born in London. Studied art in Paris under Carolus Duran. Lived in London, and died 7th November 1937.

KINSELLA, E. P. (died 1936).

Cartoonist and poster designer. Died on 8th May 1936.

KIPLING, J. Lockwood (died 1911).

Illustrator. Spent 28 years in India, where he was architectural sculptor at Bombay School of Art, and later Principal of Mayo School of Industrial Art, Lahore. Illustrated several books by son Rudyard Kipling (1865–1936). Died at Tisbury, Wiltshire aged 74 years.

*KIRK, Eve (1900–1969).

Lived in London, and exhibited with the N.E.A.C.

KIRKPATRICK, Joseph (born 1872–*c.* 1930).

Genre and landscape painter; aquatinter. Born in Liverpool. Studied at Liverpool School of Art under John Finnie, and in Paris at the Académie Julian. Exhibited at the R.A., and in the provinces. Lived in London, and at Arundel in Sussex.

KIRKSHAW, Frederick (died 1913).

Lancaster water-colour painter.

*KITSON, Robert Hawthorn, R.B.A. (died 1947).
Exhibited mainly in the 1920s.

KNIGHT, Charles, Snr. (1865–1948).
Landscape painter in water-colour. Born at Slinfold, near Horsham, Sussex. Worked widely in Sussex, North Wales and Somerset. Member of Brighton Arts Club, and is represented in Brighton Art Gallery. Father of the artist Charles Knight, R.W.S. Died in May 1948, and a memorial exhibition held at Brighton Art Gallery 1949.

KNOX, Miss Madeline (1890–1975).
Painter and needleworker. Met Sickert 1909, and studied etching under him. Assisted Sickert in his teaching activities, and later married Arthur Clifton, proprietor of the Carfax Gallery. Lived in London, and died 5th February 1975 aged 84.

KOE, Laurence (1868–1913).
Portrait painter and sculptor. Studied at Brighton School of Art, then at St. John's Wood School of Art, and at the R.A. Schools from 1889 having been admitted as a sculptor. Received the Landseer Prize, and gained distinctions in painting, sculpture and drawing. Took a studio in London, and began to accept portrait commissions. Exhibited at the R.A. from 1891, and obtained a gold medal at the Paris Salon 1897. Died on 8th January 1913 aged 44. A memorial exhibition was held at Brighton Art Gallery 1913.

KOSSOFF, Leon, L.G. (born 1926).
Landscape and figure painter in oil. Born in London on 7th December 1926. Studied at St. Martin's School of Art 1948–53, during the evenings under Bomberg at the Borough Polytechnic 1950–52, and at the R.C.A. 1953–56. Represented in the Tate Gallery, and elected L.G. 1962.

L

LACEY, Mrs. Enid H., W.I.A.C. (*fl. c.* 1925–1955).
Wood engraver of figure subjects. Exhibited at the R.P., W.I.A.C., and lived in London.

*LAING, Frank James, A.R.E. (1862–1907).
Exhibited at the R.A. from 1893.

*LAMB, Charles Vincent, R.H.A. (1893–1964).
Represented in Belfast Art Gallery, and other public collections in Ireland.

LAMOND, W. B. (died 1924).
Dundee artist, who exhibited at R.S.A., G.I. Died 3rd December 1924 aged 67.

LANGDALE, Miss Stella (*fl. c.* 1910–1930).
Aquatinter and book illustrator. Lived in Brighton.

LANGLEY, William (*fl. c.* 1880–1920).
Landscape painter in oil. Worked under the influence of Joseph Thors. Painted in South-East England.

LASCELLES, Frank (died 1934).
Sculptor. Died 23rd May 1934 aged 58.

LATCHFORD, Miss Alice, R.M.S. (*fl. c.* 1905–1925).
Miniature painter. Lived in London, and exhibited at R.M.S.

*LAUDER, Charles James, R.S.W., G.I. (1841–1920).
Exhibited at the R.B.A. from 1890. Died in Glasgow.

LAURENCE, Sydney M., R.B.A. (*fl. c.* 1890–1902).
Landscape painter. Exhibited a scene of Venice at the R.B.A. 1890. Lived at St. Ives in Cornwall.

*LAW, David, R.B.A., R.E. (1831–1901).
Born in Edinburgh on 25th April 1831. Died in Worthing 29th December 1901.

*LAWRENCE, Alfred Kingsley, R.A., R.P. (1893–1975).
Died in Kensington on 5th April 1975.

*LAWSON, John (1868–'1909).
Born in Glasgow. Exhibited at the R.S.A., G.I., and in Manchester. Died at Carmunnock on 9th August 1909.

LEADER, B. Eastlake (died 1916).
Landscape painter. Son of B. W. Leader, R.A., and Mary Eastlake, his parents having married in 1877. Served in World War I as a 2nd Lieut. in the Royal West Surrey Regiment.

LE FANU, Brinsley (born 1854).
Illustrator and landscape painter. Born in Dublin. Studied art at the Royal Dublin Society and the R.H.A. Schools. Later settled in London, and received further training at Heatherley's Art School. Exhibited at the R.A. from 1881, also at the R.B.A., R.I., in the provinces, and at the Paris Salon. Contributed to magazines such as *The Sketch* and *Vanity Fair*, also illustrated books. He is recorded at a London address in 1922.

LEGGATT, Miss Rowley (*fl. c.* 1910–1925).
Painter in oil of genre and interiors. Exhibited with the N.E.A.C. Lived at Fittleworth in West Sussex.

LEIGH, Phillipa (born 1913).
Painter of landscapes and coastal scenes. Studied at St. Martin's School of Art, at Cambridge Technical College, and under John Cherrington. Exhibited at the R.A., and in the provinces. One-man shows held in Cambridge. Works chiefly in East Anglia.

*LEIGHTON, Alfred Crocker (1901–1965).
Born at Hastings in Sussex. Studied at Hastings School of Art, Hornsey School of Art, and in Paris. Died at Calgary, Canada.

*LEIST, Frederick William, R.O.I., R.B.A. (1878–1945).
Landscape painter in oil and water-colour. Born in Sydney, Australia. Studied art under Julian Ashton. At the age of 20 came to England, contributing illustrations to *The Graphic*. Exhibited at the R.A. from 1911 and the Paris Salon from 1912. Official war artist with the A.I.F. in the Great War. Painted murals in America, and returned to Australia 1925. Member of the Australian Watercolor Institute and the Royal Art Society of New South Wales. Represented in many public collections in Australia.

LETT HAINES (born 1894).
Painter and art teacher. Studied art at Chelsea, Newlyn, and in Paris at the Académie Colarossi. One-man shows held at Casa d'Arte Bragalia, Rome 1922; Gallerie Levan Palais Royal, Paris 1925; St. Georges Gallery, London 1935; Brook Street Gallery, London 1939; The Minories, Colchester 1966. Founded the

Ixion Society 1935, and the East Anglian School of Painting and Drawing 1936.

LEVICK, Miss Ruby (Mrs. Bailey) (*fl. c.* 1895–1930).

Figure sculptor. Studied art for eight years at the R.C.A. under Lanteri, winning a free scholarship a year after joining. In 1897 she received the Princess of Wales Scholarship, and the British Institution Scholarship for Modelling 1896. Exhibited at the R.A. Works include *Sea Urchin* and *Asleep in the Arms of the Slow Swinging Seas.* Lived in London.

LEWIS, John Hardwicke (1841–1927).

Painter of landscapes, figure subjects and miniatures. Born at Hyderabad in India, son of F. C. Lewis. Studied art under his father, and in Paris. Exhibited at the leading London galleries from 1867, including the R.A., R.B.A. Worked in Britain, America and Switzerland, where he died on 3rd October 1927.

LEWIS, Miss Mabel Terry (Mrs. Batley) (died 1957).

Miniature painter; actress. Exhibited at the R.A., the New and Grafton Galleries, and in the provinces. Lived at Shepton Beauchamp in Somerset, and died 28th November 1957.

LEWIS, Tobias (died 1916).

Brighton oil painter. Exhibited at the R.O.I. and taught at Brighton School of Art. Served in World War I in the Royal Sussex Regiment and was killed in action.

LILLY, Marjorie (born 1891).

Oil painter of portraits and figure subjects. Studied art at the Slade School. A follower of Walter Sickert, she was represented in the "Sickert Women and the Sickert Girls" exhibition held at the Parkin Gallery, London 1974. Exhibited at the R.A. Lived in London.

LINDSAY, C. T. (died 1916).

Member of Chelsea Arts Club. Killed in action in World War I.

LINDSAY, Miss Ruby (1887–1919).

Painter in water-colour and gouache; illustrator. Born at Creswick, Victoria, Australia. Sister of Norman, Lionel and Daryl Lindsay. Contributed illustrations to magazines under the name Ruby Lind. Married the artist Will Dyson 1909, and settled in London. Died in Chelsea.

LING, Rita M. (born 1922).

Sculptor. Born in Wolverhampton on 7th November 1922. Studied at Wolverhampton College of Art, and the R.C.A. 1946–50. Taught at Farnham School of Art 1950, and at the R.C.A. from 1955. Represented in the Tate Gallery.

LINNELL, James Thomas (1826–1905).

Landscape painter. Son of the artist John Linnell. Exhibited at the R.A. from 1850. Lived at Redhill in Surrey.

LINTON, James Walter Robert (1869–1947).

Landscape and genre painter in water-colour. Born in London. Son of Sir James Linton, P.R.I. Studied art at the Slade School under Legros and at Westminster School of Art under Fred Brown. Exhibited at the leading London galleries from 1890, chiefly the R.I. Settled in Western Australia 1902, and taught art at Perth for 29 years.

*LINTOTT, Edward Barnard, N.P.S. (1875–1951).

Painted several London scenes, including *Bankside*, a work illustrated in *The Artist's London.*

LINTOTT, Henry Chamen, R.M.S. (born *c.* 1880–died 1918).

Painter of portraits and miniatures. Exhibited at the R.A. from 1900, also in America. Joined the army as a volunteer shortly after the outbreak of World War I, and went to France with the Artists Rifles January 1915. Invalided home 18 months later, but returned to France early in 1917. Died from wounds on 22nd March 1918, when leading his platoon into action on the Western Front.

LIPSCOMBE, Guy (*fl.* 1909–1936).

Landscape and genre painter in oil. Exhibited at the R.A. During World War I he was an ambulance driver with the Red Cross on the Italian Front and four paintings by him, of this theatre of the war, are in the Imperial War Museum. Lived in London.

LISMER, Arthur, R.Canadian A. (1885–1969).

Painter of landscapes and figure subjects. Born in Sheffield. Studied at Sheffield School of Art, and the Académie Royale des Beaux Arts in Antwerp. Settled in Canada 1911, and elected A.R.Canadian A. 1919, full member 1946. Taught at Ontario College of Art 1915–16, Principal of Nova Scotia College of Art 1916–19, and Vice Principal Ontario College of Art 1919–27. Member of the "Group of Seven" of Canadian painters. Lived in Montreal, and died there 23rd March 1969.

*LITTEN, Sydney Mackenzie, N.S., A.R.C.A.(Lond.) (1887–1949).

Etchings include *Gate of Justice, Granada* and *Night and the Salute, Venice.*

LLOYD, Ernest H. D., S.M. (*fl.* 1895–1905).

Miniature painter. Exhibited at the R.A., G.I., S.M. and Walker Art Gallery in Liverpool. Lived in London.

LONG, Nat (born 1893).

Etcher and aquatinter of landscapes and figure subjects. Born in Bournemouth, and received his initial art training in the town. Served in World War I in Mesopotamia, Persia and Russia. Then spent two years studying at St. Martin's School of Art. Works include *Misty Morn, Sea Nymph* and *Summer Days.*

LONGE, William Verner (1857–1924).

Painter in water-colour of landscapes and horses. Born on 27th April 1857 at Coddenham in Suffolk. Studied at Ipswich School of Art, and in Brussels. A member of Ipswich Art Club, he contributed to *The History of the Grand National.*

LONGHURST, Joseph (1874–1922).

Landscape painter. Born in Brighton. Exhibited at the R.A. and Walker Art Gallery, Liverpool. Lived at Cranleigh in Surrey, where he died.

*LORD, Miss Elyse Ashe, R.I. (died 1971).

Exhibited at the R.I. and Walker Art Gallery, Liverpool. Works include *A Spring Dream* and *The Hunchback.*

LOUDAN, Terence (born *c.* 1900).

Oil painter of portraits and flower subjects. Son of the artist W. Mouat Loudan. Exhibited at the R.A., R.P., R.O.I., R.W.A. Lived in London.

LOWNDES, Alan (born 1921).

Oil painter. Born at Stockport, Cheshire. Served

in World War II in the Middle East, Italy and Austria. Then studied painting at night school. He has held several one-man shows, and was included in the "Artists of Fame and Promise" exhibition held at the Leicester Galleries. Represented in Plymouth Art Gallery.

*LOWRY, Laurence Stephen, R.A., R.B.A., L.G., N.S. (1887–1976).

Died near Manchester on 23rd February 1976. Important retrospective exhibition held at the Tate Gallery 1966.

LUCAS, Denis (born 1918).

Oil painter. Studied at Beckenham School of Art and at the R.C.A., where he received a travelling scholarship 1949. Exhibited at the R.A., N.E.A.C., L.G. Taught at Ravensbourne College of Art, St. Martin's School of Art, and the R.A. Schools. Represented in Plymouth Art Gallery by *Clockhouse Road, Winter.*

LUCAS, Miss Marie Ellen Segmont (Mrs. Grubbe) (died 1951).

Miniature painter. Daughter of John Seymour Lucas R.A. Exhibited at the R.A. from 1910. Died at Blythburgh in Suffolk on 4th November 1951.

LUCCHESI, Edmund (1870–1964).

Colour woodcut artist. Born in London on 28th December 1870, of Italian and Scottish parents. His father was a well-known opera singer, who died when the boy was five years of age. His mother, also on the operatic stage, sent him and his sister to a boarding school in Italy. While there he received a commission from a Jesuit to draw religious subjects. At 17 he came to London, and worked with his uncle who was property master at a circus. He never had real art training, but said that his work on pantomine masks at the circus helped him greatly. Some years later went to Berlin and worked in the studios of a number of artists. Exhibited at the R.A., also in Rome, Paris, Munich, and held a one-man show. As he grew older, he became interested in woodcuts and linocuts, and executed illustrations and book jackets. He had a cousin, Giorgio Lucchesi, who was a still life painter and sent all of his work to America. Lived in Brighton for many years, where he died 30th August 1964.

LYNCH, Julia (died 1975).

New Zealand portrait painter. Studied art at the Slade School, and received first prize for portrait painting. Then became a nun, and as Sister Mary Lawrence was with the Sisters of Mercy for 51 years. Much of her later work was sold for charity. Died at Wellington, New Zealand, aged 79.

LYNN, William H., R.H.A. (died 1916).

Irish architect. Lived in Belfast and later Dublin. Died on 12th September 1916.

LYON, J. H. (died 1921).

Scottish painter in oil and water-colour. Exhibited at R.S.A., R.S.W., G.I., and Walker Art Gallery, Liverpool. Lived in Edinburgh and at Strathyre Perthshire. Died February 1921.

M

MACCARTHY, Mrs. Clara (*née* Christian) (died 1906).

Landscape and genre painter. Lived in Dublin, and died at an early age.

McCLOY, Samuel (1831–1904).

Landscape and figure painter. Born at Lisburn in Ireland on 13th March 1831. Apprenticed to a firm of Belfast engravers, and then became a master at Waterford School of Art. Exhibited at the leading London galleries from 1859, including the R.A., R.I., R.B.A., and at the R.H.A. from 1862. Worked in Belfast 1875–81, and later in London. Died at Balham on 4th October 1904.

McCUBBIN, Frederick (1855–1917).

Australian oil painter of landscapes, portraits and genre. Born at West Melbourne on 25th February 1855. Studied at the Art Gallery School of Victoria, and was drawing master there 1886–1917. Exhibited at the Paris Salon 1897, also at the Grafton Galleries in London. Visited Europe 1906. Member of the Australian Art Association, and President of the Victorian Art Society. Works include *A Bush Burial, On the Wallaby Track,* and *Down on his Luck.* Lived at South Yarra, Melbourne, and died 22nd December 1917.

MACDONALD, Alexander (1839–1921).

Painter of landscapes, portraits, animals and still life. Appointed by Ruskin as first Drawing Master at Oxford University 1871. Keeper of the University Galleries 1882–1908. Died in Oxford 16th October 1921.

MACDONALD, James W. G. (1897–1960)

Landscape painter in oil. Born at Thurso, Caithness. Studied at Edinburgh College of Art until 1922. Taught at Lincoln School of Art, and in 1926 settled in Vancouver, Canada. Member of the Canadian Group of Painters 1933. Visited California 1937. Died in Toronto.

McDONNELL, James (died 1911).

Painter of landscapes and animals, especially horses. Lived in Ireland, and exhibited at the R.H.A. from 1875.

*MACDOUGALL, Leslie Grahame, R.S.A (1896–1974).

Died on 3rd June 1974.

MACGREGOR, A. G. (died *c.* 1909).

Painter of landscapes and genre in oil, water-colour and tempera. Works include *Wasted Hours* and *Sorrow and Memory.*

*McGUINNESS, William Bingham, R.H.A. (*fl. c.* 1880–1930).

Elected A.R.H.A. 1882, R.H.A. 1884.

MACHELL, Reginald, R.B.A. (*fl. c.* 1880–1905).

Genre painter in oil and water-colour. Exhibited at the leading London galleries from 1881, including the R.A., R.B.A., R.I., also at the Walker Art Gallery, Liverpool. Lived in London.

*McINTYRE, Raymond (died *c.* 1927).

Born at Christchurch, New Zealand. Exhibited at

the Goupil Gallery. Represented in the National Gallery, Wellington, New Zealand.

*MACKECHNIE, Robert G. S., R.B.A. (died 1975).
Lived at Rye in Sussex for many years. Died on 20th December 1975.

MACKINNEY, Herbert Wood (born 1881).
Cartoonist. Studied at the R.A. Schools. After being articled to a London architect he went to South Africa, where he painted water-colours and executed political cartoons. Lived in Cape Town.

MACKINTOSH, Colin J. (died 1910).
Landscape and figure painter. Exhibited at the R.S.A. Lived at Inverness, and died 1st September 1910.

*MACLAGAN, Philip Douglas (1901–1972).
Painter in oil and water-colour of landscapes, figures, portraits and still life. Born in South China, his family returned to Berwick-on-Tweed 1905. In 1918 he studied at St. John's Wood Art School, and entered the R.A. Schools 1919. First exhibited at the R.A. 1921, and was frequently represented there until 1941, also showed at the Venice Biennale 1930. Married the artist Dorothea Maclagan 1929. Taught at the City of London School and during that time studied book binding at the Central School. In 1937 he removed to the Vale of Aylesbury, and settled as a landscape painter. Served in World War II in North Africa and Italy in Photographic Intelligence. He rarely painted after the war, and on his retirement from teaching moved to Totnes, Devon in 1967.

McNICOLL, Miss Helen, R.B.A. (*fl. c.* 1910–1925).
London artist, who exhibited chiefly at the R.B.A.

MACQUEEN, Kenneth (born 1897).
Landscape painter in water-colour. Born at Ballarat, Victoria, Australia. Served with the A.I.F. in France in World War I. After the war he studied art at the Slade School and Westminster School of Art. Exhibited at the R.A., N.E.A.C. Member of the Australian Water-color Institute, and is represented in many Australian public collections.

MAGUIRE, Miss Helena J. (1860–1909).
Genre painter in water-colour. Born in London, daughter of the artist Thomas Herbert Maguire (1821–1895). Exhibited at the leading London galleries from 1881, chiefly the R.A., R.I., also at Birmingham and Liverpool. Contributed illustrations to children's books. Lived in London, and died November 1909.

MAHONEY, Frank P. (1862–1916).
Painter of landscapes and figures in oil and water-colour. Born at Melbourne, Australia on 4th December 1862. Taught at the Royal Art Society, Sydney, and contributed illustrations to several magazines. A friend of Charles Conder, he settled in London 1904. Represented in several Australian public collections.

MAIDMENT, T. (*fl.* 1940s).
Painter in oil of interior subjects. Exhibited at the R.A. Lived at Helston in Cornwall.

MALLALIEU, H. (died *c.* 1973).
Artist, and teacher at Hornsea College of Art. Removed from London to Burpham in Sussex, where he died.

MALTWOOD, Mrs. Katharine E. (died 1961).
Sculptor and author. Studied art at the Slade School. Exhibited at the R.A., S.W.A., I.S. Lived in London,

and later at Vancouver Island, Canada. Died on 29th July 1961.

MANCINI, Antonio, N.P.S., I.S. (1852–1930).
Painter of portraits in oil. Exhibited at the leading London galleries from 1893, including the R.A., I.S., Goupil Gallery, and at the R.S.A. Lived in London for a time, and is represented in the Tate Gallery.

MANLY, Charles Macdonald, A.R.Canadian A. (1855–1924).
Landscape painter in oil and water-colour. Born at Englefield Green, Surrey. Emigrated to Canada when young. Returned to London, studying at Heatherley's Art School and later at the Metropolitan School of Art in Dublin. Exhibited at the leading London galleries from 1884, chiefly the R.I., R.B.A. He taught at Ontario School of Art, and was elected a member of Ontario Society of Artists 1876, A.R.Canadian A. 1890. Died in Toronto.

MANN, H. W. (died 1918).
Painter of landscapes and town scenes; architect, with a practice at Chelmsford in Essex. During the time he served in the army in World War I he drew many subjects in Northern France, and was killed in action 30th March 1918.

MARR, Leslie (born 1922).
Painter in oil and water-colour. Born at Durham on 14th August 1922. Studied art under David Bomberg at the Borough Polytechnic, and became a member of the Borough Group, showing from the second exhibition held December 1947. Visited Cyprus with Bomberg 1948. He has held several one-man shows, and lives near Fakenham in Norfolk.

MARTIN, Arthur Edmund, A.R.C.A.(Lond.) (died 1932).
Mural painter. Exhibited at the R.A. Lived in London, and later at Rickmansworth. Died on 14th November 1932.

MARTIN, Arthur Ronald, S.G.A. (born 1904).
Landscape painter in water-colour and acrylic, wood engraver and lithographer; graphic designer for commerce and industry until 1964. Born at Eastbourne in Sussex. Studied at Eastbourne School of Art, Brighton College of Art, and the L.C.C. School of Art and Graphic Reproduction. Exhibited at the R.A., R.I., R.B.A., R.S.M.A., S.G.A., in the provinces, and has held a number of one-man shows. Elected F.S.I.A. 1968, and a member of the Society of Sussex Painters 1971. Lives in Hove, and is represented in Hove Art Gallery.

MARTIN, Henry (*c.* 1840–1908).
Oil painter of landscapes and coastal subjects. He was painting in Cornwall from the early 1870s, and lived at Newlyn for some years, later at Paul. Exhibited at the R.A. from 1874. Recorded as living at Sidcup 1880, Plymouth 1883, Saltash 1887. Represented in the exhibition "Paintings by the Newlyn School 1880–1900" held at Newlyn Art Gallery 1958.

*MARTIN, Mrs. Mary Adela, L.G., A.R.C.A.(Lond.) (1907–1969).
Represented in the Tate Gallery.

MARTIN, Max (*fl.* 1920s).
Painter in oil of figure subjects. Lived in London for a time, and was represented in the "Australian Artists" exhibition held at Brighton Art Gallery 1925.

MARTIN, Miss Rosa Plant, R.M.S. (*fl. c.* 1895–1925).

Miniature painter. Exhibited at the R.A., R.M.S. Lived at Ealing, and later at Shiplake, near Henley.

MARTIN, William Alison, L.A.A. (*fl. c.* 1900–1935).

Painter in oil and water-colour of figure subjects and landscapes; etcher and lithographer. In 1900 won a gold medal for drawing at Liverpool School of Art, and a travelling scholarship enabling him to study under Bouguereau and Ferrier in Paris. After visiting Italy, he returned to England, and in 1902 exhibited at the R.A. Also showed at the R.Cam.A., and Walker Art Gallery, Liverpool. First one-man show held in London at the Baillie Gallery 1907. Lived in Liverpool for many years.

MARX, Miss Enid Crystal Dorothy, S.W.E. (born 1902).

Painter, wood engraver, and illustrator. Born in London on 20th October 1902. Studied at the Central School of Arts and Crafts, and at the R.C.A. under Paul Nash, Leon Underwood and Bernard Adeney. Exhibited at the R.A., also on the continent and in America. Elected R.D.I. 1944. Represented in several public collections. She has lived in London for many years.

*MASKELL, Christopher Mark (1846–1933).

Painter in oils of animals and landscapes. Settled in Ipswich 1898, and is represented in Ipswich Museum. He was the last surviving painter of the Suffolk School.

MASON, Miss Josephine, W.I.A.C. (*fl. c.* 1915–1950).

Painter of flower subjects and still life. Exhibited at the R.A., N.E.A.C., W.I.A.C. Lived in Chelsea for many years.

MASTIN, John, R.B.A. (*fl. c.* 1895–1930).

Painter of portraits, genre and figure subjects; book illustrator. Exhibited at the R.B.A., and in Birmingham, Manchester, Liverpool. Lived in Sheffield and Pen-y-Groes, North Wales.

MATHER, John (1848–1916).

Landscape painter in oil and water-colour. Born at Hamilton, near Glasgow. Studied art in Edinburgh. Painted in England, Scotland, France, and exhibited at the G.I. Went to Melbourne, Australia 1878, and later visited New Zealand. Founder member of the Australian Art Association and President of Victorian Artists' Society.

MATTHEW, Sir Robert Hogg, A.R.S.A. (1906–1975).

Scottish architect. Born on 12th December 1906. Received many public and private commissions, and was knighted 1962. P.R.I.B.A. 1962–64. Died on 21st June 1975.

*MAUFE, Sir Edward Brantwood, R.A. (1883–1974).

Died on 12th December 1974.

MAVROGORDATO, Alexander James (*fl. c.* 1892–1935).

Genre painter in oil and water-colour, said to be a Greek extraction. Exhibited at the R.A. from 1892, also at the R.I. Subjects include scenes in Italy, Algeria and Russia. Lived in London for many years.

MAY, Frederick (born 1891).

Cartoonist. Born on 25th January 1891. Studied at Wallasey School of Art, and under Seaby at Reading University. Contributed illustrations to *Tatler, Weekly Sketch,* and *The Graphic.* An exhibition of his drawings

and paintings was held at Middlesbrough 1930. Lived at Reading for many years.

MAZE, Paul Lucien (born 1887).

Painter in oil, pastel and water-colour of landscapes, marines, figure subjects and still life. Born at Le Havre, France on 21st May 1887. He was brought up in an artistic atmosphere through his father's connection with the great French painters of that generation. Exhibited in France, Britain and America. He has held several one-man shows in London, Paris and New York, including at Wildenstein and Marlborough Fine Art. In 1934 he published *A Frenchman in Khaki.* Lives near Midhurst in Sussex.

MEAD, Dorothy (died 1975).

Painter who exhibited with the L.G.

MEAD, Miss Marion Grace, A.R.M.S. (*fl. c.* 1905–1935).

Miniature painter. Exhibited at the R.A., R.M.S., and Walker Art Gallery, Liverpool. Lived in London for many years.

MEAD, Miss Rose (1868–1946).

Painter of portraits and genre. Born at Bury St. Edmunds, Suffolk. Studied art at the Slade School, and in Paris. Exhibited at the R.A., R.P., and Paris Salon. A member of Ipswich Art Club, she lived at Bury St. Edmunds.

*MEDWORTH, Frank Charles, R.B.A. (1892–1947).

Settled in Australia 1939. Died in Mexico while attending a U.N.E.S.C.O. conference.

MEERE, Charles, A.R.C.A.(Lond.) (1890–1961).

Painter in oil of landscapes and figure subjects. Born in London. Studied at West Ham Technical School, and the R.C.A. where he received his diploma 1922. Exhibited at the R.A., and in the provinces. Settled at Sydney, Australia, and is represented in several Australian public collections.

MENZIES, John (*fl. c.* 1910–1930).

Painter of landscapes and decorative subjects. Exhibited at the R.S.A., S.S.A. Works include *Butterflies* and *Voice of the Sea.* Lived in Edinburgh.

*MERRIOTT, Jack, R.I., R.O.I., P.S., S.M.A. (1901–1968).

Member of the Society of Sussex Painters. Died November 1968.

MERTON, Owen, R.B.A. (born 1887).

New Zealand artist. Born at Christchurch, South Island, on 14th May 1887. Studied art in London, and in Paris under Percyval Tudor Hart. Exhibited in London, and on the continent. Lived in France for a time.

*METHUEN, Lord (Paul Ayshford), R.A., R.W.S., P.R.W.A., R.B.A., N.E.A.C. (1886–1974).

Died on 7th January 1974.

MEYER, Miss Sylvia (*fl. c.* 1910–1950).

Painter in oil of portraits and figure subjects. Studied art at the Slade School under Tonks, and received a portraiture prize. Married the artist Harold Gilman, whom she had met at Westminster School of Art about 1915.

MICHAELSON, Assur, R.B.A. (born 1870).

Painter in oil of genre and figure subjects. Born in London. Studied at St. John's Wood Art School, Heatherley's Art School, and the R.A. Schools. Exhibited at the R.A., R.B.A., Grafton Gallery, in the provinces, and at the Paris Salon. Painted in India, Japan and Italy. Lived in London, and at one time was Principal of the St. John's Wood Art Schools.

MIDDLETON, Horace, R.B.A. (*fl. c.* 1900–1920).
Painter of portraits and figure subjects. Born at Ladywood, Birmingham. Began in business, but turned instead to painting. Studied at Manchester Art School and at the M.A.F.A. for five years. Settled in London, and attended Chelsea Art School for two years under John and Orpen. Exhibited at the R.A. from 1904, also at the R.B.A. and Paris Salon. Painted in France and Holland.

MILLAR, Harold R. (*fl. c.* 1890–1930).
Illustrator. Exhibited at the R.A. from 1892. Illustrated works include *Fairy Tales Far and Near* 1895, *The Dreamland Express* 1927. Lived in London.

MILLARD, Jack (*fl. c.* 1900–1915).
Portrait sculptor. Born at Wigan, Lancashire. Studied at Warrington Art School, then in Paris at the École des Beaux Arts where he received a gold medal. Later settled in Wigan.

*MILLER, John, R.S.A., P.R.S.W., S.S.A. (1911–1975).
Died on 18th January 1975.

*MILLER, Mrs. Josephine Haswell, A.R.S.A., S.S.A. (1890–1975).
Christened Elizabeth Josephine Cameron. Studied at Glasgow School of Art 1909–14, and in 1914 received a travelling scholarship of £120. Also studied in Paris, and in London under Sickert. Married the artist A. E. Haswell Miller 1916. In 1919 she joined her husband on the staff of the Glasgow School of Art, and between 1919–30 was very active as a painter and etcher, executing portraits, landscapes and some classical subjects. Worked in the 1920s in France, Belgium, Germany, Austria, Italy and Spain. She produced about a dozen etchings and aquatints, but there are relatively few of her paintings extant as she destroyed a great deal of her work feeling it to be unsatisfactory.

MILLER, Harrison, R.M.S. (*fl. c.* 1890–1915).
Miniature and genre painter. Exhibited at the leading London galleries from 1891, including the R.A., R.B.A., R.M.S., also at the Walker Art Gallery in Liverpool. Lived in London, and later at Chertsey in Surrey.

*MILLS, Charles A., A.R.H.A. (died *c.* 1925).
Elected A.R.H.A. 1913.

MILNE, James (died 1918).
Aberdeen artist, who exhibited at the R.S.A. shortly before the outbreak of World War I. Died November 1918.

MILNE, Joseph (died 1911).
Landscape painter. Exhibited at the R.A. from 1887. Lived in Edinburgh and died January 1911 aged 50.

*MILNER, Miss Elizabeth Eleanor (1861–1953).
Born on 14th June 1861. Studied at the R.O.I., and Walker Art Gallery in Liverpool.

MILNER, James Hiley, A.R.W.A. (1869–1954).
Painter in oil and water-colour; designer of woodcut colour prints. Born at Huddersfield, Yorkshire, and studied at Huddersfield School of Art. Exhibited at the R.A., R.W.A., N.E.A.C. Father of the artist Donald Milner, P.R.W.A., he lived at Clifton, Bristol.

MILNER, Mrs. Mildred, R.W.A. (born 1896).
Painter in oil and water-colour; embroiderer. Born in London, *née* Dodd. Studied at Camberwell School of Arts and Crafts. Exhibited at the R.A., R.W.A., and various provincial art galleries. Held a joint show with her husband Donald Milner, P.R.W.A. at Swindon Art Gallery. Represented in the R.W.A. collection. Lives at Wotton-under-Edge, Gloucestershire.

MISKIN, Lionel (born 1924).
Painter of portraits and figure subjects. Born at Cannes, France. Studied at St. Martin's School of Art. Exhibited in London, the provinces, and abroad. Taught at Falmouth College of Art in Cornwall, and is represented in Plymouth Art Gallery by a work in tempera *Portrait of Jack Clemo*.

MITCHELL, C. L. (died 1918).
Scottish artist who lived at Dundee and later at nearby Tayport. Exhibited with the G.I. Died June 1918.

MITCHELL, Denis (born 1912).
Sculptor in bronze; painter and craftsman. Represented in the Tate Gallery. Exhibits in Cornwall, and lives at St. Ives.

MITCHELL, Mrs. Mary, R.M.S. (*fl. c.* 1885–1925).
Miniature painter. Exhibited at the R.A. from 1889. Lived at Bayswater.

MITCHELL, William Mansfield, R.H.A. (died 1910).
Irish architect. Elected A.R.H.A. 1889, R.H.A. 1890. Lived in Dublin.

MONAHAN, Hugh C. (*fl. c.* 1945–1960).
Painter of bird subjects. Born in Ireland. Entered the Army, and served with the Gurkha Regiment. Following an illness after World War II he took up painting, exhibiting in Britain and America. He was President of the Wildfowlers' Association of Great Britain and Ireland.

*MONNINGTON, Sir Walter Thomas, P.R.A. (1902–1976).
Died 7th January 1976.

MOORE, Miss Eleanor (*fl. c.* 1915–1930).
Portrait painter. Exhibited at the R.S.A., G.I. Lived at Newmilns in Ayrshire.

MOORE, Leslie L. Hardy (born 1907).
Landscape painter in water-colour. Born in Norwich. Received no formal art training. Exhibited at the R.A., in the provinces, and abroad.

MOORE, Thomas Sturge (1870–1944).
Wood engraver, book illustrator and poet. Born on 4th March 1870. Studied at Lambeth School of Art under John Sparkes. In 1895 he produced a portfolio of ten woodcuts, limited to an edition of twelve, entitled *Metamorphoses of Pan and other Woodcuts*. Illustrated books published by the Vale, Unicorn and Eragny Presses. Lived in London, and died on 18th July 1944.

MORCOM, J. Herbert, R.Cam.A. (born 1871).
Sculptor. Born at Wrexham on 31st May 1871. Studied at the School of Architecture and Applied Arts, University College, Liverpool. Exhibited at the R.A. Lived at Leicester.

MORRICE, James Wilson (1865–1924).
Landscape painter in oil. Born at Montreal, Canada on 10th August 1865. Studied art in Paris at the Académie Julian during the 1890s, and worked in France for many years, often returning to Canada. Also painted in Italy, North Africa, Cuba, West Indies. Exhibited

in London at the Goupil Gallery, and from 1901 with the I.S. Died at Tunis 23rd January 1924.

MORRIS, Edmund M., A.R.Canadian A. (born 1871).
Landscape and figure painter. Born at Perth, Ontario, Canada. Studied at the Art Students' League, New York, and at the Académie Julian in Paris. Returned to Canada 1896. Founder member of the New Canadian Art Club 1908, and elected A.R.Canadian A. 1897. Painted chiefly in Canada, also in Scotland and Holland.

MORRIS, Miss Elisabeth (born *c.* 1915).
Painter in gouache, pastel, oil and water-colour of interiors, figure subjects and coastal scenes. Born at Wimbledon. Studied at the Grosvenor School of Art under Iain Macnab. Painted subjects in Spain and France. She has exhibited her work in London and provincial galleries.

*MORRIS, William Bright, R.O.I. (1834–*c.* 1912).
Landscape painter. Born at Salford. Exhibited at the leading London galleries from 1869, chiefly the R.A., R.O.I., Grosvenor and New Galleries, and in Liverpool at the Walker Art Gallery. Lived in London.

MORTIMER, Lewis (*fl. c.* 1900–1920).
Painter of landscapes and coastal scenes in water-colour. Worked chiefly in Cornwall, Devon and Dorset.

MORTON, Alistair (1910–1963).
Abstract painter in oil. Represented in the Tate Gallery.

MOSS, Marlow (1890–1958).
Abstract painter; sculptor. Mondrian's only English pupil. Represented in the Tate Gallery, she lived at Lamorna in Cornwall.

*MOSS, Sidney Dennant, R.B.A. (1884–1946).
Exhibited at the R.A. from 1912. Elected R.B.A. 1935. After World War I he settled at Tunbridge Wells, and in 1933 removed to Pevensey. A memorial exhibition held at Brighton Art Gallery 1947.

*MOYNAN, Richard Thomas, R.H.A. (1856–1906).
Painter of portraits and figure subjects. Intended for the medical profession but took up art instead. Exhibited at the R.H.A. from 1880. Died at Rathgar, Ireland.

MUELLER, Max (born 1901).
Landscape painter; lithographer. Studied art in Leipzig. Exhibited at the R.A., R.I., and has held four one-man shows at Norwich Assembly House. Came to Norfolk after World War II, found himself drawn to the county, and has lived there ever since.

MUIRHEAD, Miss Kate Campbell (*fl. c.* 1910–1925).
Sculptor. Received the first Guthrie Award, with D. M. Sutherland. Exhibited at the R.S.A., and lived in Edinburgh.

MULLINS, Edwin Roscoe, F.R.B.S. (died *c.* 1906).
Sculptor. Exhibited at the leading London galleries from 1873, including the R.A., R.B.A., New Gallery, also at the G.I. and Walker Art Gallery, Liverpool. Lived in London.

MULOCK, Frederick Charles (1866–1931).
Landscape painter. Exhibited at the leading London galleries from 1888, chiefly the R.A., also at the R.H.A. Lived at Instow in North Devon, and in London.

*MUNCASTER, Claude Grahame, R.W.S., R.O.I., R.B.A., S.M.A. (1903–1974).
President of St. Ives Society of Artists 1955–63. Died 30th November 1974.

MUNNOCH, John (died 1915).
Landscape and genre painter. Exhibited at the R.S.A., S.S.A., and lived in Edinburgh. Served as a private in the 5th Battalion of Royal Scots in World War I, and was killed in action June 1915.

MUNRO, Leo (1878–1957).
Illustrator. Born on 17th April 1878. Studied art at Lambeth Art School, and the Academy in Antwerp. Died on 28th February 1957.

MURA, Frank, I.S. (born 1861).
Landscape oil painter and etcher. Born in Alsace, France. Went to New York as a child, and became an American citizen. At the age of 20 returned to Europe, and studied art in Munich, later at The Hague. Settled in Hampstead 1891, then to Dunmow in Essex, and later lived at Sompting in Sussex. Exhibited at G.I., I.S. Painted many Sussex landscapes.

MURA, James (died 1917).
Paisley artist, who died 3rd September 1917.

*MURRAY, Albert Edward, R.H.A. (1849–1924).
Elected A.R.H.A. 1893, R.H.A. 1910.

MURRAY, J. G., A.R.E. (*fl. c.* 1890–1906).
Etcher. Elected A.R.E. 1895, membership ceased July 1906.

*MURRAY, John Reid (1861–1906).
Born at Helensburgh. Studied art at Edinburgh, Glasgow and Antwerp. Received a gold medal at Munich 1897. Died at Prestwick.

MURRAY DIXON, Henry Edward Otto (1885–1917).
Painter of bird subjects. Born at Loughborough. An admirer of Archibald Thorburn, much of his work appeared in the *Illustrated Sporting and Dramatic News,* published weekly between 1912–15. He was killed on active service on the Vimy Ridge on 9th April 1917.

MUSGROVE, Alexander (1882–1952).
Painter in water-colour of landscapes and town scenes. Born at Edinburgh. Studied at Edinburgh University, and Glasgow School of Art. Settled in Canada, becoming Director of Winnipeg Art School and Art Gallery 1913–21. A founder member of Manitoba Society of Artists 1925. Died at Winnipeg.

MUSPRATT, Miss Aimée, A.R.M.S. (*fl. c.* 1900–1925).
Miniature painter. Exhibited at the R.A., R.M.S., and Walker Art Gallery in Liverpool. Lived at Cley in Norfolk, in Paris, then at Bournemouth, and later in London.

MUSPRATT, Miss Alicia Frances (born 1902).
Painter in oil and water-colour of portraits, landscapes and flowers. Born in Lancashire on 8th February 1902. Studied art chiefly privately, but attended twice weekly for six months at Liverpool School of Art. Exhibited at the R.A., R.O.I., R.Cam.A., Paris Salon, and held a one-man show in London 1936. Lives at Slindon in Sussex.

MYER, George Val (1883–1959).
Portrait painter; architect. Born on 14th February 1883. Articled to John Belcher, R.A. Retired from his architectural practice 1950. Late in life settled in Gibraltar, and died 25th February 1959.

MYERS, Miss Hannah, R.M.S. (*fl. c.* 1890–1915).
Miniature painter. Exhibited at the R.A. from 1893, also at the R.S.A., R.O.I., R.M.S., I.S., G.I. Lived in London.

N

NEATBY, William James, A.R.M.S. (*fl.c.* 1900–1915).
Miniature painter. Exhibited at the R.A., R.M.S., and Walker Art Gallery in Liverpool. Lived in Chelsea.

NEAVE, David S. (*fl. c.* 1900–1915).
Landscape painter in oil. Exhibited at the R.A., N.E.A.C., G.I., and Walker Art Gallery, Liverpool. Lived in Scotland, then in Chelsea, and later at Topsham in Devon. Painted some subjects in France.

NEAVE, Henry J. (*fl. c.* 1940–1960).
Painter of aviation and marine subjects. Exhibited at the R.A. A founder member of the Society of Aviation Artists 1955. Lived in London.

*NELSON, Harold S.G.A. (1871–1946).
Exhibited at the R.A. from 1899. Member of the A.W.G.

NEWBOULD, Frank (born 1887).
Poster designer. Born in Bradford, son of a chemist. Intended for his father's business, but took up art instead, entering Bradford School of Art aged 16. Influenced by the Beggarstaff Brothers, he produced many posters for the railways and the underground. Lived in London.

*NICHOLLS, Bertram, P.R.B.A., R.O.I. (1883–1974).
Died in Worthing on 23rd December 1974.

NICHOLLS, Charles Wynne, R.H.A. (1831–1903).
Genre painter. Born in Dublin on 20th October 1831. Studied at the Royal Dublin Society's Schools, and the R.H.A. Schools. Exhibited at the R.H.A. from 1859, and elected A.R.H.A. 1861, R.H.A. 1869. In 1864 he settled in London, exhibiting at the R.A., R.B.A. Died in London on 24th January 1903.

* NICHOLLS, John E., N.S. (*fl. c.* 1925–1955).
Painter and etcher. Exhibited at the Twenty-One Gallery, London.

NICHOLSON, Hugh, R.B.A., R.M.S. (*fl. c.* 1890–1925).
Miniature painter. Exhibited at the R.A. from 1893. Lived in Wimbledon.

NICHOLSON, Miss Kate (born 1929).
Oil painter. Born in Cumberland, daughter of the artists Ben and Winifred Nicholson. Studied at Bath Academy of Art. One-man shows held in London at the Waddington Gallery. A member of the Penwith Society, she is represented in Plymouth Art Gallery by *Fern Colour*.

NICKAL, John, R.B.A. (*fl. c.* 1910–1925).
London artist, who appears to have exhibited chiefly at the R.B.A.

NIELSEN, Kay (1886–1957).
Book illustrator. Born in Denmark. Studied art in Paris at the Académies Julian and Colarossi 1904–11. Lived in London 1911—16, exhibiting at Dowdeswells and the Leicester Galleries. His work was shown in New York, and after designing stage sets in Copenhagen 1918–22 settled in America. Illustrated a number of books, including Hans Andersen's fairy tales.

NISBIT, Tom, R.H.A. (born 1909).
Irish painter in water-colour.

*NIVEN, William, A.R.E. (1846–1921).
Born in Southern Scotland on 6th November 1846.

NOCKOLDS, Roy Anthony (born 1911).
Painter in oil, water-colour and acrylic of landscapes, trout and salmon fishing subjects, and vintage motoring scenes. Born in London on 24th January 1911. Self-taught in art, apart from some private lessons in figure drawing. Began sketching and painting motoring subjects in the mid 1920s contributing illustrations to *Autocar*, *Motor* and *Motor Sport*. During World War II he worked for the Ministry of Information, served in the R.A.F. and was ultimately a war artist. Exhibited at the R.A., R.P., R.O.I., R.S.M.A., Society of Wildlife Artists, Society of Aviation Artists and Guild of Aviation Artists. One-man show held at Kensington Art Gallery 1953, and also showed at the Exhibition of British Motoring Achievements in New York 1960. Chairman of the Guild of Aviation Artists 1975. Lives near Farnham in Surrey.

NOEL, John Bates (1870–1927).
Landscape painter. Born at Malvern, son of the artist David Bates. In order not to trade on his father's reputation he altered his surname from Bates to Noel, originally his second christian name. Exhibited at the R.A. 1894–1907. Painted scenes in the West Country, especially Worcestershire, also in France and Switzerland. Works include *Birth of Spring*, *Game Keepers* and *Nature's Carpet*.

*NORRISS, Miss Bess (Mrs. Tait), R.M.S. (1878–1939).
Australian artist, settling in London 1905. Exhibited in Australia with the Victorian Artists' Society.

NORTON, R. D. (*fl. c.* 1910–1940).
Landscape painter. Works include *The Cornfield*, *Rye*.

O

O'BRIEN, J. H. (died 1917).
A member of Huddersfield Art Society. Killed in April 1917.

O'CONNOR, Andrew (1874–1941).
Irish sculptor in bronze of portraits and figure subjects. Represented in the Tate Gallery.

O'DONOHOE, Francis Joseph, A.R.H.A. (1878–1911).
Landscape and figure painter. Born in Dublin on 30th April 1878. Studied art in Dublin at the Metropolitan School of Art from age 11. In 1896 he was sent to the South Kensington Schools, also studied at the R.H.A. Schools and the Académie Julian in Paris.

Exhibited at the R.H.A. from 1899. Died on 23rd November 1911 as a result of a motor accident in Dublin.

OFFICER, Edward Cairns, R.B.A. (1871–1921).

Landscape painter in oil. Born in Australia at Murray Downs, Swan Hill, Victoria. Studied art at the Victorian Art Gallery Schools, and the Academie Julian in Paris. During the time he was in Europe he exhibited at the R.O.I. and Paris Salon, and became a member of the R.B.A. President of the Australian Art Society 1912–21, he died at Mount Macedon in Victoria.

*ORCHARDSON, Charles M. Q., R.B.A., R.O.I. (1873–1917).

Painter of portraits and figure subjects. Born on 24th December 1873, eldest son of Sir William Q. Orchardson, R.A. Studied art at the R.A. Schools. Exhibited at the R.A., R.B.A., R.O.I., G.I., at Birmingham and the Walker Art Gallery, Liverpool. One of the Principals of the St. John's Wood Art Schools. Lived in London. During World War I he was attached to a camel corps in the East, and died of wounds received.

*ORCHARDSON, Sir William Quiller, R.A. (1831–1910).

Visited Holland and Germany c. 1859–60, Venice 1870. Elected a member of the Society of Portrait Painters 1897, President 1905.

*O'RORKE, Edward Brian, R.A. (1901–1974).

Died on 1st March 1974.

ORR, Arthur Anselm (1868–1949).

Stained glass designer; craftsman in metal and wood. Born at Chiswick on 21st October 1868. Studied at Westminister School of Art, and the R.C.A. Exhibited at the R.A. from 1896. Designed windows for several churches. Lived at Harrow for many years and died 9th November 1949.

OSBORN, Mrs. Dorothy (fl. c. 1900–1910).

Painter in water-colour of urban scenes and figures.

Exhibition held in London at the Ryder Gallery 1905. Worked in London, especially Chelsea.

OSBORN, William E. (died 1906).

Landscape painter in oil. Exhibition held 1906 at Paterson's Gallery in Bond Street, London. Died in Chelsea at an early age.

OSBORNE, Stuart John, A.R.B.S., A.R.C.A.(Lond.) (born 1925).

Sculptor in wood, clay, stone and wax. Born on 20th May 1925 at Weston-Super-Mare, Somerset. Studied at Bristol Art School 1948–53, and the R.C.A. He made sculpture from the time he left school, but did not begin to show outside student exhibitions until 1953, when he won a prize in the International Competition for the Monument to the Unknown Political Prisoner. Exhibited at the R.B.A., R.W.A., Society of Portrait Sculptors, Free Painters and Sculptors, also in Paris, Biarritz, New York. Elected A.R.B.S. 1969. He runs a three-year sculpture course at Stafford College of Further Education.

*O'SULLIVAN, Sean, R.H.A. (1906–1964).

Member of the Senefelder Club.

*OTTEWELL, Benjamin John, H.R.I. (died 1937).

Exhibited at the leading London galleries from 1885.

OYLER, Miss Judith Audrey Allenby (fl. from late 1920s).

Landscape painter in water-colour. Born at Wychbold, Worcestershire. Studied at Grimsby School of Art, and Leicester College of Art. Exhibited at the R.A., R.I., R.B.A., W.I.A.C., and Goupil Gallery. Member of the committee of the Lincolnshire and South Humberside Artists Society. Taught at Harrogate School of Art 1930–35, and Head of the Art Department at Christ's Hospital Girls High School, Lincoln 1935–70. Lives in Lincoln.

OYSTON, George Dean (fl. c. 1890–1930).

Landscape and genre painter in water-colour. Exhibited at the R.I. from 1891. Lived at King's Norton, Birmingham in the 1920s.

P

PAGET, Walter Stanley (died 1935).

Figure painter. Exhibited at the leading London galleries from 1878, including the R.A., R.B.A. Lived in London, and died 29th January 1935 aged 72.

*PALMER, James Lynwood (1867–1941).

Born January 1867. Began in the diplomatic service, and received no formal art training. Settled in Canada, where he worked on a ranch, drawing horses in his spare time. Removed to New York and there achieved some measure of success as a painter. Returned to England after an absence of eleven years, and received a number of important commissions.

PAN, Arthur (fl. c. 1920–1960).

Portrait painter in oil. Born in Hungary. Studied at the Budapest Academy of Art, and in Paris at the Académie Julian. Lived in England for many years, and received commissions in this country and America. Painted Queen Elizabeth II and Sir Winston Churchill.

PASCAL, Leopold, R.O.I., N.E.A.C., S.M.A. (born 1900).

Painter in oil of landscapes, seascapes and still life. Born at Morlaix in Brittany. Studied art and worked in Paris, and became a member of the Salon d'Automne, the Salon des Indépendants, and the Salon des Tuileries. Came to England in June 1940, and served as a war correspondent and artist to the Free French Navy. Settled in Chelsea, and exhibited at leading galleries in London, the provinces, and abroad. Married the artist Lucette de la Fougère.

PATERSON, Hamish C. (1890–1955).

Portrait painter. Born on 1st February 1890, son of James Paterson, R.S.A. Served in World War I in 9th Royal Scots, as a private, and was shot through both wrists. Exhibited at the R.A., R.S.A., R.S.W., G.I., S.S.A. Lived in Edinburgh, and died 23rd September 1955.

PEAKE, Mervyn (1911–1968).

Author, poet, painter and illustrator. Born in China on 9th July 1911. Published *Rhymes Without Reason* 1944, *Titus Groan* 1946, *The Rime of the Flying Bomb* 1962, and other works. Lived in London, and at Burpham in Sussex. Died on 17th November 1968.

*PEARSE, Alfred (died 1933).

Painted some battle scenes, also portrait miniatures; magazine illustrator. Lived in London, and was aged 79 at the time of his death.

PEARSON, H. G., A.R.W.A. (*fl. c.* 1910–1930).

Bristol artist. Exhibited at the R.W.A.

PEDDIE, James Dick (*fl. c.* 1890–1920).

Scottish portrait painter. Exhibited at the R.A., R.S.A., New Gallery, and Walker Art Gallery, Liverpool. Lived in London and Edinburgh.

*PELLEW, Claughton (1890–1966).

Painter and engraver of landscapes and figure subjects. Spent much of his childhood in Canada. Studied art at the Slade School under Tonks, Steer and Brown. Settled in Norfolk 1919. Exhibited with the Modern English Water-colour Society. Represented in the British Museum and the Victoria and Albert Museum. A memorial exhibition was held at the Assembly House, Norwich 1967.

PENN, Audrey (born 1897).

Landscape painter. Received no formal art training. Exhibited at the R.I., R.W.S. Art Club, and in the provinces. One-man shows held at the Deben Gallery, Woodbridge, and elsewhere. She has lived in East Anglia for many years.

PENTLAND, J. Howard, R.H.A. (*fl. c.* 1885–1915).

Irish architect. Elected A.R.H.A. 1894, R.H.A. 1895. Lived in Dublin.

PERCIVAL, Harold Stanley, A.R.E. (1868–1914).

Etcher and lithographer of landscapes and town scenes. Born at Bickley, Kent on 6th September 1868. Followed a career as an engineer until 1897 and was involved in the construction of the Manchester Ship Canal. Worked in Sussex and East Anglia. Elected A.R.E. 1905. Died on 6th October 1914, a memorial exhibition held the following year at Brighton Art Gallery.

PETERS, William (*fl. c.* 1895–1915).

Painter of landscapes and figure subjects. Worked in Norway 1905.

PETHERICK, Miss Rosa C. (died 1931).

Illustrator of children's books. Lived at Croydon and died 20th December 1931.

PETO, Miss Gladys Emma (Mrs. Emmerson) (born 1890).

Book illustrator, poster designer and water-colourist. Born at Maidenhead on 19th June 1890. Studied at Maidenhead Art School 1908, and London School of Art 1911. Contributed to *The Sketch* 1915–26, and published several books including *Gladys Peto's Children's Annual*, *Malta and Cyprus*, *Gladys Peto's Sunshine Tales*. Painted water-colours in Malta, Cyprus, Egypt, India and Ireland. Lives in County Derry, Northern Ireland.

PHILLIPS, Walter Joseph, A.R.Canadian A. (1884–1963).

Water-colour painter and etcher of landscapes and genre. Born at Barton-upon-Humber, Lincolnshire. Studied at Birmingham School of Art 1899–1902. Settled in Canada, and lived at Winnipeg 1913–24 later removing to Calgary. Elected A.R.Canadian A. 1922.

PICKING, F. H. (*fl.* 1920s).

Australian landscape painter. Represented by a water-colour *Gum Trees in Moonlight* at the "Australian Artists" exhibition held at Brighton Art Gallery 1925.

PICKUP, Jack (born 1910).

Oil painter. Born at Rossendale, Lancashire. Studied at Manchester School of Art, where he later taught painting and studied glass design. Settled in Plymouth 1938, and became a lecturer at Plymouth College of Art also a member of Plymouth Society of Artists. Represented in Plymouth Art Gallery by *Citadel Road*.

PIERCE, Robert, A.R.Cam.A. (born 1884).

Architect. Born on 3rd April 1884. Studied at the Architectural Associated School. Exhibited at the R.A., R.Cam.A. Lived at Caernarvon, North Wales, for many years.

PIETERSEN, Miss Jacqueline (*fl. c.* 1920–1960).

Painter of still life in oil. Married Charles Cundall, R.A., 1923. Exhibited at the R.A., N.E.A.C. Lived at Fairlight, near Hastings, in Sussex.

PIKE, W. H., R.B.A. (born 1846).

Landscape painter in oil and water-colour. Born at Plymouth. Exhibited at the leading London galleries from 1874, including the R.A., R.B.A., R.I., R.O.I. Lived in London, and appears to have exhibited regularly up to about 1907.

PILKINGTON, Sydney (died 1905).

Landscape painter. Second son of Colonel W. W. Pilkington of Prescot, Lancashire. Studied art for two years at the Slade School under Brown. Exhibited at the N.E.A.C. for several years. Lived at Salford in Worcestershire, and painted widely in that county. Died at the early age of 32.

PITE, Arthur Beresford (1861–1934).

Architect. Born in London on 2nd September 1861. Studied art at the R.C.A. Exhibited at the R.A. from 1882. Lived in London, and at Beckenham in Kent. Died on 27th November 1934.

*PLATT, John Edgar, A.R.C.A.(Lond.) (1886–1967).

Represented in the Tate Gallery by *The Port of St. Tropez*.

*POCOCK, Alfred Lyndhurst, R.M.S. (1881–1962).

Miniaturist, metalworker and sculptor. Prior to World War I he worked in Russia for Fabergé, the Russian court jewellers, and at that time, as later in life, produced some fine carvings in semi-precious materials, such as onyx and jade. Returned to this country and lived for many years at Slinfold in Sussex, where he died. Member of the Association of Sussex Artists from 1928.

*POCOCK, Geoffrey Buckingham (1879–1960).

Member of Ipswich Art Club.

POLLEN, Arthur Joseph Lawrence (born 1899).

Sculptor. Born in London on 13th October 1899. Exhibited with the L.G. Married the artist Daphe Baring, and lived in London.

POLLEN, Mrs. Daphne (born 1904).

Decorative artist. Born at Wimbledon, *née* Baring. Studied art at the Slade School. Decorated All Hallows

Church, Poplar, and the Chapel, Campion Hall, Oxford. Married the artist Arthur Pollen, and lived in London.

POLLITT, Albert (*fl. c.* 1900–1915).
Landscape and marine painter in water-colour. Worked in Lancashire and North Wales.

POWELL, Eric Walter (died 1933).
Painter and art teacher. Exhibited at the R.I. A drawing master at Eton College, he lived at Windsor. Killed with three other Eton masters in the Alps on 17th August 1933 aged 47.

POWELL, Leonard M. (*fl. c.* 1882–1922).
Landscape painter. Exhibited at the leading London galleries from 1882, including the R.A., R.I., R.B.A., New Gallery. Lived at Hertford for many years.

*POWER, Harold Septimus, R.O.I., R.I. (1878–1951).
Painter of landscapes, portraits and figures. Born at Dunedin, New Zealand. Settled in Europe 1905, and served in World War I with the A.I.F.

POWNALL, Gilbert Anthony (born 1876).
Potrait painter in oil. Born in London on 17th January 1876. Studied art at the R.A. Schools. Exhibited at the R.A., and in the provinces. He produced a considerable amount of work in London Catholic churches, and painted a portrait of Cardinal Bourne. Executed some mosaics at Westminster Cathedral 1928–35.

PRIOR, Melton (died 1910).
War artist, producing illustrations of battle scenes. Died on 2nd November 1910 aged 73.

*PROCTER, Mrs. Dod, R.A., N.E.A.C. (1892–1972).
Erratum—Surname spelt as above.

*PROCTER, Ernest, A.R.A., N.E.A.C., I.S. (1886–1935).
Erratum—Surname spelt as above.

PROPERT, John Lumsden (1835–1902).
Landscape etcher. Exhibited at the leading London galleries from 1870, chiefly the R.A. Worked in Wales, Italy and along the Thames.

PRYDE, Samuel (died 1920).
Liverpool artist. Died January 1920 aged 78.

PURSE, Reginald (died 1915).
Anglo-American artist. Died on the *Lusitania* on 7th May 1915.

*PURSER, Miss Sarah, R.H.A. (1849–1943).
Portrait and genre painter in oil; stained glass artist. Founded her studio "An Tur Gloine" 1903.

*PUSINELLI, Miss Doris, R.I., P.S. (died 1976).
Although known under the above name as an artist she was in fact Mrs. Winifred Doris Pusinelli Smith. Died in London on 19th January 1976.

Q

QUINN, Réné Robert (died 1934).
Portrait and figure painter. Son of James Quinn,

R.P. Lived at Fulham. Died on 7th June 1934 at an early age.

R

RAKOCZI, Basil Ivan (born 1908).
Oil painter and sculptor. Born in London on 31st May 1908. Studied at Brighton School of Art. His painting *Fishermen's Huts, Hastings* was included in the Wertheim Collection exhibition held at Worthing Art Gallery 1958. Represented in several public collections. Lives in France.

RALSTON, William (died 1911).
Illustrator. Exhibited in London from 1875. Contributed to *Punch* and *The Graphic*. Lived in Glasgow and died October 1911.

RAMPLING, R. E. (died 1909).
Water-colour painter. Died in April 1909 aged 73.

*RAMSAY, Lady Victoria Patricia Helena Elizabeth, R.W.S., R.W.A., N.E.A.C. (1886–1974).
Died 12th January 1974.

RAMSDEN, Omar, R.M.S., A.W.G. (1873–1939).
Craftsman, goldsmith and designer. Born in Sheffield on 21st August 1873. Studied art at the R.C.A., also in Spain, France, Italy, Germany. Exhibited at the R.A. and Paris Salon. Represented in several public collections. Lived in London, and died August 1939.

RECKITT, Miss Rachel, N.S. (*fl. c.* 1930–1950).
Wood engraver of landscapes and architectural subjects. Studied art under Iain Macnab. Exhibited at the N.S., and lived at Watchet in Somerset.

REED, Edward Tennyson (1860–1933).
Cartoonist. Born on 27th March 1860. Visited Egypt, China and Japan 1880. Exhibited at the New Gallery from 1885. Political cartoonist to *Punch* 1894–1912, he also contributed to *The Bystander*. Lived in London, and died 12th July 1933.

REID, George Agnew, R.Canadian A. (1860–1947).
Painter in oil of landscapes and genre. Born at Wingham, Ontario, Canada. Studied at Ontario School of Art, Philadelphia Academy of Fine Arts, also in Paris and Madrid. Exhibited at the Paris Salon 1889–93, and at the R.A., but chiefly in North America. Elected A.R.Canadian A. 1885, a full member 1890, and President 1906–07. President of Ontario Society of Artists 1899–1903, and President of the Canadian Society of Painter Etchers 1935–36. Principal of Ontario College of Art 1912–29. Represented in several public collections in Canada. Lived in Toronto and died 23rd August 1947.

REID, Nano (born 1910).
Irish genre painter in oil. She studied art in Dublin and Paris. First Dublin exhibition held 1933.

*REID, Miss Nina Margaret ("Winder"), R.S.M.A. (1891–1975).
Lived at Eastbourne and died 29th December 1975.

RENDLE, Arthur E., A.R.C.A.(Lond.) (died 1917).

West Country artist. Studied art at the R.C.A. Exhibited at the R.W.A. and lived at Redland, Bristol. Killed in France 6th September 1917.

REUSS, Albert (1889–1975).

Oil painter and sculptor. Born on 2nd October 1889. Educated in Vienna but self-taught as an artist. Exhibited in Britain, also on the continent, and is represented in several public collections. Lived at Mousehole, near Penzance, in Cornwall and died 4th November 1975.

REYNOLDS, Miss C. Jeannie, R.M.S. (*fl. c.* 1905–1925).

Miniature painter. Exhibited at the R.A., R.M.S., and Walker Art Gallery, Liverpool. Lived at Sunbury-on-Thames and in London.

REYNOLDS, John Patrick (1909–1935).

Illustrator and cartoonist. Died by his own hand on 25th December 1935 aged 26.

REYNOLDS, O. B. (*fl. c.* 1935–1950).

Landscape painter. Works include *Spring in Ross-shire*.

RHEAM, Henry Meynell, R.I. (1859–1920).

Genre painter. Born at Birkenhead on 13th January 1859. Studied art in London at Heatherley's, later in Paris under Bouguereau and Tony Fleury. Exhibited at the leading London galleries from 1887, including the R.A., R.I., R.B.A., also in Birmingham and at the Walker Art Gallery, Liverpool. Elected R.I. 1893. Lived at Newlyn in Cornwall, and worked chiefly in that county. Died November 1920.

RHIND, Ethel Mary (died 1952).

Irish stained glass artist.

RHIND, T. Duncan (*fl. c.* 1905–1915).

Architect, and etcher of architectural subjects. Studied at Edinburgh School of Art. Served in World War I as a Major in the 5th Battalion of Royal Scots.

RIBBANS, Albert Charles (1903–1967).

Mural painter and water-colourist. Born at Ipswich on 15th November 1903. Studied at Ipswich School of Art. Exhibited at the R.A. A member of Ipswich Art Club, he lived at Rushmere, Ipswich.

RICE, Mrs. E. Garrett (*fl.* 1920s).

Landscape etcher and colour print artist. Lived at Coventry, and exhibited at Birmingham Art Gallery.

RIDDLE, John (*fl. c.* 1920–1950).

Truro artist. Exhibited at R.A., R.S.A., R.B.A. Lived at Blackheath in the 1920s and later at Truro, Cornwall.

RIDGEWELL, William Leigh (1881–1937).

Cartoonist and book illustrator. Born in Brighton on 8th September 1881. Studied at Brighton School of Art. In 1936 he produced a book *Line and Laughter.* A member of Brighton Arts club, he lived in the town. Died by his own hand on 7th November 1937.

RITCHIE, C. E., R.O.I. (*fl. c.* 1895–1940).

Oil painter. Began as a barrister, but then took up art and studied in Paris. Exhibited at the R.A., R.O.I., R.S.A., R.W.A., New Gallery, and Walker Art Gallery, Liverpool. Lived in London, Aberdeen and St. Andrews. A member of Aberdeen Artists' Society.

RIVERS, Richard Godfrey (1859–1925).

Landscape painter in oil. Born at Plymouth. Studied art at the Slade School under Legros. Exhibited at the leading London galleries from 1879, including the R.A., R.B.A., and at the Paris Salon. Settled in Australia 1889, and became President of Queensland Art Society.

ROBERTS, Miss Dorothy F., R.B.A., A.R.M.S. (*fl. c.* 1910–1925).

Miniature painter. Exhibited at the R.A., R.B.A., R.M.S. Lived at Aston-on-Clun, Shropshire, and in London.

ROBERTS, Miss Winifred Russell (*fl. c.* 1890–1915).

Landscape painter in water-colour. Exhibited at the R.B.A. from 1893, and at Dowdeswell's 1906. Lived in London.

ROBERTSON, Arthur, A.R.E. (*fl. c.* 1876–1911).

Etcher and water-colour painter. Exhibited at the leading London galleries from 1876, including the R.A., R.B.A., R.I. Elected A.R.E. 1888, his membership ceased 10th November 1911.

ROBINSON, Miss Bay, W.I.A.C. (born 1898).

Illustrator, lithographer and painter in water-colour and gouache. Born at Hampstead on 6th August 1898, daughter of Charles Robinson, R.I. Studied at Hornsey College of Art. Exhibited at the R.A., R.I., R.B.A., S.G.A. and W.I.A.C. One-man shows held at the Walker Art Gallery in Bond Street, and at Guildford House. She has taught part time at various schools, including Downe House at Newbury, and lives at Maidenhead in Berkshire.

ROBINSON, Major Douglas F., I.S. (died 1937).

Landscape painter. Exhibited at the leading London galleries from 1890, including the R.A., R.B.A., I.S., and at the R.W.A. Lived in London and died 19th January 1937.

ROBINSON, Thomas H. (1865–1953).

Illustrator. Born in London, brother of Charles and William Heath Robinson. Studied art at the R.A. Schools. Works illustrated include *Legends from River and Mountain* 1896, *The Heroes* 1899, and *Tales from the Arabian Nights* 1914.

ROCKE, Basil (born 1904).

Painter in oil and water-colour of landscapes and figures. Born at Hampstead. Studied art at Reading University, in Vienna, and at the Euston Road School in London. Exhibited with the L.G. Lived in London.

RODMELL, Ilsa (born 1898).

Oil painter. Represented in the Wertheim Collection exhibition held at Worthing Art Gallery 1958 by *From Birth to Death* and *Lucy's Coleus.*

ROGERS, Frederick, F.R.B.S. (*fl.c.* 1885–1905).

London sculptor. Exhibited at the R.A. from 1889.

ROGERS, Mark (1848–1933).

Sculptor. Born in London. Studied art at South Kensington and Lambeth School of Art. Exhibited at the R.A. from 1880. Lived in London, and died 14th December 1933 aged 85.

ROPE, Miss Ellen Mary (1855–1934).

Sculptor. Studied art at the Slade School under Legros. Exhibited at the R.A. from 1885, also at the New Gallery. Lived in London, and at Tunstall, near Aldeburgh, in Suffolk. Died on 13th September 1934.

*ROSE, Robert Traill, S.S.A. (1863–1942).

Exhibited chiefly at the R.S.A., S.S.A., but also in France, Germany and North America.

ROSENBERG, Isaac (1890–1918).

Painter of portraits, figures and landscapes; poet. Son of Jewish immigrants from Lithuania, he was brought up in the East End of London. At age 14 he began to study engraving, and later came under the patronage of Mrs. Herbert Cohen. As a result he was sent to the Slade School, where he studied under Tonks. An acquaintance of Mark Gertler. Went to South Africa for a year, and returned to England following the outbreak of World War I. He saw active service in the army, and was killed in April 1918.

ROSKRUGE, Francis John (born 1871).

Etcher. Born on 10th August 1871 at St. Keverne, Cornwall. Served in South Africa 1899–1900, and East Africa 1914–18. Exhibited at the R.W.A. and Newlyn Society of Artists. President of St. Ives Arts Club. Lived at St. Ives, Cornwall for many years.

ROWBOTHAM, Charles (*fl.c.* 1877–1914).

Landscape painter in water-colour. Exhibited at the leading London galleries from 1877, chiefly the R.B.A., R.I. Water-colours include *Town and Bay of Sorrento; The Castle of Urquhart, Loch Ness; View of Arundel* and *MacGillycuddy's Reeks, Ireland.* Lived in Brighton for some years and later in Croydon.

ROWDEN, Thomas (died 1926).

Exeter artist, who does not appear to have exhibited extensively. Died on 15th May 1926 aged 84.

*RUSHTON, George Robert, R.I., R.B.A., R.B.S.A. (1868–1948).

Born on 1st January 1868. Elected R.I. 1929.

RUSHTON, W. C. (died 1921).

Exhibited at the G.I. and Walker Art Gallery, Liver-pool. Lived at Cambuslang in Scotland, and later at Bingley, Yorkshire. Died October 1921.

RUSSELL, Charles, R.H.A. (1852–1910).

Portrait and genre painter. Born at Dumbarton on 4th February 1852. Settled in Dublin 1874. Exhibited at the R.H.A. from 1878, and at the R.A. from 1889. Elected A.R.H.A. 1891, R.H.A. 1893. Died at Black-rock on 12th December 1910.

RUSSELL, George (1867–1935).

Irish landscape and figure painter in oil. Works include *The Gully* and *The Potato Gatherers.* Represented in the Dublin Gallery of Modern Art.

RUSSELL, G. Horne, P.R.Canadian A. (1861–1933).

Portrait painter in oil. Born at Banff in Scotland. Studied at Aberdeen School of Art and South Kensington. Settled in Montreal, Canada 1890. Elected A.R.Canadian A. 1909, a full member 1918, and President 1922–26.

RUSSELL, J. Galloway (died 1917).

Dunfermline artist. Killed in action on 3rd May 1917.

RYAN, Vivian Desmond, N.S.A. (1893–1950).

Painter in oil of portraits, landscapes and still life. Born on 7th September 1893, second son of Sir Gerald Hemmington Ryan Bt. of Hintlesham Hall, Suffolk. Studied art under Seymour Lucas. Exhibited at the R.A., R.P., R.B.A., R.W.A., Paris Salon, and elected N.S.A. 1921. One-man show held at the Beaux Arts Galleries, London. Being deaf and dumb he had a handi-cap that towards the end of his life distracted him from his painting. Father of the artist Adrian Ryan. Lived in London.

S

SAGE, Henry (1868–1953).

Little known Guildford painter.

SAINSBURY, Hesta, S.W.E. (*fl.* 1920s).

Wood engraver. Exhibited at the S.W.E. 1921, later becoming a member.

SALAMAN, Michael Jonathan (born 1911).

Painter in oil, water-colour and gouache of landscapes and portraits. Born on 8th May 1911 at Porlock in Somerset. Studied art at the Slade School, and in Paris at the Académie Ranson. Exhibited at the R.A., L.G., and Leicester Galleries. Retrospective exhibition held at the Morley Gallery 1975. Represented in the Victoria and Albert Museum, and the South London Gallery. Visiting teacher at the R.A. Schools, Chelsea School of Art, and Camberwell School of Arts and Crafts. Lives in London.

SANDERS, Henry (born 1918).

Painter, in oil and water-colour, and lithographer of figure subjects, animals and landscapes. Born at Dresden, Germany on 27th March 1918. Studied at Hornsey College of Art 1935–39, 1945. One-man shows held at the Ben Uri Gallery, Newcastle Peoples Theatre, Queenswood Gallery, and has also exhibited at the Whitechapel and Redfern Galleries. Lives in London.

SAVAGE, Ernest, P.S. (born 1906).

Landscape painter in pastel, water-colour, gouache and oil. Born in London on 14th July 1906. Studied at Cheltenham College of Education and West Ham College of Art. Exhibited at the R.I., Mall Galleries, and widely in the provinces. Elected P.S. 1958 becoming Vice-President 1974. President of the Cheltenham and Horsham Art Clubs. A council member of the Society of Sussex Painters and of the Association of Sussex Artists. Author of *Pastel for Beginners* 1965, and *Painting Landscapes in Pastel* 1971. Lives at Fittleworth in West Sussex.

SAVAGE, William Beck (*fl. c.* 1910–1915).

Painter of figure subjects. Exhibited with the N.E.A.C. Served in World War I in the Public Schools Brigade, Royal Fusiliers.

SCHMOLLE, Miss Stella (1908–1975).

Sculptor. Born in Barnes. Studied and then taught at the Central School of Arts and Crafts. Exhibited at the R.A. Executed a number of portrait commissions. Represented in the British Museum. Lived in London, and died 5th March 1975.

SCHOFIELD, Kershaw (*fl. c.* 1900–1930).

Painter in oil of landscapes and seascapes. A friend

of the artist Herbert Royle. Lived at Bradford, Yorkshire.

SCOTT, Charles (1886–1964).

Landscape painter. Born at Newmilns, Ayrshire. Studied at Glasgow School of Art, also in Belgium, Holland, Germany. Settled in Calgary, Canada 1912, and subsequently removed to Vancouver. Director of Vancouver School of Art 1925–52, and died in that city.

SCOTT, Miss J. Mary (Mrs. Finch), R.M.S. (*fl. c.* 1895–1950).

Miniature painter. Exhibited at the R.A., R.M.S., G.I., and Walker Art Gallery, Liverpool. Lived in London in the early years of the century.

SCOTT, Patrick (born 1921).

Irish oil painter of abstracts and landscapes.

SCOTT, William, R.E. (born 1848).

Etcher of architectural subjects. Articled in 1867 to a provincial architect, he passed his R.I.B.A. examination 1870. Awarded silver medal of the R.I.B.A. 1875, the Soane medallion 1877, and the R.A. travelling scholarship 1878. Exhibited at the leading London galleries from 1876, including the R.A., R.E., R.B.A. Elected R.E. 1881, but withdrew from the society 1896. Etched several Venetian subjects, also worked in Rome and on the Italian Riviera.

SCOTT-MOORE, Mrs. Elizabeth, R.W.S., R.I., N.E.A.C. (born 1906).

Painter in water-colour and oil of landscapes, portraits and figure subjects. Born October 1906 at Dartford in Kent, *née* Brier. Studied at Goldsmiths' College School of Art, the Central School of Arts and Crafts, and in Italy. Exhibited at the R.A., R.W.S., R.I., R.P., N.E.A.C., and has held fourteen one-man shows (two in London, twelve in the Home Counties). Received a Gold Medal at the Paris Salon 1962. Member of the Society of Chelsea Artists, now disbanded. Lives in Surrey.

*SCULLY, Harold,** R.H.A. (died 1935).

Elected A.R.H.A. 1900, R.H.A. 1906.

*SEGAL, Arthur** (1875–1944).

Represented by an oil painting—*Bornholm Harbour*—in the Tate Gallery.

SELLERS, James Henry (1861–1954).

Artist, craftsman, furniture designer and architect. Born at Oldham in Lancashire. First exhibited at the R.A. 1891, his work was still being shown there fifty years later. A partner of Edgar Thomas Wood, he lived in Manchester for many years.

*SEVERN, Walter,** R.Cam.A. (1830–1904).

Erratum—Christian name correctly listed above.

SHACKLETON, Keith Hope, P.R.S.M.A. (born 1923).

Painter in oil of marine subjects and wildlife. Born at Weybridge in Surrey on 16th January 1923. Received no formal art training. Exhibited at the R.A., Mall Galleries, and abroad. One-man shows held in London at Rowley Gallery, Tryon Gallery, Rowland Ward Gallery. Early member of the Society of Aviation Artists, and now Hon. Vice President of the Guild of of Aviation Artists. Elected R.S.M.A. 1960, President 1973, and a founder member of the Society of Wildlife Artists 1964. Represented in the National Maritime Museum at Greenwich, City of Belfast Art Gallery, City of Birkenhead Art Gallery, and in the Diploma Collection at the R.S.M.A. He has painted, and carried out wildlife field work, in many parts of the world. Lives in London.

SHAKESPEAR, Miss Dorothy (born 1886).

Vorticist painter. Contributed illustrations to *Blast*. Married Ezra Pound 1914.

SHARLAND, E. W. (*fl.* 1915–1940).

Etcher of architectural subjects. He took up art, instead of entering his father's cabinet making business, and was influenced by Frank Brangwyn. Exhibited at the R.W.A. Works include *Toledo; Burgos Cathedral; Bridge of Sighs, Venice;* and *Piccadilly Circus.* Lived at Bristol.

SHAW, Mrs. Evelyn Caroline Eunice Byam (1870–1960).

Genre and portrait painter. Studied at St. John's Wood School of Art and the R.A. Schools. Exhibited at the R.A. from 1894, initially under her maiden name of Pyke-Nott. Married John Byam Shaw 1899. By the outbreak of World War I she had abandoned painting owing to deteriorating eyesight.

SHELDON, Miss Pearl (*fl.* 1920s).

Painter in water-colour of landscapes and architectural subjects. Exhibited with the "Australian Artists" at Brighton Art Gallery 1925.

SHELDON-WILLIAMS, Inglis (1870–1940).

Landscape and genre painter. Studied art at the Slade School, and in Paris at the École des Beaux Arts. Lived in Canada for some years, firstly in Saskatchewan and later at Regina.

*SHEPARD, Ernest Howard** (1879–1976).

Died at Midhurst, Sussex on 24th March 1976.

*SHEPHERD, F. H. S.,** N.E.A.C. (1877–1948).

Landscape and genre painter. Born at Stoke-sub-Hamdon, near Yeovil, in Somerset.

SHEPPARD, Benjamin, F.R.B.S. (*fl. c.* 1905–1910).

London sculptor. Exhibited at the R.A., G.I., and New Gallery. Lived in Chelsea.

*SHEPPARD, Oliver,** R.H.A., F.R.B.S. (1864–1941).

Portrait sculptor. Elected A.R.H.A. 1898, R.H.A. 1901. One-time modelling master at Nottingham School of Art.

SHEPPARD, R., F.R.B.S. (*fl. c.* 1905–1915).

London sculptor. Exhibited at the R.A.

SHERMAN, Albert John (born 1882).

Flower painter in oil. Born at Truro in Cornwall on 30th June 1882. Studied at Truro Central Technical School. Settled in Australia after World War I, and in 1934 was elected an associate of the Royal Art Society of New South Wales.

*SHORE, Robert S.,** R.H.A. (died 1931).

Elected A.R.H.A. 1894, R.H.A. 1895.

SHORT, Frederick Golden (*fl. c.* 1885–1907).

Landscape painter in oil. Exhibited at the leading London galleries from 1885, including the R.A., R.B.A., R.I., R.O.I., New Gallery. Lived at Lyndhurst, Hampshire, for some years, and painted New Forest subjects.

SHORT, William (died 1921).

Suffolk artist. Died April 1921 aged 93.

SIMMONS, S. Noel (*fl. c.* 1900–1915).

Painter in oil and water-colour of interior subjects and town scenes. Influenced by William Nicholson. Exhibited with the N.E.A.C., also at the Stafford and Chenil Galleries in London. Served in World War I in the Royal Wiltshire Yeomanry.

SITWELL, Pauline C. M., S.W.E. (born 1916).

Painter, wood engraver, lithographer, aquatinter of landscapes, floral subjects and people at work; poet and writer. Born in Malta on 5th October 1916. Studied at St. John's Wood Art School, and at the R.A. Schools 1933–37. Exhibited at R.E., S.W.E., P.S., R.S.M.A., S.G.A. One-man show held 1973 under the auspices of Westminster City Council, and a shared exhibition with Diana Hills held in Suffolk. Elected S.W.E. 1969. Represented in collections in Italy, France, Holland and Belgium. A well known ski-mountaineer, her wood engravings of mountain subjects are of interest to enthusiasts. Similarly, as a long-shore fisherwoman, co-owning a boat at Southwold for some three years after the war, her boat subjects reflect her love of the sea. She was married to the artist Peter Stebbing, and lives in London.

SMALLFIELD, Miss Beatrice C., R.M.S. (*fl. c.* 1895–1925).

Miniature painter. Exhibited at the R.A., R.M.S., G.I., and Walker Art Gallery, Liverpool. Lived at St. John's Wood and later at Finchley. Probably a daughter of Frederick Smallfield, A.R.W.S.

SMITH, David T. (born 1920).

Oil painter of war subjects. Served in the R.A.F.

*SMITH, Erik, R.W.S., R.B.A., R.E., A.R.C.A.(Lond.) (1914–1973).

Died aged 58.

SMITH, Lindsay (died 1915).

Member of Chelsea Arts Club. Served in World War I as a 1st Lieut. in the 8th Battalion of Gordon Highlanders, and was killed 10th November 1915.

SMITH, Mrs. Mary W., W.I.A.C. (born 1904).

Oil painter of still life, interiors and portraits. Born at Bury, Lancashire on 29th February 1904, *née* Parker. Studied art at the Slade School 1923–26, where she won prizes for drawing, painting and composition. Exhibited at the R.A., N.E.A.C., W.I.A.C., in the provinces, and with two other artists at the Beaux Arts Gallery 1933. Represented in Manchester City Art Gallery and Bury Art Gallery. Lives at Barcombe, near Lewes, in Sussex.

SMITH, Neville (died 1916).

Illustrator and cartoonist. Contributed to *Punch*. Killed on 26th January 1916.

SMITH, Phil W. (*fl. c.* 1900–1935).

Etcher of landscapes, genre and horses. Lived at Chorlton-on-Medlock, Manchester, and later in London. His work was published by Colnaghi's.

SMITH, Sidney (born 1912).

Self taught oil painter. Took up art in 1937.

SMITH, Sydney Ure (1887–1949).

Etcher and water-colour painter. Born at Stoke Newington, London, January 1887. Studied art under Julian Ashton. Elected President of Sydney Society of Artists 1922, he is represented in several Australian public collections. Lived in Sydney for many years, and died 11th October 1949.

SMITH, Thomas Reynolds (1839–1910).

Miniature painter and sculptor. Born at Newcastle-upon-Tyne.

SMITHARD, G. S. (died 1919).

Landscape and genre painter in oil. A native of Derby, he made his reputation in South Africa. Died July 1919.

SOLOMON, William Ewart Gladstone (1880–1965).

Mural decorator. Exhibited at the R.A., and Walker Art Gallery, Liverpool. Lived in Kensington for some years, and later in Cape Province, South Africa. Died on 18th December 1965.

SOLON, Leon Victor, R.B.A. (born 1872).

Decorative painter, illustrator and author. Born at Stoke-on-Trent. Studied art at the R.C.A., where he won a scholarship and medal. Exhibited at the R.A. and Paris Salon. Settled in America, and lived at Lakeland, Florida.

SOMERVILLE, Miss Edith Œ. (1858–1949).

Landscape painter in oil and water-colour, illustrator and writer. Studied art in Paris at the Académies Colarossi and Délécluse. Exhibited at the R.H.A., and Walker Art Gallery, Liverpool. Lived at Skibbereen, County Cork.

SOMERVILLE, J. Whyte (died 1916).

Scottish artist. Exhibited at the R.S.A., G.I. Lived in Edinburgh, and was killed 22nd June 1916.

SOORD, Alfred U. (died 1915).

Figure painter. Exhibited at the R.A. from 1893, also at R.I., R.W.A., G.I., New Gallery, Birmingham, and Walker Art Gallery, Liverpool. Lived at Bushey for some years, and died 10th August 1915 aged 47.

*SORRELL, Alan, R.W.S., A.R.C.A.(Lond.) (1904–1974).

Died following a road accident on 21st December 1974.

SPARROW, Dr. Geoffrey, A.R.E. (1887–1969).

Etcher, illustrator, caricaturist and writer. Born on 13th July 1887. Member of the Society of Sussex Painters. His autobiography *Foxes and Physic* was published 1962. Died February 1969.

SPARTALI, Miss Marie (Mrs. Stillman) (died 1927).

Figure painter. Exhibited at the leading London galleries from 1867, including the R.A., R.B.A., R.I., New and Grosvenor Galleries. Influenced by Burne-Jones. Died 1st March 1927 aged 83.

*SPRADBERY, Walter Ernest (1889–1969).

Produced some posters. Chairman of Essex Art Club.

*SPRING-SMITH, Miss Effie, R.B.A. (1907–1974).

Member of Ipswich Art Club.

SPRUCE, Edward Caldwell (*c.* 1865–1925).

Portrait and figure sculptor in bronze. Born at Knutsford, Cheshire. Employed at a local tile factory, he spent his lunch breaks making portrait busts. Settled in Leeds, became head designer and modeller at Burmantofts Art Pottery, and also taught modelling at Leeds School of Art. Went to Paris for further study, and first exhibited at the Paris Salon 1905. His work was also shown at the R.A.

SQUIRRELL, Martin (1926–1950).

Water-colour painter. Son of the artist Leonard Squirrell. Exhibited at the R.A. from 1944. A member of Ipswich Art Club, he lived in that town. Died on 13th December 1950.

STABB, Charles (*fl. c.* 1900–1925).

Figure painter in oil. Exhibited with the N.E.A.C., and lived in London.

STACY, H. E., R.W.A. (died 1915).

Painter in oil of landscapes and coastal subjects. Exhibited at the R.B.A. in 1872, but more frequently at the R.W.A. Lived at Weston-super-Mare, and later at Willsbridge, near Bristol. Died October 1915 aged 77.

*STEPHEN, Douglas George (born 1909).

Now lives at Mainridge, Victoria, Australia.

*STEPHENSON, John Cecil (1889–1965).

Represented in the Tate Gallery.

STEWART, Miss Janet Agnes Cumbrae (died 1960).

Painter in pastel and water-colour of landscapes, portraits and figure subjects. Born at Brighton, Victoria, Australia. Worked in several European countries, including England and France, and exhibited at the R.A. also in the provinces. Received an Hon. Mention at the Paris Salon, and was represented in the "Australian Artists" show held at Brighton Art Gallery 1925. Lived in Australia for much of her life.

STOBART, John, R.S.M.A. (born 1929).

Painter in oil of marine and aviation subjects, specialising in historical subjects such as *Savannah—Worlds First Steam Ship Leaving Savannah, Georgia May 20th 1819*, which was available in America as a limited edition print. Born in Leicester on 29th December 1929. Studied at Derby College of Art and the R.A. Schools. where he received a medal and the Landseer Scholarship. Exhibited at the R.A., R.B.A., R.S.M.A., and in North America, including five shows at the Kennedy Galleries, New York City. Lives in America at Potomac.

STOKES, A. G. Folliott (died 1939).

Landscape painter and author. Exhibited at the R.B.A. from 1892, also at R.A., New Gallery, and in the provinces. Wrote books on Cornwall, including *The Cornish Coast and Moors.* Lived at St. Ives, and later at Henley-on-Thames. Died on 17th October 1939.

STONE, H. Mulready (*fl. c.* 1905–1925).

Etcher of architectural subjects. Worked in Cornwall, London and Denmark.

STRAHAN, Geoffrey, R.B.A. (died 1916).

Member of the London Sketch Club. Exhibited at the R.B.A., R.I., R.O.I., and New Gallery. Lived in London and at Tatsfield in Surrey. Killed in the Great War.

STRATTEN, Miss Lucy A., R.M.S. (*fl. c.* 1890–1925).

Miniature painter. Exhibited at the R.A. from 1890, also at R.M.S. and Walker Art Gallery, Liverpool. Lived at Hessle in East Yorkshire, and later in Chelsea.

STRATTON, Fred (*fl. c.* 1900–1930).

Painter in oil and water-colour of landscapes, genre and portraits. Studied figure drawing in London for three years. Influenced by the Barbizon painters. Exhibited at the R.A. Works include *The Woodland Stream; The River Bank; Summer;* and *The Picnic.* Lived at Amberley in Sussex, and in London. Father of the sculptor Hilary Byfield Stratton.

STREVENS, F. John L. (*fl.* from *c.* 1935).

Painter in oil and water-colour of portraits and figure subjects, especially children. Born in London. Received no formal art training. Exhibited at the R.A., R.B.A. and at the Paris Salon. A member of the London Sketch Club. Lives at Loughton in Essex.

STROBL, Kisfaludy Sigismund De (1884–1975).

Portrait sculptor. Born at Alsorajk, Hungary. Studied art at the Budapest Royal Academy, also in Vienna, Paris and Italy. Professor at the Royal Academy, Budapest from 1924, and received Hungary's Order of Merit 1954. Worked in London extensively between the wars, and executed busts of the Queen when a child, George Bernard Shaw, Lady Astor, Field Marshall Allenby. Exhibited at the R.A., and held a one-man show in London at the White Allom Gallery 1935. Died in Budapest aged 91.

STROUDLEY, L. James, R.B.A., A.R.C.A.(Lond.) (*fl. c.* 1930–1960).

Oil painter of figure subjects. Exhibited at the R.B.A., and in the provinces. A painting *Rowing Men* was shown at Brighton Art Gallery 1936.

STURGEON, Miss Kate (*fl. c.* 1880–1910).

Genre painter in oil and water-colour. Exhibited at the leading London galleries from 1882, including the R.A., R.B.A., R.I. Member of the Norwich Art Circle.

SULLIVAN, James Frank (died 1936).

Illustrator and author. Brother of the artist E. J. Sullivan, he studied at South Kensington School of Art. Exhibited at the leading London galleries from 1875. Contributed to a number of magazines, and wrote several books, including *Queer Side Stories, From Fog to Fairyland.* Lived in London, and died 5th May 1936 aged 83.

SUTHERS, Leghe (*fl. c.* 1885–1907).

Genre painter. Studied art in Antwerp under Verlat. Exhibited at the R.A. from 1885, he settled about that time at Newlyn in Cornwall and became friendly with Stanhope Forbes and Norman Garstin. Later lived at Porlock, near Taunton, in Somerset.

SWAIN, Ned, R.E. (*fl. c.* 1876–1902).

Etcher. Exhibited at the leading London galleries from 1876, including the R.A., R.B.A. Elected R.E. 1882, his membership ceased 9th January 1902.

*SWAISH, Frederick George, R.W.A. (*fl. c.* 1905–1930).

Painter of classical figure subjects. Exhibited at the R.A.

SWANZY, Miss Mary (born 1882).

Landscape and genre painter in oil. Her painting *Reading the Employment Offered Column* is in the Ulster Museum, Belfast. Lived at Coolock, near Dublin.

SWINSTEAD, Miss Eulalia Hillyard (Mrs. Weld), A.R.C.A.(Lond.) (born 1893).

Miniature painter. Born at Hornsey on 17th November 1893, daughter of the artist George Hillyard Swinstead. Studied art at the R.C.A. Exhibited at the R.A. and R.Cam.A. Lived in London for many years.

SWYNNERTON, Joseph William (died 1910).

Sculptor. Exhibited at the leading London galleries from 1873, including the R.A. and New Gallery. Married the artist Annie Swynnerton 1883. Lived in London, and Rome. Died 8th August 1910 aged 62.

SYKES, Aubrey F., P.R.I., P.S. (*fl.* from *c.* 1930).

Painter in oil, water-colour and pastel of landscapes. He has exhibited at the major London galleries, and in the provinces.

SYKES, Miss Dorcie (born 1908).

Painter of flowers and figure subjects in water-colour. Born in Sheffield on 16th May 1908, daughter of the artist J. G. Sykes. Studied art in Cornwall at the Harvey and Proctor School of Painting. Exhibited at the R.W.A., and with the Newlyn Society of Artists. Lives at Newlyn.

*SYKES, John Guttridge (1866–1941).

Father of the artists Dorcie and Melville Sykes.

SYKES, Melville (*c.* 1900–1930).

Marine painter in oil. Son of the artist J. G. Sykes. He died at an early age.

SYKES, Mrs. Saida Elizabeth (*née* Ward) (*fl. c.* 1895–1930).

Genre painter in oil. Wife of the artist J. G. Sykes, and mother of Dorcie and Melville Sykes. Lived at Newlyn, Cornwall.

SYMONS, George Gardner, R.B.A. (1865–1930).

American landscape painter in oil. Born in Chicago. Studied art at the Art Institute of Chicago later in Munich, London and Paris. Painted in Cornwall and other parts of England. Exhibited at the R.A., R.B.A., R.W.A., Walker Art Gallery in Liverpool, and in Birmingham. Returned to America 1909. He worked extensively in Massachusetts and California, and almost every year visited Europe. Elected N.A. 1911, and is represented in many American Museums. Died at Hillside, New Jersey on 12th January 1930.

*SYNGE, Edward Millington. A.R.E. (1860–1913).

Born at Great Malvern on 17th April 1860. Began as a land agent, but took up etching at Westminster School of Art 1891. Received advice from Seymour Haden and Frank Short. Exhibited at the R.A. from 1899, and at the Paris Salon from 1901. Worked in France, Italy and Spain.

T

TABOR, G. H. (died 1920).

Teddington artist, husband of Mrs. H. G. Tabor. Exhibited at the London Salon. Died May 1920 aged 63.

TABOR, Mrs. H. G., A.R.W.A. (*fl. c.* 1900–1930).

Teddington artist, wife of G. H. Tabor. Exhibited at the London Salon and R.W.A.

TARBET, J. Henderson (*fl. c.* 1910–1935).

Landscape painter in oil. Exhibited at the R.A., R.S.A., R.W.A., S.S.A., and Walker Art Gallery, Liverpool. Lived in Edinburgh.

TATE, Mrs. Barba, R.M.S., S.W.A. (born 1927).

Painter in oil of genre, flowers and still life. Born at Uxbridge, Middlesex. Studied drawing at Ealing School of Art. Exhibited at the R.A., R.P., R.B.A., R.O.I., R.M.S., in the provinces, also at Paris Salon, Salon du Comparaisons, Salon Terres Latines and the 8th Grand Prix de Peinture de la Cote d'Azur. One man show held in Paris 1969. Elected S.W.A. and Associate of the Société des Artistes Français 1970, A.R.M.S. 1971, R.M.S. 1972. Four works reproduced as prints, namely *Golden Girl, The Green Shawl, Clematis* and *Nasturtiums*, the latter selected amongst the Top Ten Prints of 1974. Left London to live in Switzerland 1975, and is married to the artist James Tate.

*TATE, James, A.R.M.S. (born 1914).

Exhibited at the R.A., R.I., R.O.I., R.B.A., R.M.S., U.A., N.S. and F.P.S. "Trends" exhibitions in London, and abroad at the Paris Salon, Ville Eternal Rome, the 4th Concours International de la Palme d'Or des Beaux Arts Monte Carlo, and was Laureat at the 8th Grand Prix de Peinture de la Cote d'Azur Nice. Represented in the U.K. touring exhibition "Contemporary Painters" 1972. Elected an Associate of the Société des Artistes Français 1970, A.R.M.S. 1973. His working life spent in London until 1975, he now lives in Switzerland.

TAYLER, Laurie (*fl.* 1920s).

Landscape painter in oil. Represented in the "Australian Artists" exhibition held at Brighton Art Gallery 1925.

TAYLOR, Sir Andrew Thomas, R.Canadian A. (1850–1937).

Architect and water-colour painter. Born in Edinburgh on 13th October 1850. Studied art at the R.A. Schools. Exhibited at the R.A. from 1875. Settled in Canada 1883, and had a practice at Montreal. Returned to London 1904. Chairman of the Bartlett School of Architecture, London University. Died on 5th December 1937.

TAYLOR, Ernest E. (1863–1907).

Portrait and figure painter. Born at Bournemouth. Exhibited in London from 1882, and at the R.H.A. from 1890. Lived in Ireland for some years. Died of pneumonia at Greenock on 31st January 1907.

TEED, Henry Samuel, R.B.A. (1883–1916).

Landscape painter in oil. Exhibited at the R.A., R.B.A., R.O.I., N.E.A.C., New Gallery, Walker Art Gallery at Liverpool, and in Birmingham. Director of Whitechapel Art Gallery, he lived in London. Received a commission in the Berkshire Regiment in August 1915, and was killed in action 25th July 1916.

TELBIN, William Lewis (died 1931).

Landscape painter; scenic artist. Exhibited at the R.B.A. 1875. Died on 3rd December 1931 aged 85.

TENISON, Arthur Heron Ryan (died 1930).

London artist, who exhibited at the R.A. Died 22nd September 1930 aged 69.

TEW, Ernest Frederick, R.W.A. (born 1905).

Architect. Born at Bedale, Yorkshire. Studied at Glasgow School of Architecture. Elected R.W.A. 1951. Lives at Bath.

THIRKETTLE, R. Frank (died 1916).

Yorkshire artist. Lived at Headingley, Leeds, and died 30th May 1916.

*THOMAS, Bert, P.S. (1883–1966).

Produced some posters.

THOMPSON, Sir Matthew William Bt. (1872–1956).

Painter. Born on 28th June 1872. Studied at Trinity College, Cambridge. Exhibited at the R.A. Lived in London, and died 25th November 1956.

THOMPSON, Wilfred H., A.R.E. (*fl. c.* 1884–1902).

Painter and etcher of landscapes, genre and historical subjects. Exhibited at the leading London galleries from 1884, including the R.A., R.I., R.B.A. Elected A.R.E. 1895, his membership ceased 9th January 1902.

*THOMSON, John Murray, R.S.A., R.S.W., P.S.S.A. (1885–1974).

Died on 16th October 1974.

THOMSON, Sinclair, A.R.S.A., R.S.W. (born 1914).

Represented in Glasgow Art Gallery.

THOMSON, William, R.B.A., A.R.C.A.(Lond.) (born 1926).

Painter in oil, water-colour and acrylic of portraits, figure subjects, landscapes and still life; etcher and lithographer. Born on 24th January 1926 at Hamilton, Ontario, Canada. In 1947 he received a gold medal from the Ontario College of Art in Toronto, and was influenced by his teacher John Alfsen. He came to England to study, and travelled to Holland, Belgium, France. Studied at the R.C.A. 1949–52. In 1953 he was commissioned to paint a mural for Johnson-Matthey at Wembley Park, and the following year held his first one-man show in London at St. George's Gallery. Exhibited at the R.A., R.B.A., and Artists of Fame and Promise at the Leicester Galleries. Elected R.B.A. 1966. Lives in London, and teaches at the Central School of Art and Design.

THOMSON, Miss Winifred Hope (died 1944).

Miniature painter. Exhibited at the leading London galleries from 1890, chiefly the R.A. and New Gallery. Lived in London, and died 15th August 1944.

THORNLEY, D'Arcy, U.A., B.W.S. (*fl.* 1930s).

Landscape painter in oil and water-colour. He had a studio in Chelsea, and was a member of the South Wales Art Society.

THORNTON-CLARKE, Miss E., R.M.S. (*fl. c.* 1895–1925).

Miniature painter. Exhibited at the R.A., R.I., R.M.S., and Walker Art Gallery, Liverpool. Lived in London.

THORNYCROFT, Miss Helen (died 1937).

Painter of figure subjects and still life; sculptor. Exhibited at the leading London galleries from 1864, including the R.A., R.B.A., R.I., New Gallery. Lived at Kensington, and died 11th November 1937 aged 89.

THOROGOOD, Stanley (1873–1953).

Potter. Born at Ripley, Surrey on 1st June 1873. Studied at Brighton School of Art, at the R.C.A., also in France and Italy. Exhibited at the R.A., in the provinces, and at the Paris Salon. Head of Burslem School of Art for many years, and Principal of Camberwell School of Arts and Crafts 1920–38. Died on 7th November 1953.

*THORPE, John Hall, R.B.A. (1874–1947).

Represented in several public collections.

*TIBBLE, Geoffrey Arthur (1909–1952).

Represented in the Tate Gallery.

TILY, Eugene James (1870–1950).

Etcher, engraver and aquatinter of portraits; painter in oil and water-colour. Although intended for the medical profession, he instead went to Bedford Park School of Art, and later studied under Arthur Stock and Walter Williams. Exhibited at the R.A., Paris Salon, and received a gold medal at the St. Louis International Exhibition. Lived at Sutton in Surrey.

TIMMIS, Robert (*fl. c.* 1920–1960).

Painter in oil of landscapes, portraits and still life. Born at Leek in Staffordshire. Studied at the Allan Fraser School of Art at Arbroath. Lived in Liverpool for many years, and exhibited chiefly in Lancashire.

*TISDALL, Henry C., R.H.A. (*fl. c.* 1890–1950).

Elected A.R.H.A. 1892, R.H.A. 1893.

*TITTENSOR, Harry, R.I. (1887–1942).

Water-colours include *Vannes, Brittany; The Gateway, Wells; Old Houses Boston;* and *Leaving Church, Trequir.* Exhibited at a number of provincial art galleries.

*TOD, Murray Macpherson, R.S.W., R.E., G.I., S.S.A., A.R.C.A.(Lond.) (1909–1974).

Died on 13th August 1974.

TOLANSKY, Miss Ottilie, R.O.I., N.E.A.C., W.I.A.C. (born 1914).

Painter in oil of portraits, flowers and still life. Born in Vienna on 30th May 1914. Studied at Berlin Municipal Academy of Art and Hammersmith School of Art. Exhibited at the R.A., R.O.I., and in the provinces. She was elected R.O.I., N.E.A.C., W.I.A.C. and to the Contemporary Portrait Society in the mid 1960s. Has held six London one-man shows, and lives at Richmond in Surrey.

TOMKINS, Charles Algernon, A.R.E. (*fl. c.* 1872–1903).

Etcher and engraver. Exhibited at the R.A. from 1872. Elected A.R.E. 1899, his membership ceased 12th November 1903.

*TONKS, Myles Denison Boswell, R.I. R.B.A., P.S. (1890–1960).

Member of Chelsea Arts Club. Qualified as a surgeon.

TOOBY, Charles Richard (1863–1919).

Animal painter. Born in London. Went to Weimar to study painting, and in the years leading up to the Great War had a high reputation in Germany. Once war broke out he was sent to Ruhleben, and this undermined his health, leading to his death.

TOPPING, James (born 1879).

Landscape painter in oil; lithographer. Born at Cleator Moor, Cumberland. Studied art under George Adamson and Richard Herd. Exhibited for some years in America, where he received a number of prizes for his work.

TOSELAND, Peter, A.R.C.A.(Lond.) (born 1917).

Landscape painter in oil and water-colour; illustrator, scribe and picture restorer. Born on 15th June 1917 at Broughton, near Kettering, in Northamptonshire. Studied at Northampton School of Art 1931–37, where he received Drawing and Industrial Design Certificates, and at the R.C.A. 1937–40. Exhibited at R.A., R.W.S., R.I., Britain in Water-colours, and from 1950–62 twice yearly at Eton College. One-man shows held at Slough 1950, 1955, Windsor 1960, Fletching 1966, 1971, Brighton 1972, Hove 1974, Charleston Manor Festival 1975. Lives in Brighton.

TOWNSEND, Miss S. Thompson (*fl.* 1920s).

Painter in oil of figure subjects. Lived in London.

*TOWNSEND, William, L.G. (1909–1973).

Represented in the Tate Gallery.

TRANGMAR, Charles Frank, A.R.C.A.(Lond.) (born 1889).

Landscape painter and etcher. Born in Brighton on 22nd August 1889. Studied at Brighton School of Art, and at the R.C.A. where he received his diploma 1913. Lived in London, and does not appear to have exhibited extensively.

TREGLOWN, Ernest (died 1922).

On the staff at Birmingham School of Art. Died on 26th February 1922.

TRESILIAN, S., S.G.A. (*fl. c.* 1915–1950).

Painter in water-colour of portraits and figure subjects. During World War I he was a prisoner of war at Rastatt, near Karlsruhe, and made drawings of life in camp. Represented in the Imperial War Museum. Lived in London for many years.

TRIER, Hans A., R.B.A. (born 1877).

Oil painter. Born in London on 20th May 1877. Exhibited at the R.A., R.B.A., R.O.I. In World War I he served initially in the Artists Rifles, and later in France with the R.A.F. His wife Adeline was also an artist. Lived in London.

TRINGHAM, Holland, R.B.A. (*fl. c.* 1891–1901).

Genre painter. Exhibited at the leading London galleries from 1891, including the R.A., R.B.A. Lived at Streatham.

TROBRIDGE, George (1857–1909).

Landscape painter. Born in Exeter. Studied art at South Kensington 1875–80. Exhibited at the R.B.A. from 1884, also in Ireland. Headmaster of Belfast School of Art 1880–1901. Died at Gloucester.

TRUMAN, W. Herbert (*fl. c.* 1910–1960).

Painter in oil of landscapes and figure subjects. Brought up at Dawlish in Devon. Studied at South London School of Art and St. Martin's School of Art. Exhibited at the R.A. from 1912, also at the R.W.A. Represented in Plymouth Art Gallery. Lived at St. Ives in Cornwall, and later in Bristol.

TSCHUDI, Lill (born 1911).

Colour linocuts of figure subjects. Studied under Claude Flight at the Grosvenor School of Modern Art 1929.

*TUCKER, James Walker, A.R.W.A., A.R.C.A.(Lond.) (1898–1972).

Lived at Upton St. Leonards in Gloucestershire for many years.

TUCKER, Tudor St. George (1862–1906).

Oil painter. Born in London. Studied art in Paris, and at the Victorian Art Gallery School in Australia. Founder of Melbourne Art School in conjunction with E. Phillips Fox. Returned to England, exhibiting at the R.A. and in the provinces.

TURNER, J. Doman (*fl. c.* 1910–1925).

Member of the Camden Town Group. Exhibited with the I.S. Lived at Streatham for some years.

TWIDLE, Arthur (died 1936).

Illustrator. Exhibited at the R.A. Lived at Sidcup in Kent, and later at Godstone Green in Surrey. Died 26th April 1936 aged 71.

*TYRRELL, Thomas, F.R.B.S. (1857–1929).

Erratum—Surname correctly listed above.

U

*UDEN, Ernest Boye, R.I. (born 1911).

Painter of urban scenes. A work in chalk and wash, *Off Oxford Street,* was exhibited at Brighton Art Gallery 1936.

*UNDERWOOD, Leon (1890–1975).

In 1961 he began exhibiting again after a lapse of 22 years. Died on 9th October 1975.

URQUHART, Miss Annie Mackenzie (*fl. c.* 1905–1935).

Painter of decorative subjects. Born in Glasgow. Studied at Glasgow School of Art, and on the continent.

Exhibited at the R.A., and in the provinces. Works include *Spring* and *Blossoms.* Lived at Clarkston, Glasgow.

*URQUHART, Murray McNeel Caird, R.B.A. (1880–1972).

His water-colour *Fishing Boats, Concarneaux,* was illustrated in *Water-colour Painting of Today,* a Studio Special 1937.

*URWICK, William H., R.E. (died 1915).

Exhibited chiefly at the R.E.

V

*VAN DER WEYDEN, Harry H. (born 1868).
Born at Boston in the U.S.A. Studied art at the Slade School, and at the Académie Julian in Paris. Received gold medals at exhibitions in Paris, Munich, Vienna and Atlanta. Represented in several public collections.

*VAN SOMEREN, Edmund Lawrence, R.O.I. (1875–1963).
Member of Ipswich Art Club.

VARLEY, Fleetwood C. (born 1875).
Miniature painter. Exhibited at the Walker Art Gallery, Liverpool. Lived in London.

VARLEY, Frederick H., A.R.Canadian A. (1881–1969).
Sheffield born artist. Studied at Sheffield School of Art, and at the Antwerp Academy. Settled in Toronto, Canada 1911. Elected A.R.Canadian A. 1922. Taught art in Toronto and Vancouver.

VARLEY, Illingworth, A.R.C.A.(Lond.) (1869–1942).
Painter in oil and water-colour of landscapes, often including figures and animals, and portraits. Born at Saltaire in Yorkshire on 11th April 1869. Trained at the art schools of Saltaire and Shipley, and then joined the staff. In 1893–94 he studied in London at St. John's Wood and Hampstead Art Schools, where he received national awards and medals. Then spent three years teaching in Maccledfield. Returned to London, and obtained his A.R.C.A. 1901. He held several teaching posts in London, and in 1907 was appointed Headmaster of Malvern School of Art, a position he occupied until his retirement in 1935. Exhibited at the R.A., also at other London galleries, and in the provinces, especially Birmingham and Worcester. His wife, Eleanor Varley (1870–1951), was an accomplished craftswoman, and his two daughters Eleanor Doris Varley and Mabel Illingworth Varley are both artists. He died in Malvern on 14th January 1942.

VARLEY, John (died 1933).
Landscape painter, especially of Egyptian subjects. A grandson of the famous water-colour painter of the same name. Exhibited at the leading London galleries from 1870, chiefly the R.A., R.I., R.B.A. In 1904 a show of his work was held at the Hanover Gallery and included *Nile Craft, Gizeh; From the Foot of the Pyramids Looking East.* Died July 1933 aged 83.

VERESMITH, Emile (c. 1865–1935).
American born painter and engraver, brother of the artist Daniel Albert Veresmith. Brought up in Cleveland, Ohio. Began as designer to a firm of decorators, and then became draughtsman to a wood engraving company. In 1888 he came to England to study painting under Herkomer at Bushey. Lived in London for some years.

VERNER, Frederick Arthur, A.R.Canadian A. (1836–1928).
Painter of animal subjects in oil and water-colour. Born at Sheridan, Ontario, Canada. Studied art in England 1856–60. Painted in Canada 1862–80, and then in England except for two return visits to his native country. Exhibited at the leading London galleries from 1881, including the R.A., R.I., R.B.A. Member of Ontario Society of Artists 1872, and elected A.R. Canadian A. 1893. Died in London.

VICKERY, G. Herbert (*fl. c.* 1900–1915).
Painter of decorative subjects. Son of an architect, he studied architecture at first, but abandoned this in favour of painting. Studied at the Slade School, and for several years in Antwerp. Exhibited at the R.A. and in Belguim.

VINE, Henry Charles Land (died 1918).
Illustrator. Born at Hampstead about 1887. Joined the staff of the General Register and Record Office of Shipping and Seamen 1902. Later painted subjects in water-colour, pastel, oil, and illustrated a number of books. During the Great War he served in the R.A.F. Nicknamed and latterly signed his work "Chum". Died on 3rd November 1918 at Wye in Kent of influenza.

*VOKES, Arthur Ernest (born 1874).
Erratum—First christian name as above. A native of Northampton, he had a studio in Bayswater for some time.

VYSE, Charles, A.R.C.A.(Lond.) (1882–1971).
Sculptor and potter. Born on 16th March 1882. Studied art at the R.C.A., where he won a travelling scholarship, and in Italy. Exhibited at the R.A. He often worked in conjunction with his wife, and lived in London for many years.

W

WADHAM, Percy, A.R.E. (*fl. c.* 1890–1910).
Illustrator and architect. Born in Australia, son of Hon. William Wadham of Adelaide. Studied art at Canterbury under T. S. Cooper R.A., and later under James Chapman. Originally intended to become an architect, but from 1892 worked chiefly as a book illustrator, contributing also to many magazines. Exhibited in London and in the provinces. A founder member of the London Sketch Club 1898. Elected A.R.E. 1902, his membership ceased on 10th March 1910.

*WAITE, Harold, R.B.A. (*fl. c.* 1893–1930).
Studied art at the R.A. schools, receiving the Turner Gold Medal and Creswick Prize. Works include *In the Kennet Valley* and *The Harvest.* His father and grandfather were both noted painters.

WALBOURN, Ernest, R.B.A. (*fl. c.* 1890–1920).
Landscape painter. Born at Chingford, Essex. Exhibited at the R.A. from 1897, also at Birmingham and the Walker Art Gallery, Liverpool. Travelled widely, and worked in Australia. Lived for some years at Theydon Bois, Essex.

WALKER, Richard Ian Bentham (born 1925).

Painter in all media, but chiefly oil, of portraits, landscapes, still life and imaginative subjects. Born in Croydon on 18th March 1925. Studied at Croydon Art School 1945–48, also at London University and the Slade School 1948–50. Exhibited at the R.A., R.B.A., R.P., U.A., in the provinces, and at the Paris Salon. One-man shows held at St. Hilda's College, Oxford and Fairfield Halls, Croydon. Represented in several public collections. Lives in Croydon.

WALLACE, Harold Frank (1881–1962).

Painter in water-colour of landscapes and sporting subjects; author. Born on 21st March 1881. Exhibited in London and Scotland. Publications include *Stalks Abroad* 1908, *The Big Game of Central and Western China* 1913, and *Hunting Winds* 1949. Lived in Staffordshire, and died on 16th September 1962.

WALLCOUSINS, Charles Ernest (died 1976).

Painter, illustrator and designer. Exhibited at the R.A., R.B.A., R.I. Illustrated all official programmes for Royal occasions from the 1935 Silver Wedding to the wedding of Princess Alexandra 1963. Lived in London and later at Leigh-on-Sea. Died at Rochford, Essex on 29th January 1976 aged 93.

*WARBURTON, Samuel, R.M.S. (1874–1935).

Exhibited at the Walker Art Gallery, Liverpool.

*WARD, Archibald, A.R.C.A.(Lond.) (died 1965).

Principal for a time of Ipswich School of Art, and member of Ipswich Art Club.

WARDLE, Edmund (c. 1885–1950).

Painter, engraver and etcher of figure subjects. Born in London, nephew of the artist Arthur Wardle. Studied at the Central School of Arts and Crafts. A member of the Langham Sketch Club.

WARREN, Harold B. (1859–1934).

Landscape painter. Born in Manchester on 16th October 1859. Exhibited at the R.A. Lived at Boston in America for a time, and died on 23rd November 1934.

WATKINS, John, R.E. (*fl. c.* 1876–1908).

Etcher of figure subjects. Exhibited at the R.A., R.B.A. Elected R.E. 1881, his membership ceased 5th October 1908.

WATKINS-PITCHFORD, Denys J. (born 1905).

Painter and illustrator of bird subjects; author. Born in Northamptonshire, son of the Rector of Lamport. Studied art in Paris, and at the R.C.A. under Rothenstein. Appointed to the position of assistant art master at Rugby School and during the war years took over from R. B. Talbot-Kelly as art master. He then retired to concentrate on his illustration and writing, producing such books as *Little Grey Men; Dark Estuary; Tides Ending*. Known widely under his pen name "B.B.".

WATTON, J. F. (*fl.* 1940s).

Illustrator of figure subjects. Studied art at the Slade School. Best known for his drawings of fellow prisoners in Colditz camp during World War II. These were smuggled back to this country and were published in such magazines as *Illustrated London News, Tatler, Sketch*.

*WAY, Miss Frances Elizabeth (Mrs. Thacker), R.M.S. (1871–1961).

Exhibited at the R.P., R.M.S., S.M., during the first quarter of the century.

WEBB, John Cother (died 1927).

Mezzotint engraver. Exhibited at the R.A. from 1875, also at the R.Cam.A. Lived in London, and died 19th November 1927 aged 72.

WEBB, Kenneth, N.S., A.R.W.A., A.R.U.A. (born 1927).

Painter in oil of landscapes and flower subjects. Born in London on 21st January 1927. Received the Slade Scholarship 1945. Served in the Fleet Air Arm 1945–48. Returned to the University of Wales and on graduation in 1953 was appointed Head of the Painting School at Belfast College of Art. Resigned that position in 1959 in order to devote more time to painting. He established a studio in County Down but also spent much time painting in Eire, especially on the West Coast. Exhibited at the R.A., R.I., R.B.A., R.O.I., R.H.A., N.S., R.U.A., Paris Salon, and has held many one-man shows. Elected A.R.W.A. 1956, N.S. 1958. Founded the Irish School of Landscape Painting 1956. Worked in Spain, Gibraltar and North Africa 1964–65, East Africa 1969, Canary Islands 1971, America 1972. In 1974 he removed from Ireland to Gloucestershire, where he now lives near Amberley.

WEBB, Matthew William (died 1924).

Member of Oxford Art Society. Exhibited at the Walker Art Gallery, Liverpool. Lived in London, and later in Berkshire. Died on 13th October 1924 aged 73.

WEBB, Stephen (died 1933).

Sculptor. Professor of sculpture at the R.C.A., he lived in London. Died 17th May 1933 aged 84.

WEDGWOOD, Lord Francis Charles Bowen (1898–1959).

Oil painter. Born on 20th January 1898. Studied at Burslem School of Art 1920–22 and Slade School 1922–25. Exhibited at the N.E.A.C. from 1927, and at the R.A. from 1931. Died on 22nd April 1959.

WEIR, Harrison William, R.I. (1824–1906).

Animal painter. Born at Lewes, Sussex on 5th May 1824. Studied art under George Baxter. Exhibited at the leading London galleries from 1843, chiefly the R.I. but also R.A., R.B.A. He wrote and illustrated a number of books, generally on animals. Lived at Appledore in Kent, and died 3rd January 1906.

WEISS, José (1859–1919).

Landscape painter in oil; noted experimenter with gliders. Born in Paris on 21st January 1859, he became British by naturalisation. An admirer of the Barbizon School he gave up business life in France and settled in England about 1893. Exhibited at the R.A., R.B.A. and the Paris Salon. Lived at Houghton, near Arundel, from 1897 and painted the Sussex landscape.

WESCHKE, Karl (born 1925).

Painter in oil of landscapes, figures and abstracts. One-man shows held in London at the Woodstock, Matthiesen and Grosvenor Galleries. Elected a member of the Penwith Society of Artists 1957. Represented in public collections at home and abroad. Lives in Cornwall.

WEST, Miss Nan (Mrs. Robertson) (born 1904).

London artist. Daughter of Herbert E. West, an artist, she was born in the metropolis. Studied art at the

Byam Shaw School and the Slade School. Exhibited with the N.E.A.C.

*WEST, Richard Whately (1848–1905).
Born on 18th January 1848. Exhibited at the R.I., R.B.A. Buried in Florence.

WHEELER, A. H. (died 1916).
A member of Manchester Arts Club. Killed in World War I.

WHEELER, Edward J. (died 1933).
Illustrator, contributing to *Punch*. Exhibited in London from 1872. Died November 1933 aged 85.

*WHITE, Charles Franklin (died 1975).
Born at Adelaide. Settled in England prior to World War I, and taught drawing at the Slade School for many years from 1919. Represented in the Victoria and Albert Museum, British Museum, and the Ashmolean at Oxford. Died on 2nd November 1975 aged 83.

WHITE, Miss Florence, V.P.R.M.S. (*fl. c.* 1895–1930).
Miniature painter. Exhibited at the R.A., R.M.S., Walker Art Gallery in Liverpool and at Birmingham. Lived in Kensington.

WHITE, Miss Gwen B. A.R.C.A.(Lond.) (*fl.* from *c.* 1940).
Painter in water-colour and tempera; author. Born at Exeter. Studied at Bournemouth School of Art and the R.C.A. Married the artist C. Rupert Moore. Exhibited at the R.A. She has written and illustrated thirteen books, beginning with *Ancient and Modern Dolls*, the latest being *Toys, Dolls, Automata, Marks and Labels* published October 1975. Lives at Radlett, Hertfordshire.

WHITE, Miss Mildred H. Congden (*fl. c.* 1905–1915).
Painter in oil of genre and animals. Studied art at the Calderon School of Animal Painting. Received first prize for animal composition with *The End of the Day*.

WHITFIELD, George (born 1891).
Figure painter in oil, poster designer, illustrator and art critic. Studied at Liverpool School of Art under Frederick Vango Burridge. Exhibited chiefly at provincial galleries. Lived in Cheshire and now in Wales.

WHITTET, Andrew (*fl. c.* 1890–1910).
Landscape painter in oil. Exhibited at the R.S.A., and at Manchester. Lived in Edinburgh.

WICKS, David Vaughan, R.E. (born 1918).
Engraver. Born on 20th December 1918. Studied art at the R.C.A. 1946–49, and taught there 1949–54. Elected A.R.E. 1950, R.E. 1961. Lives in Essex.

WILDEBLOOD, John Peake (1868–1956).
Landscape painter in water-colour. Studied art at the Slade School. Exhibited at the R.I. Painted subjects in Egypt and Palestine. Lived in London.

*WILDMAN, William Ainsworth, R.W.S., R.B.A. (1882–1950).
Works include *Berkeley Square* and *Rain at Mevagissey*.

WILENSKI, Reginald Howard (1887–1975).
Painter and art critic. Born in London. Studied art in London, Paris and Munich. Exhibited at the R.O.I., R.P., I.S., and Paris Salon. Lived at Marlow in Buckinghamshire, and died 19th April 1975.

WILKINSON, Norman (1882–1934).
Painter and stage designer. Studied at Birmingham School of Art and in Paris. Began designing scenery and costumes for the stage 1910. Lived at Chiswick, and died 14th February 1934 aged 51.

*WILKINSON, Reginald Charles, P.S. (1881–1939).
Exhibited with the Society of Sussex Painters for a number of years.

WILKINSON, Thomas William, A.R.B.S. (1875–1950).
Sculptor. Born in Bradford on 18th October 1875. Studied at Bradford School of Art and Ipswich Art School. Exhibited at the R.A. from 1903, and at the Paris Salon. Lived in Ipswich and was a member of Ipswich Art Club.

WILKS, Maurice Canning (born 1910).
Painter in oil and water-colour of landscapes, marines and portraits. Born in Belfast. Exhibited at the R.A., and held one-man shows in London and Ireland. He had studios in Belfast and at Cushendun, Antrim. Represented in a number of public collections.

WILLIAMS, Albert George (born 1923).
Painter in oil of flowers and portraits. Born in Hove on 20th March 1923, son of Arthur C. Williams, an artist. Studied art under his father and grandfather, also in Brighton, London and Paris. Exhibited at the R.A., R.W.S., R.O.I., R.B.A., Paris Salon. Represented in public collections in America and South Africa. His work has been widely reproduced as fine art prints. Lives in Hove.

*WILLIAMS, Miss Barbara Moray, A.R.E., A.R.C.A.(Lond.) (1911–1975).
Died in Iceland on 30th December 1975.

WILLIAMSON, Horace W. (born 1897).
Etcher of landscapes, figures and animals. Born in London. Served in World War I and was severely wounded. Studied at Sheffield School of Art and St. Martin's School af Art. Works include *Silent Pool; Winter Sunshine;* and *Dartmoor Ponies*.

WILLIS, Richard Henry Albert (1853–1905).
Landscape painter in oil, water-colour and pastel; sculptor and stained glass artist. Born at Dingle, County Kerry, Ireland on 5th July 1853. Studied at Cork School of Art and at South Kensington. Exhibited at the R.A. from 1882. Appointed Headmaster of Manchester School of Art 1882 and of Dublin Metropolitan School of Art 1904. Died at Ballinskelligs on 15th August 1905.

WILSON, Bassett (died 1972).
Oil painter. Worked in Paris in the 1930s with his wife Muriel, a flower painter. Exhibited in London and France.

WILSON, Edgar W. (1861–1918).
Genre painter and etcher. Exhibited at the leading London galleries from 1886, including the R.A., R.I. Lived in London and died February 1918.

WILSON, Miss Helena (1836–1923).
Head of the Royal Female School of Art for nearly fifty years. Exhibited flower paintings at the R.A. Died at Ballinger, Buckinghamshire on 8th January 1923 aged 86.

WILSON, John (*fl. c.* 1910–1940).
Landscape painter in oil. Born in Halifax, and studied at Halifax School of Art. Lived near Preston, and painted in Lancashire and the Lake District.

WILSON, Patten (born c. 1868).

Illustrator, especially of historical and classical subjects. Born at Cleobury Mortimer in Shropshire. At about age 19 he went to Kidderminister School of Art but left disenchanted a few months later. Worked in Liverpool and then in London, where he became assistant to a wallpaper manufacturer. During the evenings he studied at Westminister School of Art under Fred Brown. Took up book illustration and contributed to the *Yellow Book*.

*WILSON, Scottie (1889–1972).

Represented in the Tate Gallery by *The Tree of Life* and *The Bowl of Life*.

WILSON, Sydney Ernest (born 1869).

Mezzotint engraver. Born at Isleworth on 13th June 1869. Exhibited at the R.A., New Gallery, and Walker Art Gallery in Liverpool. Lived at Harpenden.

*WIMPERIS, Edmund, Jnr. (died 1946).

Architect and painter. Exhibited at the Walker Art Gallery, Liverpool.

WINDER, W. Smallwood, R.B.A. (*fl. c.* 1900–1910).

Little known member of the R.B.A., who exhibited there and at the Dudley Gallery. Lived at Stanwix near Carlisle, and later at Kendal.

WITCOMBE, John, R.B.A. (*fl. c.* 1908–1915).

Bath artist. Exhibited at the R.B.A., R.W.A., G.I.

WITHYCOMBE, John G., R.B.A. (*fl. c.* 1910–1915).

Landscape painter in oil. Exhibited chiefly at the R.B.A. Lived at Dedham in Essex and later at East Bergholt.

WOLFE, Miss Edith Grace, R.M.S. (born 1883).

Miniature painter. Exhibited at the R.I., R.M.S., R.H.A., and Walker Art Gallery, Liverpool. Lived in London.

WOOD, A. J. Carter (died 1915).

Oil painter. Exhibited at the R.A. and Walker Art Gallery, Liverpool. Lived at Newlyn in Cornwall, and later at Silloth in Cumberland. Died on 1st February 1915.

WOOD, Edgar Thomas (1860–1935).

Artist and craftsman. Exhibited at the R.B.A. from 1885. Lived in Manchester for many years and founded the Northern Art Workers Guild. A prominent member of the Arts and Crafts movement.

WOOD, James (died 1975).

Portrait painter and author. Educated at Jesus College, Cambridge 1908–11, and studied painting under Tudor Hart. He exhibited little, painting mainly for his own pleasure. Co-author of *Mayvale* 1915 and *The Foundation of Aesthetics* 1922, also published *New World Vistas* 1926. Lived in Hampstead, at Llanthony near Abergavenny, and later at Grafton, Clanfield where he died on 25th May 1975 aged 86.

WOOD, James F. R., R.M.S. (died 1920).

Miniature painter. Lived in London for some years, and died July 1920.

WOOD, J. Barlow (1862–1949).

Landscape and genre painter in water-colour. A member of Ipswich Art Club, he lived at Woodbridge and later in Ipswich.

WOOD, Kenneth, N.S. (*fl.* 1940s).

Landscape painter. Lived near Witham in Essex, and later in London.

WOOD, Stanley L. (died 1928).

Illustrator, and painter of military subjects. Exhibited at the leading London galleries from 1885, including the R.A., R.I., R.O.I., also at Manchester. Lived in London and died 1st March 1928 aged 62.

WOOD, Starr (1870–1944).

Caricaturist. Born in London on 1st February 1870. Known as "The Snark", he published *The Snark's Annuals*. Lived at Rickmansworth in Hertfordshire, and died 2nd September 1944.

*WOOD, Wilfred Rene (1888–1976).

Died at Barnack, near Stamford, in Lincolnshire on 18th February 1976.

WOODHOUSE, Basil (*fl. c.* 1905–1915).

Landscape painter in oil. Exhibited with the I.S. Works include *Kirkcudbright Castle*.

*WOOLLASTON, Leslie Alfred (1900–1976).

Founder of the Renart Studio. Died on 20th February 1976 aged 75.

WOOLRICH, E. (died 1916).

London artist, member of the London Sketch Club.

WOOLRIDGE, Harry Ellis (died 1917).

Painter of figure subjects. Exhibited at the leading London galleries from 1867, including the R.A., R.B.A. Slade Professor at Oxford 1895–1903. Died on 13th February 1917 aged 72.

WORK, George O. (died 1921).

Exhibited at the Walker Art Gallery, Liverpool, as did his wife Mrs. C. Orkney Work. Lived for some years in Liverpool, and later at Skipton in Yorkshire. Died October 1921.

*WORKMAN, Harold, R.B.A., R.O.I., R.Cam.A., S.M.A. (1897–1975).

Died on 18th May 1975.

WORRALL, Miss Ella (born 1863).

Painter of miniatures and landscapes. Born in Liverpool on 7th November 1863. Exhibited at the R.A. from 1903, also at the Walker Art Gallery, Liverpool. Lived at Liverpool for many years.

WORSFOLD, Miss Maud Beatrice, R.M.S. (*fl. c.* 1895–1935).

Painter of portraits and miniatures. Studied art at the R.A. Schools. Exhibited at the R.A., R.M.S., and Walker Art Gallery, Liverpool. Lived near Dover and later in London.

WRAGG, Arthur (born 1903).

Illustrator. Born near Manchester on 3rd January 1903. Studied at Sheffield School of Art from 1916, and settled in London 1923. Visited Stockholm 1930. Illustrated *The Psalms for Modern Life* 1933, and *Jesus Wept* 1935.

WRIGHT, Henry Charles Seppings (died 1937).

Painter of military subjects; illustrator. Exhibited at the leading London galleries from 1883, including the R.B.A., R.I., and in the provinces. Contributed from abroad to the *Illustrated London News*. Lived at Harrow and died 7th February 1937 aged 88.

*WYLLIE, Harold, S.M.A. (1880–1973).

Died on 22nd December 1973.

*WYNDHAM, Guy Richard Charles (1896–1948).

Works include *Portrait of a Negress*.

*WYNTER, Bryan Herbert, L.G. (1915–1975).

Died in Penzance on 11th February 1975.

Y

*YATES, Frederic (1854–1919).
    Erratum – Christian name as above.
YOUNG, A. Stanley, A.R.B.S. (*fl. c.* 1905–1940).
    Sculptor. Lived in Chelsea for many years.
YOUNG, John (born 1930).
    Painter in oil of transport subjects, especially aircraft. Born at Bristol on 2nd June 1930. Studied at High Wycombe School of Art 1946–48. Exhibited at the R.S.M.A., and is represented in the R.A.F. Museum, Hendon. Member of the Guild of Aviation Artists, and its predecessors the Society of Aviation Artists and the Kronfeld Aviation Art Society. His work for the R.A.F. and various airlines has taken him to South America and Kenya, and he has flown in military aircraft in Aden, Singapore, Malaysia, Hong Kong. Illustrated a number of books on transport subjects. Lives at Chesham, Buckinghamshire.

*YOUNG, William Blamire, R.I., R.B.A. (1862–1935).
    Painter in oil and water-colour of landscapes and figures. Born in Yorkshire, he went to Australia 1885. Returned to England 1893, and studied at Herkomer's School, Bushey. In 1896 he went back to Australia, and designed some posters. About 1912 he had resettled in England, and finally returned to Melbourne 1923.

YULE, Winifred J. (*fl. c.* 1905–1915).
    Scottish portrait painter. Exhibited at the R.S.A. Lived at Edinburgh.

Societies and Groups

Reference has been made in the biographical section to a great number of Art Societies and groups, some of which are still flourishing others only being short lived. The majority of these are London societies, but there are of course several provincial groups of note, including for example the R.W.A., R.G.I., R.B.S.A. The following list indicates the dates the societies were formed, and may prove useful when making reference to the biographies.

Allied Artists Association   1908
Artists International Association   1934
Arts and Crafts Exhibition Society   1888
Art Workers Guild   1883
Australian Painter Etchers Society   1921
Birmingham Art Circle   1879
Borough Bottega   1953
Borough Group   1947
British Society of Master Glass-Painters   1921
Camden Town Group   1911
Cheltenham Group of Artists   1920
Colour Woodcut Society   1920
Crypt Group   1946
Cumberland Market Group   1915
Dublin Sketching Club   1874
East London Group   1925
Emotionist Group   1923
English Surrealist Group   1936
English Wood Engraving Society   1925
Federation of British Artists   1961
Free Painters and Sculptors   1953
Glasgow Art Club   1867
Glasgow Society of Painters and Sculptors   1919
Group of Seven   1920
Grubb Group   1928
Guild of Aviation Artists   1971
Industrial Painters Group   1957
International Society of Sculptors,
    Painters and Gravers   1898
Ipswich Art Club   1874
Lake Artists Society   1904
Langham Sketch Club   1838
Liverpool Academy of Fine Arts   1810
Liver Sketching Club   1872
London Artists Association   1925
London Group   1913
London Portrait Society   1928
London Sketch Club   1898
Manchester Academy of Fine Arts   1859
Monarro Group   1919
National Academy of Design (New York)   1825
National Portrait Society   1911
National Society of Painters,
    Sculptors and Gravers   1930
New Art Club, Glasgow   1940
New English Art Club   1886
Newlyn Society of Artists   1884
New Scottish Group   1942
New Society of Artists   1921
Old Dudley Art Society   1861
Ontario Society of Artists   1873
Pastel Society   1898
Penwith Society of Artists   1949
Rhythm Group   1912

Ridley Art Club   1889
Royal Academy   1768
Royal Birmingham Society of Artists   1812
Royal British Colonial Society of Artists   1887
Royal Cambrian Academy   1881
Royal Canadian Academy   1880
Royal Drawing Society   1888
Royal Glasgow Institute of Fine Arts   1862
Royal Hibernian Academy   1823
Royal Institute of British Architects   1834
Royal Institute of Oil Painters   1883
Royal Institute of Painters in Water-colours   1831
Royal Scottish Academy   1826
Royal Scottish Society of Painters in
    Water-colours   1878
Royal Society of British Artists   1823
Royal Society of British Sculptors   1904
Royal Society of Marine Artists   1939
Royal Society of Miniature Painters   1895
Royal Society of Painter-Etchers and Engravers   1880
Royal Society of Painters in Water-colours   1804
Royal Society of Portrait Painters   1891
Royal Ulster Academy   1879
Royal Water-colour Society Art Club   1884
Royal West of England Academy   1845
St. Ives Society of Artists   1927
Scottish Society of Women Artists   1924
Senefelder Club   1910
Seven and Five Society   1919
Society of Artist Printmakers   1921
Society of Aviation Artists   1955
Society of Eight   1912
Society of Graphic Art   1920
Society of Graver Printers in Colour   1909
Society of Industrial Artists   1930
Society of Mezzotint Engravers   1898
Society of Miniaturists   1895
Society of Modern Portrait Painters   1907
Society of Mural Painters   1939
Society of Portrait Sculptors   1953
Society of Scottish Artists   1891
Society of Sussex Painters   1924
Society of Twelve   1904
Society of Twenty-Five Painters   1905
Society of Wildlife Artists   1963
Society of Women Artists   1855
Society of Wood Engravers   1920
South London Group   1921
South Wales Art Society   1887
United Artists (as New Society of Artists)   1921
Vorticist Group   1913
Wapping Group of Artists   1938
Women's International Art Club   1899

Bibliography

There are certain standard works of reference for those interested in the art of the period, and undoubtedly the most extensive is *The Studio*. This magazine of the fine arts was issued monthly, and is often to be found in bound form, although a complete set of these highly prized volumes is now likely to be prohibitively costly. However, the reference departments of public libraries usually carry a set. In addition information about artists may be obtained from *The Year's Art* (which appeared annually), *Thieme Becker* (in German), *Benezit* (in French), *Dictionary of National Biography, The Art Journal, Who's Who* and *Who's Who in Art*, first published in 1927.

The following books may also repay study:

Armfield, M.   *Tempera Painting Today*   1946
Arnold, B.   *A Concise History of Irish Art*   1969
Baker, D. V.   *Britain's Art Colony By the Sea*   1959
Baron, W.   *Sickert*   1973
Bertram, A.   *A Century of British Painting 1851–1951*   1951
Bott, A.   *The Londoner's England*   1947
Bradshaw, M.   *R.B.A. exhibitors 1824–1892*   1973
,,   *R.B.A. exhibitors 1893–1910*   1975
,,   *R.B.A. exhibitors 1911–1930*   1975
Brockway, M.   *Charles Knight R.W.S.*   1952
Brown, G. H. and Keith, H.   *New Zealand Painting—An Introduction*   1969
Browse, L.   *Sickert*   1943 and 1960
,,   *William Nicholson*   1956
Buckle, R.   *Epstein Drawings*   1962
,,   *Jacob Epstein, Sculptor*   1963
Bunt, C. G. E.   *The Water-colours of Sir Frank Brangwyn R.A.*   1958
Burbidge, R. B.   *A Dictionary of Flower, Fruit and Still Life Painters—Volume II 1850–1950*   1974
Cahill, H. and Barr, A. H.   *Art in America in Modern Times*   1934
Castle, John (publishers)   *The Artists' London*   1924
Caw, Sir J.   *Scottish Painting 1620–1908*   1908
Chamot, M.   *Modern Painting in England*   1937
Charteris, E.   *John Sargent*   1927
Clark, K.   *Henry Moore Drawings*   1974
Clifford, D.   *Collecting English Water-colours*   1970
Coombs, D.   *Churchill, His Paintings*   1967
Dale, R.   *Louis Wain the man who drew Cats*   1968
Downes, W. H.   *John S. Sargent His Life and Work*   1926
East, A.   *Brush and Pencil Notes in Landscape*   1914
Easton, M. and Holroyd, M.   *The Art of Augustus John*   1974
Eates, M.   *Paul Nash—Memorial Volume*   1948
Emmons, R.   *The Life and Opinions of Walter Sickert*   1942
E.P. Publishing   *Royal Academy Exhibitors 1905–1970—Volume I*   1974
Etheridge, K.   *Collecting Drawings*   1970
Fisher, S.   *A Dictionary of Water-colour Painters 1750–1900*   1972
Foskett, D.   *Dictionary of British Miniature Painters* 2 volumes   1972
Fry, R.   *Duncan Grant*   1930
Furst, H.   *L. Campbell Taylor R.A.—His Place in Art*   1945

Garrett, A.   *Wood Engravings and Drawings of Iain Macnab of Barachastlain*   1973
Gaunt, W.   *The Etchings of Frank Brangwyn R.A.*   1926
Grant, H. M.   *Dictionary of British Landscape Painters*   1952
Graves, A.   *A Dictionary of Artists 1760–1893*   1901
,,   *Royal Academy Exhibitors 1769–1904*   1906
Grohmann, W.   *The Art of Henry Moore*   1960
Hall, M.   *The Artists of Northumbria*   1973
Halliday, F. and Russell, J.   *Matthew Smith*   1962
Hammacher, A. M.   *Barbara Hepworth*   1968
Hardie, M.   *Water-colour Painting in Britain* 3 volumes   1967–69
Harper, J. R.   *Painting in Canada*   1966
Hartrick, A. S.   *A Painter's Pilgrimage Through Fifty Years*   1939
Hind, A. M.   *The Etchings of D. Y. Cameron*   1924
Holden, D.   *Whistler Landscapes and Seascapes*   1969
Hudson, D.   *Arthur Rackham, his Life and Work*   1960
,,   *James Pryde*   1949
Hurst, A. A.   *Arthur Briscoe—Marine Artist*   1974
Hutchison, S.   *History of Royal Academy 1768–1968*   1968
Ironside, R.   *Wilson Steer*   1943
Konody, P. G. and Dark, S.   *Sir William Orpen*   1932
Kroeger, J.   *Australian Artists*   1968
Lamb, Sir W.   *The Royal Academy—A Short History of its Foundation and Development*   1935 and 1951
Laver, J.   *Paintings by Michael Ayrton*   1948
Levy, M.   *The Paintings of L. S. Lowry*   1975
Lewis, J.   *Heath Robinson, Artist and Comic Genius*   1973
Lilly, M.   *Sickert. The Painter and his Circle*   1971
Linder, E. and L.   *The Art of Beatrix Potter*   1955
Lines, V.   *Mark Fisher and Margaret Fisher Prout*   1966
Lipke, W.   *David Bomberg*   1967
Littlejohns, J.   *British Water-colour Painting and Painters of Today*   1931
Maas, J.   *Victorian Painters*   1969
MacColl, D. S.   *Steer*   1945
MacInnes, C.   *Sidney Nolan*   1961
Macnab, I.   *The Student's Book of Wood Engraving*   1938
Marriott, C.   *Laura Knight—A Book of Drawings*   1923
Mayne, J.   *Barnett Freedman*   1948

Michel, W.   *Wyndham Lewis*   1971

Morris, S. and K.   *A Catalogue of Birmingham and West Midlands Painters of the Nineteenth Century*   1974

Mullins, E.   *Alfred Wallis Cornish Primitive Painter*   1967

„   *Josef Herman*   1967

Munnings, Sir A. J.   *An Artist's Life; The Second Burst; The Finish*   1950–52

Newbolt, Sir F.   *History of the Royal Society of Painter-Etchers and Engravers 1880–1930*   1930

Newton, E.   *Christopher Wood 1901–1930*   1938

„   *Stanley Spencer*   1947

„   *War Through Artists Eyes*   1945

Ormond, R.   *Sargent Paintings, Drawings and Watercolours*   1970

Palmer, A.   *More than Shadows—A Biography of W. Russell Flint R.A.*   1943

Paviere, S. H.   *Dictionary of Victorian Landscape Painters*   1968

Peppin, B.   *Fantasy—Book Illustration 1860–1920*   1975

Physick, J.   *The Engraved Work of Eric Gill*   1963

Postan, A.   *The Complete Graphic Work of Paul Nash*   1973

Read, H.   *Henry Moore—Sculpture and Drawings*   1944

„   *Henry Moore*   1965

Reynolds, G.   *Victorian Painting*   1966

Rothenstein, Sir J.   *British Artists and the War*   1931

„   *Augustus John*   1946

„   *British Art since 1900*   1962

„   *Modern English Painters* 3 volumes 1952, 1956, 1974

Rothenstein, W.   *Men and Memories, Recollections of William Rothenstein* 2 volumes   1931, 1932

Russell, J.   *Francis Bacon*   1971

Sewter, A. C.   *Glyn Philpot*   1951

Strickland, W. G.   *A Dictionary of Irish Artists*   1913

Sutton, D.   *Nocturne—The Art of James NcNeill Whistler*   1963

„   *James McNeill Whistler*   1966

Tate Gallery   *Modern British Paintings Drawings and Sculpture* 2 volumes   1964

„   *The Tate Gallery Collections*   1975

Victoria and Albert Museum   *Catalogue of Watercolour Paintings*   1927

Ware, D.   *A Short Dictionary of British Architects*   1967

Wheeler, Sir C.   *High Relief*   1968

Wilenski, R. H.   *Stanley Spencer Resurrection Pictures*

Wilkinson, N.   *A Brush with Life*   1969

Wilson, A.   *Dictionary of British Marine Painters*   1967

Wood, C.   *Dictionary of Victorian Painters*   1971

Woodeson, J.   *Mark Gertler*   1972

Index of Plates

THE PLATES

All dimensions are in inches,
height precedes width.

I. SIR ALFRED JAMES MUNNINGS   Oil 18 × 24.
Under Starter's Orders, Newmarket.

Courtesy of Richard Green (Fine Paintings)

II. EDWARD BRIAN SEAGO   Oil $22 \times 36\frac{1}{4}$.
Midsummer, Norfolk.

Courtesy of Marlborough Fine Art (London) Ltd.

III. PHILIP WILSON STEER   Oil   24 × 30.
Boulogne Sands.

IV. LAURENCE ATKINSON   Pencil and coloured crayons $31\frac{1}{2} \times 21\frac{1}{2}$.   Courtesy of Anthony d'Offay
Abstract Composition.

1. DOD PROCTER   Oil   29 × 24.   Courtesy of The Fine Art Society Ltd.
Burmese Woman.

2. WALTER RICHARD SICKERT   Oil $19\frac{1}{4} \times 23\frac{1}{4}$.
Place Nationale, Dieppe.

Courtesy of Thos. Agnew and Sons Ltd.

3. **SPENCER FREDERICK GORE**   Oil   19×23.
Richmond Park, Winter 1913–14.

4. ALFRED REGINALD THOMSON   Oil $23\frac{1}{2} \times 20$.   Courtesy of Michael Parkin Fine Art Ltd.
The Poon.

5. MALCOLM DRUMMOND   Oil   20 × 16½.   Courtesy of Tate Gallery
Girl with Palmette.

7. CLAUDE MAURICE ROGERS   Oil $35\frac{3}{4} \times 23\frac{3}{4}$.
Mrs. Richard Chilver.   Courtesy of Tate Gallery

6. KEITH STUART BAYNES   Oil $13\frac{1}{2} \times 10$.
Nude and Still Life.   Courtesy of Phillips and Sons

8. SIR WILLIAM MENZIES COLDSTREAM   Oil   40×50.
Seated Nude.

10. GEOFFREY ROBERT RUSSELL Oil $19\frac{1}{2} \times 15\frac{1}{2}$.
Eric Gill in his Studio. Courtesy of Andrew Leslie, Leva Art

9. RAYMOND JAMES COXON Oil 24×20.
Portrait of Jacob Epstein. Courtesy of Michael Parkin Fine Art Ltd.

11. **ROBERT GEMMELL HUTCHISON**   Oil $10 \times 6\frac{1}{2}$.
On the Zuider Zee.   Courtesy of Mrs. W. F. Wilson

12. **MARJORIE LILLY**   Oil $13 \times 9\frac{1}{2}$.
Portrait of a woman, seated, against a window.
Courtesy of Michael Parkin Fine Art Ltd.

13. WILLIAM GEORGE ROBB   Oil   16 × 17.
Still life and Flowers.   Courtesy of Reynolds Gallery

14. MARJORIE MOSTYN   Oil   36 × 24.
Flowers.   Courtesy of Reynolds Gallery

15. ITHELL COLQUHOUN   Oil $20\frac{1}{2} \times 15\frac{1}{2}$.   Courtesy of Andrew Leslie, Leva Art
Lily.

16. ALFRED J. WARNE BROWNE   Oil   8 × 14.
Evening Waves, Cornwall.   Courtesy of Bourne Gallery

17. JULIUS OLSSON   Oil   18 × 24.   Courtesy of Reynolds Gallery
Sunset over the Sea.

18. SIR WILLIAM MACTAGGART   Oil   10 × 14.
Rocky Shoreline.   Courtesy of Reynolds Gallery

19. ADRIAN KEITH GRAHAM HILL   Oil   20 × 24.
Off the Coast at Rock, Cornwall.   Courtesy of Phillips and Son

20. ALEXANDER JAMIESON   Oil   28 × 36.
The Christening.

Courtesy of Reynolds Gallery

21. FREDERICK MARRIOTT   Oil   14 × 18.
Chateau at Laval, France.

22. ARNOLD VICTOR BEAUVAIS   Oil $18\frac{1}{2} \times 14\frac{1}{2}$.   Courtesy of Peter Phillips
Mirrored Self Portrait.

23. ALAN EDMUND BEETON   Oil $11\frac{1}{2} \times 15\frac{1}{2}$.
Reposing.   Courtesy of The Fine Art Society Ltd.

24. SIR WILLIAM ORPEN   Oil $25\frac{1}{2} \times 32$.
Tea Table.   Courtesy of The Fine Art Society Ltd.

25. WALTER JOHN BAYES   Oil   40¼×57.
The Ford.   Courtesy of Tate Gallery

26. GEORGE AIKMAN   Oil   12×18.
The Road Home.   Courtesy of Phillips and Sons

27. PARKER HAGARTY   Oil   20×30.
The Ogmore Valley, Glamorgan.
                 Courtesy of Cambridge Fine Art

28. JAMES AUMONIER   Oil   24×36.
On the Thames.   Courtesy of Phillips and Sons

29. ABRAHAM HULK, Jnr.   Oil   20×30.   Courtesy of Eastbourne Fine Art
Surrey Landscape.

30. FRANK HIDER   Oil   20×30.   Courtesy of Phillips and Sons
Homeward Bound.

31. TOM MOSTYN   Oil   20×30.   Courtesy of Reynolds Gallery
St. Ives.

32. CHARLES JAMES FOX   Oil   30×50.
A Cornish Landscape.   Courtesy of Reynolds Gallery

33. WILFRED STANLEY PETTITT Oil 25×30.
The Cornfield. Courtesy of Cambridge Fine Art

34. FERDINAND E. GRÖNE Oil 35½×49½.
In the Heart of the Countryside. Courtesy of Peter Phillips

35. JAMES McINTOSH PATRICK Oil 22×30.
The Stackyard, Benvie.

36. PATRICK DOWNIE Oil 10×14.
Harvest in Lanarkshire. Courtesy of Phillips and Sons

37. EDWARD HARRY HANDLEY-READ   Oil   28 × 36.
The Dutch Girl. 1920.

38. JOHN DUNCAN FERGUSSON   Oil $13\frac{3}{4} \times 10\frac{3}{4}$.   Courtesy of The Fine Art Society Ltd.
Carnations and Narcissus. 1903.

39. SIR MATTHEW ARNOLD BRACY SMITH   Oil   30 × 25.   Courtesy of Tate Gallery
Peonies.

40. TOM ROBERTSON   Oil $15\frac{1}{2} \times 19\frac{1}{2}$.   Courtesy of Mrs. W. F. Wilson
A Scottish Loch.

41. E. AUBREY HUNT   Oil 22×35.   Courtesy of Bourne Gallery
A Still Evening, Offshore.

42. FRANK WILLIAM BOURDILLON   Oil   8 × 10.
Newlyn Harbour.   Courtesy of Mrs. W. F. Wilson

43. ARTHUR A. FRIEDENSON   Oil   16 × 22.   Courtesy of Peter Phillips
Swinging.

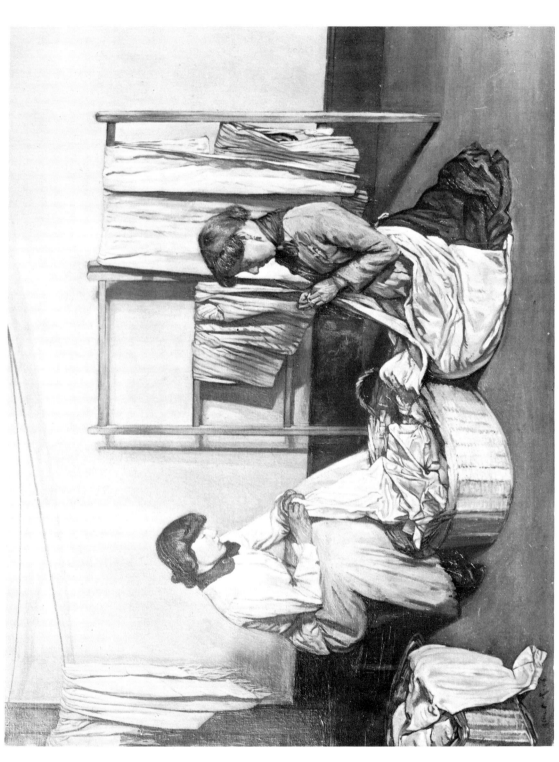

44. ALBERT DANIEL RUTHERSTON   Oil   36 × 46.
Laundry Girls, 1906.

46. **ANNA KATRINA ZINKEISEN**   Oil   88 × 52.
H.R.H. Prince Philip.   Courtesy of the artist

45. **CHARLES SPENCELAYH**   Oil   18 × 12.
Her Favourite Flower.   Courtesy of Phillips and Sons

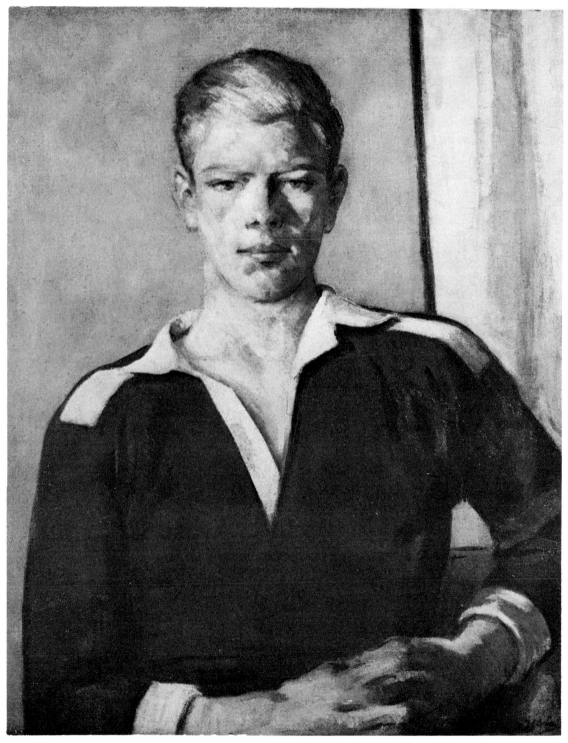

47. FRANCIS CAMPBELL BOILEAU CADELL   Oil   30 × 25.   Courtesy of Reynolds Gallery
The Rugby Player.

48. GLYN WARREN PHILPOT   Oil   50×40.   Courtesy of Andrew Leslie, Leva Art
Young Girl in Clown Costume.

49. HAROLD ING Oil 18 × 25. Courtesy of Cambridge Fine Art
Shell Tanker Hyalina.

50. PRESTON CRIBB Oil 8 × 10. Courtesy of Cambridge Fine Art
Full Steam Ahead.

51. WILLIAM LEE-HANKEY   Oil   27 × 35.   Courtesy of Reynolds Gallery
Blue Sails at Concarneau.

52. WILLIAM ERIC THORP   Oil   20 × 24.   Courtesy of Reynolds Gallery
Thames Barge on the River Crouch.

53. ALEXANDER KELLOCK BROWN   Oil   21 × 28.
Heather Burning, Loch Lomondside.   Courtesy of Phillips and Sons

54. WILLIAM FRANK CALDERON   Oil   6 × 10.   Courtesy of Reynolds Gallery
Sand Gatherers.

55. NEILS H. CHRISTIANSEN   Oil 20 × 30.   Private Collection
Winter Scene.

56. ALEC CARRUTHERS GOULD   Oil 52 × 70.
View from Porlock Hill.   Courtesy of Phillips and Sons

57. LAURENCE STEPHEN LOWRY   Oil   45 × 60.
The Pond. 1950.

58. CHRISTOPHER RICHARD WYNNE NEVINSON Oil $11\frac{1}{2} \times 16$. Courtesy of Michael Parkin Fine Art Ltd.
The Harbour.

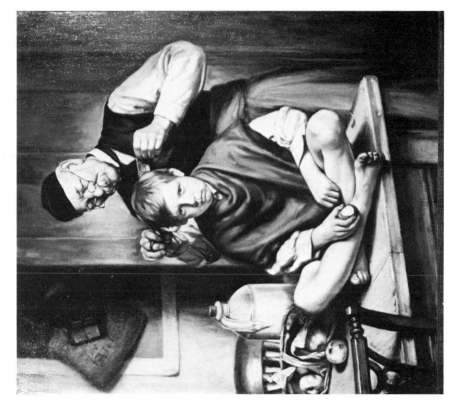

60. WILLIAM MERRETT HODGES   Oil   44 × 39.
The Amateur Barber.   Courtesy of Phillips and Sons

59. CHARLES HASLEWOOD SHANNON   Oil   31 × 26.
Portrait of a Lady. 1928.   Courtesy of The Fine Art Society Ltd.

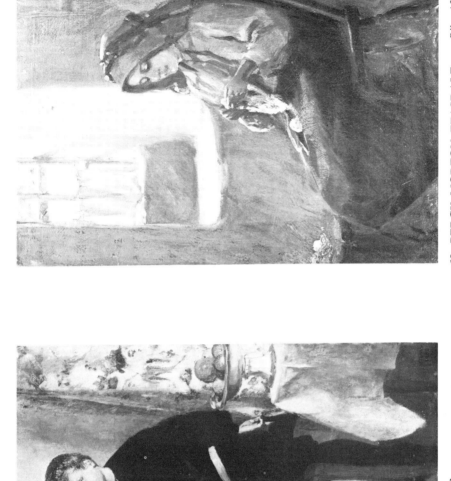

61. HENRY TONKS Oil 36×28.
The Temptation. 1908. Courtesy of The Fine Art Society Ltd.

62. PERCY MORTON TEASDALE Oil 13½×10.
A Staithes Fisherwoman. Courtesy of Phillips and Sons

63. ROBERT BUCHAN NISBET   Oil   10 × 13.   Courtesy of Phillips and Sons
Macduff Harbour.

64. FREDA MARSTON   Oil   20 × 24.   Courtesy of Reynolds Gallery
The Redentore, Venice.

65. WILLIAM A. THORNLEY   Oil   12 × 18.   Private Collection
View of Rochester.

66. JAMES CAMPBELL NOBLE   Oil   12 × 20.   Courtesy of Peter Phillips
North Queensferry.

67. ARTHUR HAYWARD   Oil $10 \times 14\frac{1}{2}$.
Beached Fishing Boats, St. Ives.

68. RONALD OSSORY DUNLOP   Oil   18 × 15.   Courtesy of Phillips and Sons
Portrait of Stanley Spencer. 1922.

69. REGINALD GRENVILLE EVES   Oil   20 × 16.   Courtesy of Andrew Leslie, Leva Art
Portrait of Thomas Hardy.

70. FRANK POTTER Oil 60×40. Courtesy of Andrew Leslie, Leva Art
Warden overlooking St. Paul's.

71. ALGERNON CECIL NEWTON Oil 24 × 36.
Houses in Regents Park. Courtesy of The Fine Art Society Ltd.

72. BERTRAM NICHOLLS Oil 24 × 36.
The Tower of London. 1959. Courtesy of The Fine Art Society Ltd.

Robert Bevan

73. ROBERT POLHILL BEVAN   Oil   31×48.
Horse Sale at the Barbican.

74. GILBERT SPENCER Oil $55\frac{1}{2} \times 72\frac{1}{2}$.
A Cotswold Farm.

76. ROBERT DUCKWORTH GREENHAM Oil 11×9.
Portrait of a Girl. 1937. Courtesy of Henry Towner

75. G. W. LENNOX PATERSON Oil 31×22.
Frank Tweedie and the Birds. 1946.
Courtesy of Andrew Leslie, Leva Art

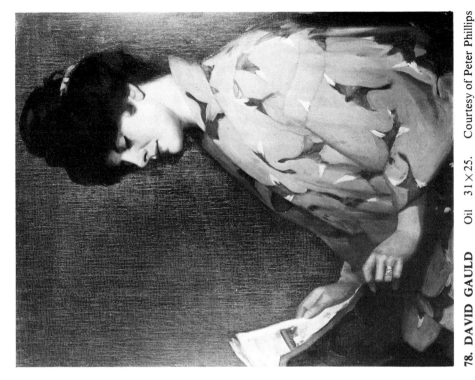

78. DAVID GAULD   Oil   31×25.   Courtesy of Peter Phillips
Irene Vanburgh.

77. HAROLD JOHN WILDE GILMAN   Oil $12\frac{1}{2} \times 9\frac{1}{2}$.
My Landlady.   Courtesy of The Leger Galleries Ltd.

79. FRANK WOOTTON   Oil   20 × 30.
Winter Landscape.

80. LUCY ELIZABETH KEMP-WELCH   Oil   28 × 36.
Ben. 1914.

81. WILLIAM HEATH WILSON   Oil 4 × 7.   Courtesy of Mrs. Ann Hobden
Ploughing.

82. GEORGE THOMAS ROPE   Oil 19 × 28.
Suffolk Punches in a Meadow.   **Courtesy of Eastbourne Fine Art**

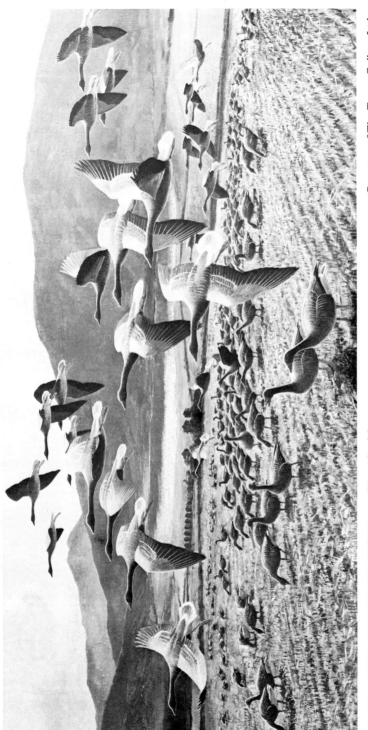

83. SIR PETER MARKHAM SCOTT Oil 48 × 96.
Greylags.

84. AUGUSTUS EDWIN JOHN   Oil   77×38.
The Smiling Woman.   Courtesy of Tate Gallery

85. CHRISTOPHER WOOD   Oil $34\frac{1}{2} \times 19$.
Portrait of J. A. Gandarillas.   Courtesy of Reynolds Gallery

86. ANNE REDPATH   Oil $20\frac{1}{4} \times 24\frac{1}{4}$.
Tulips in a Blue and White Jug.

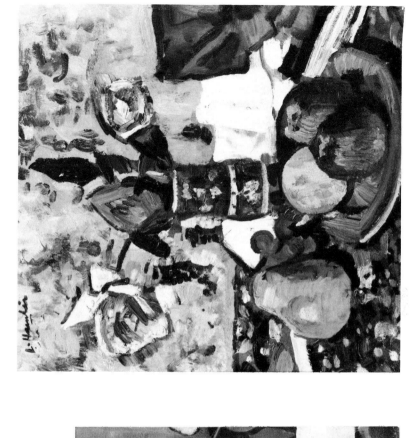

88. GEORGE LESLIE HUNTER   Oil $16 \times 13\frac{1}{4}$.
Apples, Pears and Roses.   Courtesy of The Fine Art Society Ltd.

87. SAMUEL JOHN PEPLOE   Oil 20×20.
Roses and Oranges.   Courtesy of The Fine Art Society Ltd.

89. GERALD JUDAH OSOSKI   Oil   26 × 33.
The Fair, Hampstead Heath. 1931.   Courtesy of Andrew Leslie, Leva Art

90. JOHN LOCHHEAD   Oil   25 × 30.   Courtesy of Cambridge Fine Art
Houghton Mill, Huntingdon. 1912.

91. LESTER SUTCLIFFE   Oil   18 × 24.   Courtesy of Phillips and Sons
Gathering Wood.

92. PHILIP CONNARD   Oil   21½ × 26½. Courtesy of Andrew Leslie, Leva Art
Figures Strolling in a Park.

93. P. MACGREGOR WILSON   Oil   12×18.
Loch Fyne.   Courtesy of Phillips and Sons

94. A. MARJORIE SHERLOCK   Oil   24×30.
Dorset Harbour. 1920.   Courtesy of Andrew Leslie, Leva Art

95. ROBERT BACK   Oil   20×24.   Courtesy of The Artist
Wavetree.

96. TERRICK JOHN WILLIAMS   Oil   20×26.
View of the Dogana, Venice.

97. WILLIAM TEULON BLANDFORD FLETCHER Oil 15 × 22.
Wells Next The Sea.
Courtesy of Bourne Gallery

98. ALFRED WALLIS Oil 13 × 25½.
Steamer.
Courtesy of Towner Art Gallery

99. RALPH BULLOCK Oil 11½ × 17½.
Alnmouth, Northumberland from the South.
Private Collection

100. MARK SENIOR Oil 34 × 39.
Away to the Sea, Walberswick.
Courtesy of Michael Parkin Fine Art Ltd.

101. SIR ROLAND PENROSE   Oil   30 × 39¼.
Le Grand Jour. 1938.

102. JOHN ARMSTRONG   Oil   28 × 36.
A Desolate Shore. 1951.

Courtesy of Honor Blackman

103. ROGER FRY   Oil   15 × 18.   Courtesy of Reynolds Gallery
Provencal Landscape.

104. IVON HITCHENS   Oil   16 × 29¼.   Courtesy of Tate Gallery
Damp Autumn.

105. ADRIAN PAUL ALLINSON   Oil $27\frac{1}{2} \times 38$.
Landscape with Melting Snow.   Courtesy of The Fine Art Society Ltd.

106. DAVID BOMBERG   Oil $28\frac{1}{2} \times 36\frac{1}{2}$.
San Pedro and the Old City, Cuenca-Morning. 1934.
                                      Courtesy of The Fine Art Society Ltd.

107. JAMES WALLACE   Oil   15 × 18.   Courtesy of Andrew Leslie, Leva Art
At Dordrecht. 1907.

108. SIR JOHN ALFRED ARNESBY BROWN   Oil 25 × 30.
Passing Storm.   Courtesy of The Fine Art Society Ltd.

109. CHARLES SIMS   Oil   24 × 36.   Courtesy of The Fine Art Society Ltd.
Chiswick Reach.

110. LEONARD RICHMOND   Oil   18 × 24. Courtesy of Eastbourne Fine Art
View in Jersey.

112. DAME LAURA KNIGHT   Oil 20 × 16.
The Principal Boy.   Courtesy of Andrew Leslie. Leva Art

111. THERESE LESSORE   Oil 30 × 25.
The Equestrienne.   Courtesy of Andrew Leslie. Leva Art

113. ALLAN GWYNNE-JONES   Oil   18 × 24.
A Fairground by Night.

115. W. B. FORTESCUE Oil 17×13.
Girl Driving Geese. Courtesy of Mrs. Ann Hobden

114. SIR GEORGE CLAUSEN Oil 33×26.
The Gleaners Returning. Courtesy of Tate Gallery

116. PHILIP WILSON STEER   Oil $40\frac{1}{4} \times 50$.
The Music Room.

117. MARIANNE STOKES   Oil   33 × 40. Courtesy of Reynolds Gallery
Lantern Light.

118. LEONARD JOHN FULLER   Oil   30 × 40.
Sunday.   Courtesy of Reynolds Gallery

119. R. C. WEATHERBY   Oil   20 × 23½.   Courtesy of Mrs. Ann Hobden
Girl with Sleeping Baby.

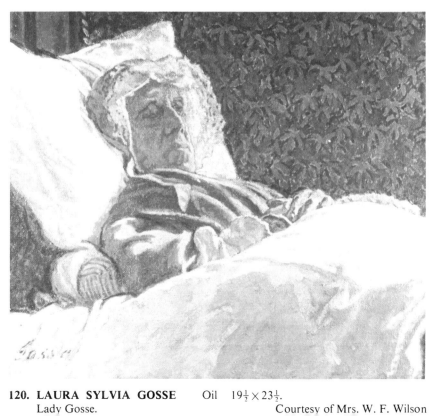

120. LAURA SYLVIA GOSSE   Oil   19½ × 23½.
Lady Gosse.   Courtesy of Mrs. W. F. Wilson

122. CHARLES EDWARD CONDER   Oil   34 × 44.
The Blue Settee.   Courtesy of The Leger Galleries Ltd.

121. CHARLES BUCHEL   Oil   36 × 24.
Gladys Cooper.   Courtesy of Reynolds Gallery

123. **EDWARD ATKINSON HORNEL**   Oil   20 × 24.
By the Sea. 1917.

124. NINA COLMORE Oil 35 × 40. Courtesy of Peter Colmore
Young's Brewery Team.

125. WILLIAM EVANS LINTON Oil 20 × 24.
Cattle by Moonlight. Courtesy of Phillips and Sons

126. ALEXANDER MACLEAN   Oil   11 × 15.   Courtesy of Phillips and Sons
The Cabbage Patch.

127. EDWARD STOTT   Oil $24\frac{1}{4} \times 31\frac{1}{2}$.   Courtesy of Towner Art Gallery
Saturday Night.

128. STUART SCOTT SOMERVILLE   Oil $9\frac{3}{4} \times 12\frac{3}{4}$.
Flower Arrangement.   Courtesy of Eastbourne Fine Art

129. VERNON de BEAUVOIR WARD   Oil 16×20.   Private Collection
Ducks and Swans.

130. CAREL VICTOR MORLAIS WEIGHT Oil $47\frac{1}{2} \times 35\frac{1}{2}$. Courtesy of Towner Art Gallery
The Old Woman in The Garden No. 2.

131. ERNEST PROCTER   Oil, with gold and silver $37\frac{1}{4} \times 35\frac{1}{2}$.   Courtesy of The Fine Art Society Ltd.
Flora and the Flying Horse.

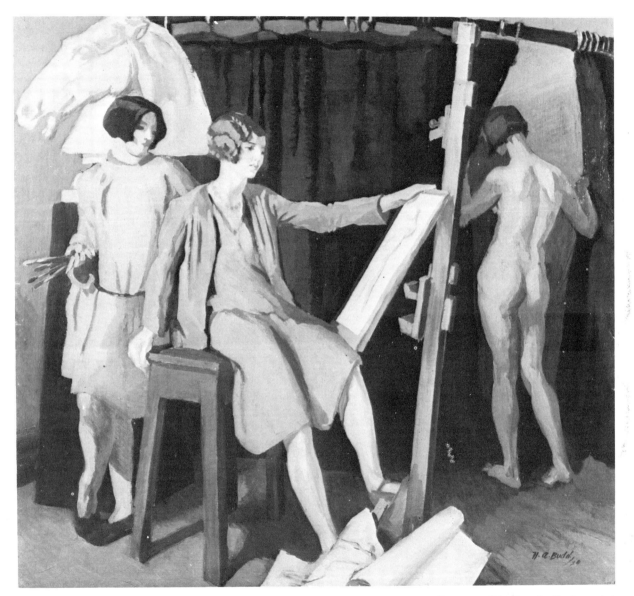

132. HERBERT ASHWIN BUDD   Oil   34 × 36.   Courtesy of Andrew Leslie, Leva Art
Helen Mackenzie in her Fulham Studio. 1929.

133. DERWENT LEES   Oil $12\frac{1}{2} \times 16$.   Courtesy of The Fine Art Society Ltd.
Girl Seated on a Sandy Bank.

134. SIR ALFRED JAMES MUNNINGS   Oil 20×24.
Maurice Codner at Flatford Mill.   Courtesy of The Leger Galleries Ltd.

135. OWEN BOWEN   Oil   17 × 21.   Courtesy of Phillips and Sons
In the Dales.

136. FREDERICK WILLIAM JACKSON   Oil $11\frac{1}{2}$ × 13.
Springtime in Runswick.   Courtesy of Peter Phillips

137. SIR FRANK WILLIAM BRANGWYN   Oil $75\frac{1}{2} \times 50\frac{1}{2}$.
Fisherfolk.   Courtesy of Andrew Leslie, Leva Art

138. ALEXANDER YOUNG JACKSON   Oil $25\frac{1}{2} \times 31\frac{3}{4}$.
The Entrance to Halifax Harbour.   Courtesy of Tate Gallery

139. ARCHIBALD STEVENSON FORREST   Oil 15×17.
Boats of Dominica. 1904.   Courtesy of Mrs. Ann Hobden

140. EDMUND DULAC Oil 25 × 30.   Courtesy of Peter Garner
The Boatyard. 1935.

141. WILLIAM WHITEHEAD RATCLIFFE Oil 20 × 24.
Bodinnick, Fowey.   Courtesy of Andrew Leslie, Leva Art

142. ARTHUR WILDE PARSONS Oil 34 × 52.
Ship Leaving Bristol Docks. Courtesy of Reynolds Gallery

143. ELLIOTT SEABROOKE Oil 32 × 32. Courtesy of Tate Gallery
Old Ship in Heybridge Basin. 1947.

144. CHARLES ERNEST CUNDALL   Oil   40 × 50.

145. SIR GERALD FESTUS KELLY   Oil   42 × 50.
Burmese Market, Taungwingyi.

146. EDWIN JOHN VICTOR PASMORE   Oil   42 × 46.
The Quiet River, the Thames at Chiswick.   Courtesy of Tate Gallery

147. SIR WILLIAM NICHOLSON   Oil   25 × 30.
Ballroom of the Piccadilly Hotel during an Air-Raid. 1918.
                    Courtesy of Michael Parkin Fine Art Ltd.

148. GRAHAM VIVIAN SUTHERLAND Oil $37\frac{3}{4} \times 37\frac{3}{4}$.
Lord Goodman.

149. ALVARO GUEVARA Oil 20¼ × 31¼.
Tête à Tête.

150. MARK GERTLER Oil 20×30.
The Virgin and St. Anne.

151. JAMES WILLIAM BOOTH   Oil $8\frac{1}{2} \times 12$.   Courtesy of Phillips and Sons
Tinkers Ponies.

152. ARTHUR WARDLE   Oil $27\frac{1}{2} \times 35\frac{3}{4}$.
Jaguar and Boa—The Duel.   Courtesy of The Moorland Gallery Ltd.

153. PETER BIEGEL   Oil   Courtesy of The Moorland Gallery Ltd.
Cantering—Winter Crop by Winter Halter.

154. MAUD EARL   Oil   Courtesy of The Tryon Gallery Ltd.
Retrieving.

155. MONTAGUE DAWSON   Oil   20 × 24

156. HENRY SCOTT TUKE   Oil   18 × 24.   Courtesy of Reynolds Gallery
Boys Bathing.

157. THOMAS COOPER GOTCH   Oil   48 × 84.   Courtesy of Reynolds Gallery
Golden Youth.

159. DOROTHEA SHARP   Oil $17\frac{1}{2} \times 14\frac{1}{2}$.
Baby with Toy Rabbit.   Courtesy of Mrs. W. F. Wilson

158. GARNET RUSKIN WOLSELEY   Oil $10\frac{1}{2} \times 8\frac{1}{4}$.
Boy Paddling.   Courtesy of Mrs. Ann Hobden

161. ROWLAND HENRY HILL   Oil   14 × 11.
Runswick Fishergirl.   Courtesy of Phillips and Sons

160. STANHOPE ALEXANDER FORBES   Oil   8 × 6.   Private Collection
Child on Seashore.

162. ALFRED AARAN WOLMARK   Oil   Courtesy of Natan Amizlev
Portrait of a Young Girl Wearing a Headband.

163. WILLIAM STRANG   Oil   45 × 39.   Courtesy of The Fine Art Society Ltd.
The Listener.

164. SIR JOHN LAVERY Oil 25 × 30.
Troops Embarking. Southampton. 1916.

165. JOHN ANTHONY PARK   Oil $13\frac{1}{2} \times 17$.
Boats at St. Ives.   Courtesy of Mrs. W. F. Wilson

166. KERSHAW SCHOFIELD   Oil 14×18.
Full Sail.   Courtesy of Cambridge Fine Art

167. MASON HUNTER   Oil $10 \times 12\frac{1}{2}$.
Union Canal at Ratho.   Courtesy of Phillips and Sons

168. BERTRAM PRIESTMAN   Oil 20×24.
Surrey Landscape. 1930.   Courtesy of Andrew Leslie, Leva Art

170. JOHN EMMS Oil
Setter, Spaniel and Pointer.

Courtesy of The Tryon Gallery Ltd.

169. HENRY HERBERT LA THANGUE Oil 55 × 39½.
The Cow Girl.

Courtesy of Andrew Leslie. Leva Art

171. OROVIDA CAMILLE PISSARRO Oil
Zebras.

172. EDWARD IRVINE HALLIDAY   Oil 41 × 51.
The Phases of Mercury. 1928.   Courtesy of Andrew Leslie, Leva Art

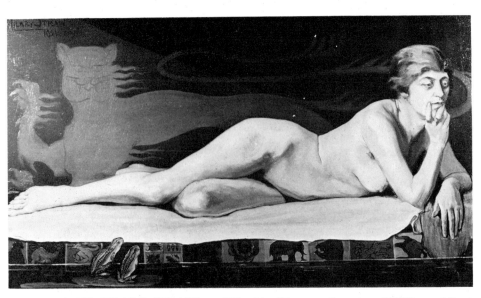

173. EUPHANS HILARY STRAIN   Oil 24 × 32.   Courtesy of Phillips and Sons
Suzannah.

174. IAIN MACNAB   Oil   36 × 28.   Courtesy of Peter Bowles
Nude in a Chair.

175. JOHN WILSON   Oil   18 × 24.
Cumberland Landscape.   Courtesy of Reynolds Gallery

176. CAVENDISH MORTON   Oil   12 × 16.
Monks Eleigh Church. Suffolk.   Private Collection

177. JOHN NOBLE BARLOW   Oil   30 × 40.
An October Morning.   Courtesy of L. S. Mungean

178. GUY LIPSCOMBE   Oil   16 × 24.
The Mill House.   Courtesy of Phillips and Sons

179. ARTHUR A. DIXON   Oil $47\frac{1}{2} \times 60$.
The Black Prince. 1915.

Courtesy of John Constable

181. JAMES FERRIER PRYDE   Oil   36 × 29.
Bed in a Studio.   Courtesy of Michael Parkin Fine Art Ltd.

180. GLADYS HYNES   Oil   48 × 36.
Private View. 1937.   Courtesy of Michael Parkin Fine Art Ltd.

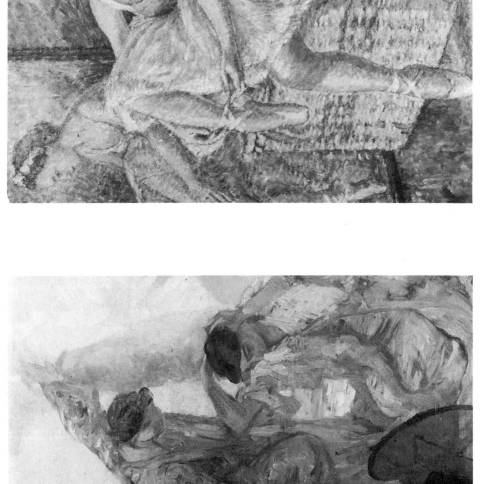

183. GRACE ENGLISH　　Oil　$35\frac{1}{2} \times 27\frac{1}{2}$
The Little Dancer. 1937.　　Courtesy of Andrew Leslie, Leva Art

182. RUPERT CHARLES WOLSTEN BUNNY　　Oil　$21\frac{1}{2} \times 15$.
Bathers Dressing.　　Courtesy of Dr. R. K. Constable

184. NINA HAMNETT   Oil   32 × 24.   Courtesy of The Fine Art Society Ltd.
The Student.

185. JAMES DICKSON INNES   Oil   62 × 45.   Courtesy of Andrew Leslie, Leva Art
The Guitarist.

186. SAMUEL WARBURTON   Oil   24×36.   Courtesy of Reynolds Gallery
Cornfield by Moonlight.

188. JULIAN OTTO TREVELYAN   Oil   21×26.   Courtesy of The Fine Art Society Ltd.
The Potteries. 1938.

187. ADAM SLADE   Oil   10×14.   Courtesy of Henry Towner
Extensive Landscape.

189. HANS HANSEN   Oil   14×18.
The Market Place. Oran. Algeria.

191. HAROLD KNIGHT Oil
Cornish Fishermen. Courtesy of Andrew Leslie. Leva Art

190. ERNEST HIGGINS RIGG Oil 18 × 12.
A Helping Hand. Courtesy of Phillips and Sons

193. ERNEST BOROUGH JOHNSON Oil 10×13¾.
The Onion Seller. 1909. Courtesy of Mrs. W. F. Wilson

192. GEORGE HILLYARD SWINSTEAD Oil 60×40
The Vision. Courtesy of Phillips and Sons

194. HAROLD C. HARVEY   Oil   30 × 30.
Gathering Pussywillow.

195. DUNCAN JAMES CORROWR GRANT   Tempera $89\frac{1}{2} \times 77\frac{1}{2}$.   Courtesy of Tate Gallery
Football.

196. MAXWELL ASHBY ARMFIELD   Tempera   18 × 16.   Courtesy of Alan M. Fortunoff
Self Portrait. 1916.

197. THOMAS ALFRED LIVERTON   Water-colour $14\frac{1}{4} \times 21\frac{3}{4}$.
The Somme at St. Valery.   Private Collection

198. WILLIAM GRANT MURRAY   Water-colour $10\frac{1}{4} \times 15$.
Coastal Landscape. 1927.   Private Collection

199. CHARLES HARRINGTON Water-colour 15 × 22.
Passing Storm, Newhaven. Sussex.   Courtesy of Gallery 33

200. ARTHUR TUCKER Water-colour 12 × 18.
Ben Nevis.   Courtesy of John Constable

202. **SIR HERBERT HUGHES-STANTON**
Scene in Normandy.
Water-colour $12\frac{1}{2} \times 19\frac{1}{2}$.
Courtesy of Mrs. W. F. Wilson

204. **JAMES HERBERT SNELL**
Pastoral Scene.
Water-colour $12 \times 17\frac{1}{2}$.
Private Collection

201. **HENRY B. WIMBUSH**
Whippingham Church, Isle of Wight.
Water-colour $7 \times 11\frac{1}{2}$.
Courtesy of Eastbourne Fine Art

203. **FRANK SPENLOVE-SPENLOVE**
Wind and Cloud. 1916.
Water-colour $11\frac{1}{4} \times 17\frac{1}{4}$.
Private Collection

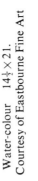

205. **L. VAN STAATEN** Water-colour 14 × 18.
Dutch River Scene. Courtesy of Eastbourne Fine Art

206. **JAN VAN COUVER** Water-colour 14½ × 21.
Near Terneuzen. Courtesy of Eastbourne Fine Art

207. **FREDERICK JAMES ALDRIDGE** Water-colour 6 × 8.
Off the South Foreland. Private Collection

208. **CHARLES FREDERICK ALLBON** Water-colour 12 × 19.
On the Zuider Zee. Courtesy of Eastbourne Fine Art

210. ARCHIBALD THORBURN   Water-colour   20 × 16.
Golden Eyes.   Courtesy of The Tryon Gallery Ltd.

209. JOHN GUILLE MILLAIS   Water-colour   20½ × 16.
King Eider. 1913.   Courtesy of The Moorland Gallery Ltd.

212. CHARLES WHYMPER   Water-colour   12 × 8.
Hoopoe.   Courtesy of The Moorland Gallery Ltd.

211. ROLAND GREEN   Water-colour
Mallard Rising.   Courtesy of The Moorland Gallery Ltd.

214. CLIFFORD ERIC MARTIN HALL Coloured Chalks $17\frac{1}{2} \times 10\frac{1}{2}$.
Coco. 1935. Courtesy of Andrew Leslie, Leva Art

213. MERVYN LEVY Pencil 10×7.
Dylan Thomas. Courtesy of Michael Parkin Fine Art Ltd.

216. GEORGE SHERINGHAM Pencil and wash $14\frac{1}{4} \times 9\frac{3}{4}$.
Sketch for Donna Clara in "The Duenna".
Courtesy of Tate Gallery

215. GEORGE FREDERICK ARTHUR BELCHER $10\frac{1}{4} \times 7\frac{3}{4}$.
Charcoal and wash
Alabaster Busks, Lidy, 2d. each. Courtesy of Tate Gallery

217. SIR WILLIAM RUSSELL FLINT   Water-colour $19\frac{1}{4} \times 26\frac{1}{4}$.
Isabelle, Nicolette and Jane.

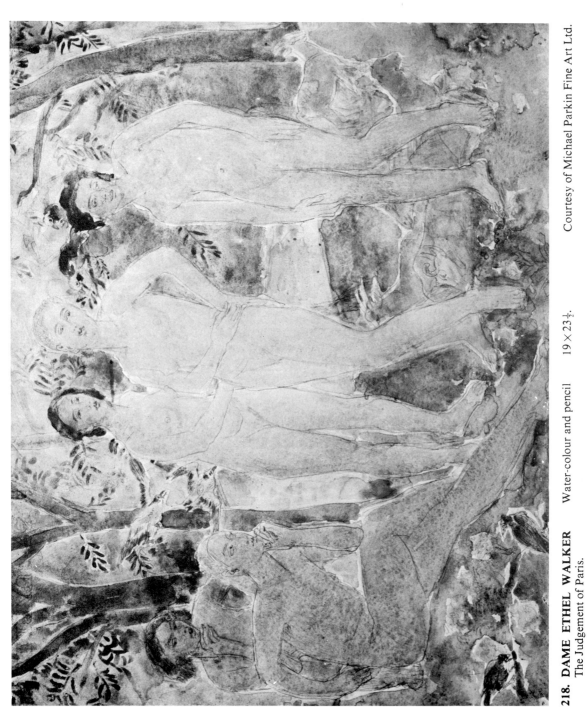

218. DAME ETHEL WALKER Water-colour and pencil 19 × 23½. Courtesy of Michael Parkin Fine Art Ltd.
The Judgement of Paris.

219. ROBERT ANNING BELL
The Listeners. 1906.   Water-colour and body-colour $19\frac{1}{2} \times 29\frac{1}{2}$.
Courtesy of Tate Gallery

220. SIR WALTER THOMAS MONNINGTON   Tempera $109\frac{1}{2} \times 49\frac{1}{2}$.   Courtesy of Tate Gallery
Allegory.

221. CHARLES ROBINSON   Water-colour $12\frac{1}{2} \times 9\frac{1}{4}$.   Courtesy of The Fine Art Society Ltd.
The Lady of Shalott.

222. AUGUSTUS OSBORNE LAMPLOUGH Water-colour 9 × 24.
Cairo and Citadel from the Desert.

Private Collection

223. W. STUART LLOYD Water-colour 12 × 26.
River Scene.

Courtesy of Eastbourne Fine Art

224. SIR DAVID YOUNG CAMERON Pencil and water-colour $10\frac{1}{2} \times 15$.
Traquair House, Peebleshire.

225. MICHAEL ANDREWS   Acrylic   60 × 84.
The Pier Pavilion.   Courtesy of Anthony d'Offay

226. CLAUDE BUCKLE   Water-colour   15 × 17¼.   Courtesy of Gallery 33
Moorings.

227. JOHN ERNEST AITKEN   Water-colour   13 × 19.   Private Collection
North Sea Fishers.

228. FRANK H. MASON   Water-colour   16 × 21.   Private Collection
The Lincolnshire.

230. ERIC HENRI KENNINGTON   Chalk   21¼ × 14¼.
An Infantryman.   Courtesy of The Fine Art Society Ltd.

229. JACOB KRAMER   Pastel and chalk   21 × 11.
Sarah, The Artist's Sister. 1916.
Courtesy of Michael Parkin Fine Art Ltd.

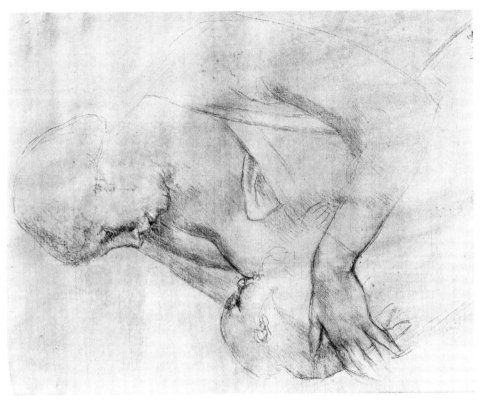

232. JOHN LAVIERS WHEATLEY   Chalk   22 × 17½.   Courtesy of Tate Gallery
Mother and Child.

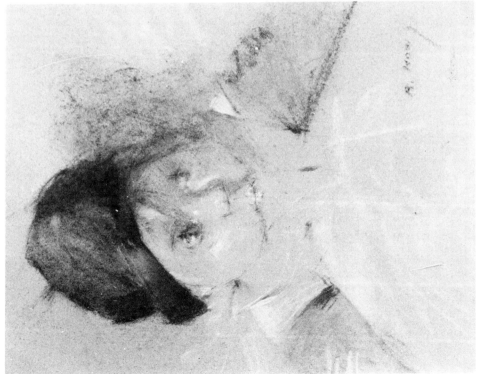

231. JULIA BEATRICE HOW   Water-colour, pastel and chalks
14 × 11.
Courtesy of Mrs. Ann Hobden
Study of a Baby.

THE TOWN BY THE RIVER

233. JESSIE MARION KING   Pen and ink   7 × 8.
The Town by the River.

Courtesy of Eastbourne Fine Art

234. LOUIS WILLIAM WAIN   Pen and ink   20 × 30.
The Cats' Diamond Jubilee.

235. THOMAS BARCLAY HENNELL   Water-colour $11 \times 18\frac{1}{2}$.
The Farm Labourers Dinner Time.   Courtesy of Mrs. W. F. Wilson

236. WILLIAM MARK FISHER   Water-colour $12\frac{1}{4} \times 19$.
The Hammock.   Courtesy of Eastbourne Fine Art

237. ALFRED WILLIAM RICH   Water-colour   5 × 9.   Private Collection
Rolling Landscape.

238. BERNARD WALTER EVANS   Water-colour   11 × 21.   Private Collection
Threatening.

240. ALEXANDER MAVROGORDATO   Water-colour   10 × 14½.
A Fish Stall.   Courtesy of Gallery 33

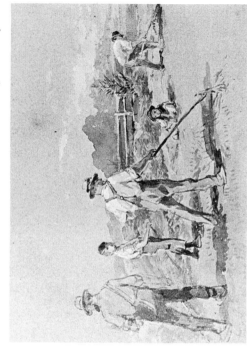

242. NORMAN GARSTIN   Water-colour   7 × 9¼.
Haymakers.   Courtesy of Mrs. W. F. Wilson

239. CARLTON ALFRED SMITH   Water-colour   12 × 18.
Feeding Chicks.   Courtesy of Bourne Gallery

241. G. FINCH MASON   Water-colour   10 × 14.
Oh! for the Comforts of Home.   Courtesy of Eastbourne Fine Art

243. ROBERT THORNE WAITE   Water-colour $14\frac{1}{4} \times 21$.
Cornstooks near Lower Beeding, Sussex.   Courtesy of Bourne Gallery

244. ROBERT WRIGHT STEWART   Water-colour 11×15.
Village Scene.   Private Collection

246. HENRY CHARLES FOX   Water-colour $20 \times 29\frac{1}{2}$.
Cattle in a Lane. 1905.   Courtesy of Eastbourne Fine Art

245. CHARLES JAMES ADAMS   Water-colour 15×22.
The Noon Time Rest.   Courtesy of Bourne Gallery

247. WILLIAM PATRICK ROBERTS   Pencil $8\frac{3}{4} \times 6\frac{1}{4}$.   Courtesy of Anthony d'Offay
Study for "Theatre."

248. PERCY WYNDHAM LEWIS Pen and ink, and pencil $13\frac{1}{2} \times 10\frac{1}{2}$.
Timon of Athens. 1913.   Courtesy of Anthony d'Offay

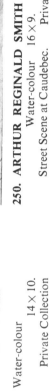

250. ARTHUR REGINALD SMITH
Water-colour   16×9.   Private Collection
Street Scene at Caudebec.

249. VICTOR NOBLE RAINBIRD   Water-colour
14×10.
A Procession, Bruges. 1926.
Private Collection

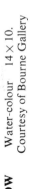

252. WALTER FREDERICK ROOFE TYNDALE   Water-colour   18 × 14.
Venice.   Courtesy of Bourne Gallery

251. ANDREW CARRICK GOW   Water-colour   14 × 10.
News of the Day.   Courtesy of Bourne Gallery

253. W. CLAUDE FLIGHT   Water-colour $15 \times 13\frac{1}{4}$.   Courtesy of Michael Parkin Fine Art Ltd.
Washing Up.

254. SIR HENRY GEORGE RUSHBURY   Water-colour   12 × 16.
Boat Building.   Courtesy of Bourne Gallery

255. EDITH MARY LAWRENCE   Water-colour   14 × 20.
Swanage Beach.   Courtesy of Michael Parkin Fine Art Ltd.

256. HENRY JOHN YEEND KING   Water-colour   11 × 17½.
Summer Fishing.   Courtesy of Eastbourne Fine Art

257. HENRY JOHN SYLVESTER STANNARD   Water-colour   10 × 14.
Landscape with Harvesters.   Private Collection

258. T. W. MORLEY   Water-colour   7 × 11.   Courtesy of Gallery 33
A Church Procession.

259. JUDITH ACKLAND   Water-colour $10\frac{1}{2} \times 14\frac{1}{2}$.
The Village from the Beach (Bucks Mill). 1939.
               Courtesy of Mary Stella Edwards and B. J. Gray

260. JOHN NORTHCOTE NASH Water-colour $16\frac{1}{4} \times 23$. Private Collection
Landscape in France. 1955.

261. ERIC WILLIAM RAVILIOUS Water-colour $17\frac{1}{2} \times 22$.
Downs in Winter. Courtesy of Towner Art Gallery

262. CHARLES KNIGHT Water-colour 15 × 22. Courtesy of Henry Towner
The Cuillins and Loch Brittle, Isle of Skye.

263. SAMUEL JOHN LAMORNA BIRCH Water-colour 12 × 16.
The Quarry Road. Private Collection

265. ARTHUR RACKHAM   Water-colour $9\frac{3}{4} \times 6$.
The Sorrowing Undine. 1909.
Courtesy of The Fine Art Society Ltd

264. KAY NIELSEN   Water-colour 14×9.
La Vision. 1914.   Courtesy of The Fine Art Society Ltd.

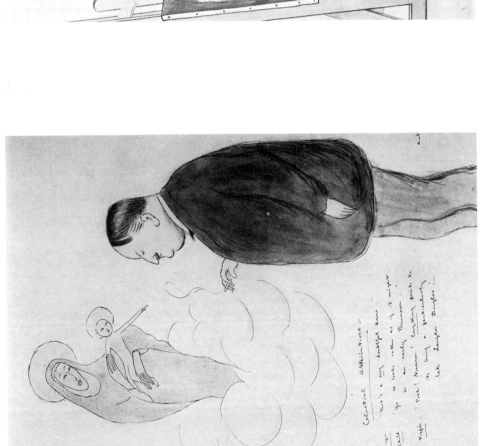

266. SIR MAX BEERBOHM Water-colour 15½ × 11¼.
Celestial Attributions. Private Collection

267. HENRY MAYO BATEMAN Water-colour 13 × 9.
Member of the Society for the Suppression of any satisfac-
tion or joy you may have in your work. 1915.
Courtesy of The Fine Art Society Ltd.

268. EDWARD ALEXANDER WADSWORTH Tempera 25 × 35. Fecamp. 1939.

269. TRISTRAM PAUL HILLIER Tempera $23\frac{3}{4} \times 32$.
Harness. 1944.

270. NORA DAVISON   Water-colour   8 × 14.   Private Collection
Brigs at their Moorings.

271. FRANK LEWIS EMANUEL   Water-colour $5\frac{1}{2}$ × 9.   Private Collection
Dutch River Scene.

272. PHILIP NAVIASKY   Water-colour   13 × 19.   Private Collection
Ibiza. 1933.

273. ROBERT JOHNSTON   Water-colour $12\frac{1}{2}$ × 18.   Private Collection
Pescador Con Linea Espanol.

274. HORACE BRODZKY   Pen and ink   11 × 21.
Reclining Female Nude. 1937.

275. WILLIAM GAUNT Pen and ink, and water-colour $8 \times 12\frac{1}{2}$.
At the Café Royal. 1929.   Courtesy of Michael Parkin Fine Art Ltd.

276. EDMOND XAVIER KAPP Pen and ink $9\frac{1}{2} \times 12$.
Blackmail in the Café Royal.   Courtesy of Michael Parkin Fine Art Ltd.

277. GEORGE DENHOLM ARMOUR   Chalk   6½ × 11.
Baying Hounds.   Courtesy of Henry Towner

278. FREDERICK PEGRAM   Pen and ink   10 × 14.   Courtesy of Henry Towner
Sheep Entering Field.

279. JOHN CYRIL HARRISON   Water-colour   22 × 30.
Grouse flying from an Eagle.   Courtesy of The Tryon Gallery Ltd.

280. PHILIP RICKMAN   Water-colour   Courtesy of The Moorland Gallery Ltd.
Grey Partridges.

281. KARL HAGEDORN   Water-colour $13\frac{1}{2} \times 20$.   Courtesy of John Constable
The Queens Hall, London. 1930.

282. WILLIAM SIDNEY CAUSER   Chalks and water-colour 6×8.
Carlton House Terrace, London.   Courtesy of Southgate Gallery

283. EDWARD BAWDEN   Pen and ink, and water-colour $18\frac{1}{2} \times 23$.
Houses at Ironbridge.   Courtesy of Tate Gallery

284. ROBERT MACBRYDE   Pen and ink, chalks, and water-colour $22\frac{3}{4} \times 27\frac{1}{4}$.
The Bombed Kitchen. 1941.   Courtesy of The Fine Art Society Ltd.

285. BERNARD ADENEY Casein or wax 89¼ × 120.
Toy Sailing Boats (The Round Pond).

286. PAUL NASH   Water-colour, pen and ink $22\frac{1}{2} \times 19$.   Courtesy of Tate Gallery
The Orchard.

287. SIDNEY HERBERT SIME   Monochrome $19 \times 13\frac{1}{2}$.   Courtesy of The Fine Art Society Ltd.
On the bank of the Styx.

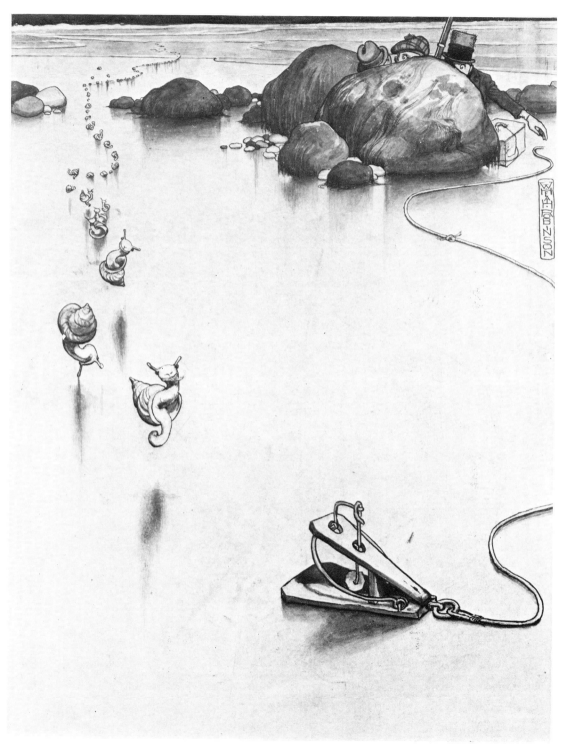

288. WILLIAM HEATH ROBINSON   Water-colour $15 \times 10\frac{1}{2}$. Courtesy of The Fine Art Society Ltd.
The Gentle Art of Catching Things—Trapping the Wily Whelks on the Shores of the Caspian Sea.

289. GEORGE CHARLES HAITÉ   Coloured Crayons $4\frac{1}{4} \times 6\frac{3}{4}$. Private Collection
Neatisbead.

290. A. MOULTON FOWERAKER   Water-colour 9×11.
Moonlight—San Roque.   Courtesy of John Constable

291. ARTHUR HENRY KNIGHTON-HAMMOND Water-colour 19 × 26.
Menton Old Town. 1929. Courtesy of Southgate Gallery

292. HUGH GRESTY Water-colour 17 × 19. Courtesy of Bourne Gallery
The Alcantara Bridge, Toledo.

294. W. H. PEARSON
View in Sussex.   Water-colour 15×21.
Private Collection

296. FREDERICK JOHN WIDGERY
Sydford Moor.   Water-colour and gouache $20 \times 29\frac{1}{2}$.
Courtesy of Eastbourne Fine Art

293. EDWARD HAMILTON CHETWOOD-AIKEN
Harvesting Scene with Harbour in Distance.
Water-colour $13\frac{3}{4} \times 20\frac{3}{4}$.   Courtesy of Gallery 33

295. GEORGE EDWARD ALEXANDER
Rye.   Water-colour 9×12.
Private Collection

298. BERNARD SLEIGH Water-colour 9 × 11.
An Isolated Community. Courtesy of Southgate Gallery

300. THOMAS LEON COOK Water-colour 8 × 16.
Grand Hotel. Eastbourne. Private Collection

297. EDITH MARY GARNER Water-colour 7¾ × 9.
The House Opposite. Private Collection

299. EDWARD WESSON Water-colour 13 × 20.
Chichester Cathedral. Courtesy of Gallery 33

301. CHARLES GODDARD NAPIER   Water-colour $20 \times 15\frac{1}{2}$.   Private Collection
Glamis Castle.

302. ANTHONY GROSS   Water-colour $7\frac{1}{2} \times 12\frac{3}{4}$.
Lookout near St. Paul's. 1940.   Courtesy of Michael Parkin Fine Art Ltd.

303. ROWLAND SUDDABY   Water-colour 12×18.
Barns near Fordham, Essex.   Courtesy of The Leger Galleries Ltd.

304. MARJORIE HOARE   Water-colour and pencil $10\frac{1}{2} \times 15$.
Ditchling Horse Fair.   Courtesy of Mrs. W. F. Wilson

305. CONRAD HEIGHTON LEIGH   Water-colour 14×18.
At the Gallop.   Courtesy of Mrs. W. F. Wilson

306. LIONEL DALHOUSIE ROBERTSON EDWARDS   Water-colour
Hunting Scene.   Courtesy of The Tryon Gallery Ltd.

307. ROBERT LITTLE   Water-colour $8\frac{1}{2} \times 10\frac{1}{2}$.   Courtesy of Mrs. W. F. Wilson
Pastoral Scene.

308. CHARLES WALTER SIMPSON   Water-colour 19×23.
Cattle Grazing.   Courtesy of Mrs. W. F. Wilson

309. CHARLES FREDERICK TUNNICLIFFE   Water-colour $13\frac{3}{4} \times 18\frac{3}{4}$.
Puffins.   Courtesy of The Moorland Gallery Ltd.

310. WINIFRED MARIE LOUISE AUSTEN   Water-colour $11\frac{1}{2} \times 15$.
Field Fare.   Courtesy of The Moorland Gallery Ltd.

311. WILLIAM AYERST INGRAM   Water-colour   16 × 24.
The Port of Leith.   Private Collection

312. WILLIAM MINSHALL BIRCHALL   Water-colour   10 × 14.
Off Lizard Head. 1921.   Courtesy of Gallery 33

313. BERNARD CECIL GOTCH   Water-colour 8×12.
View on the Itchen.   Courtesy of Eastbourne Fine Art

314. ALBERT GORDON THOMAS   Water-colour $18\frac{1}{2} \times 23\frac{1}{2}$.
Canting. 1943.   Courtesy of Jeremy Wood Fine Art, Cranleigh

316. JOHN A. AUSTEN Water-colour 7×5.
Emma and Rodolph. Courtesy of Bourne Gallery

315. ANNIE FRENCH Water-colour 9×8.
Peacock and Rose. Courtesy of The Fine Art Society Ltd.

317. ARTHUR AMBROSE McEVOY
Water-colour 21 × 12½.
Portrait of a Girl. Courtesy of Mrs. W. F. Wilson

318. BERNARD DUNSTAN
Standing Girl.
Pen and ink, and Water-
colour 14 × 9½.
Courtesy of Henry Towner

Noel H. Leaver A.R.W.A.

319. **NOEL HARRY LEAVER**   Water-colour $10\frac{1}{2} \times 15$.
An Eastern Street.

Private Collection

320. ARTHUR GEORGE BELL   Water-colour   14 × 21¼.   Courtesy of Gallery 33
Broadquay, Bristol.

321. PERCY LANCASTER   Water-colour   20 × 24.   Courtesy of Harold Day
Wells.

322. SIDNEY HAROLD METEYARD   Charcoal   14 × 18¼.
Cartoon for a Stained Glass Window.

323. LOUIS B. DAVIS Charcoal 42 × 25. Courtesy of John Constable
King David, Daniel and Miriam.

324. SIR DAVID MUIRHEAD BONE   Pencil $10\frac{1}{2} \times 15$.
St. Germain's, Auxerre. 1929.   Courtesy of The Fine Art Society Ltd.

325. WILLIAM WALCOT   Pencil and gouache 13×19.
The Victory Parade, passing The National Gallery, Trafalgar Square. 1919.
Courtesy of The Fine Art Society Ltd.

326. STANLEY ROY BADMIN   Pen, ink and Water-colour   9 × 12.
Jackson's Sawmill, Uley, Gloucestershire. 1933.

Courtesy of The Fine Art Society Ltd.

327. ALAN SORRELL   Pen, water-colour and crayon. $20\frac{1}{2} \times 24\frac{1}{2}$.
Southampton Dock. 1944.

Courtesy of Tate Gallery

329. WILLIAM TATTON WINTER   Water-colour   14 × 10.
Tunbridge Wells.   Courtesy of Eastbourne Fine Art

328. THERESA SYLVESTER STANNARD   Water-colour $14\frac{1}{4} \times 10\frac{1}{4}$.
Old Mill Garden.   Private Collection

330. LAWSON WOOD   Water-colour $13 \times 7\frac{1}{4}$.   Courtesy of Harold Day
Sailor's Return. 1908.

331. THOMAS PYNE   Water-colour   14 × 21.
View of Dedham.   Courtesy of Eastbourne Fine Art

333. CLAUDE HAYES   Water-colour   20 × 30.
Landscape with Timber Wimb.   Private Collection

332. W. E. BARRINGTON-BROWNE   Water-colour   15 × 22.
Fishing Scene.   Courtesy of The Tryon Gallery Ltd.

334. HAROLD SUTTON PALMER   Water-colour   14 × 21.
Near Amberley, Sussex.   Courtesy of Bourne Gallery

337. GEORGE E. LODGE   Tempera.
Gyr Falcon. Courtesy of The Tryon Gallery Ltd.

335. FRANK SOUTHGATE   Water-colour 11 × 18.
Mallard.   Courtesy of The Moorland Gallery Ltd.

336. VINCENT R. BALFOUR-BROWNE   Water-colour.
Stags.   Courtesy of The Moorland Gallery Ltd.

338. STEVEN SPURRIER Gouache. 24 × 21. Courtesy of John Constable
Limbering (Behind the scenes at Bertram Mills Circus on a Tour of Scotland. 1936).

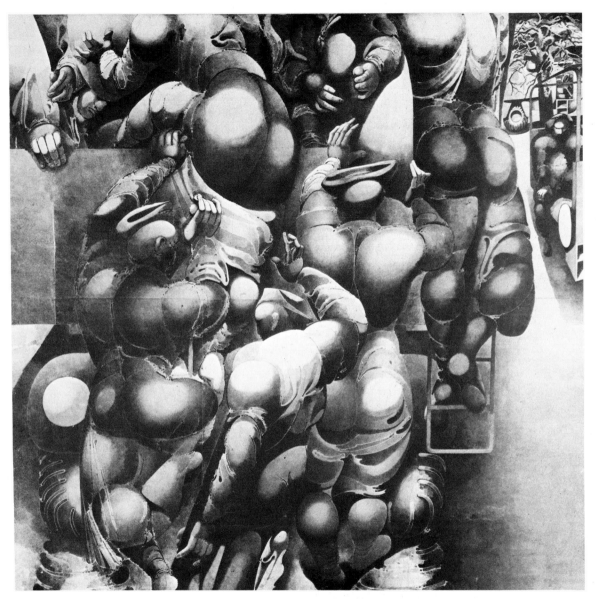

339. EDWARD BURRA   Water-colour   44 × 46.   Courtesy of Towner Art Gallery
Soldiers' Backs.

340. EDWARD JOHN GREGORY   Water-colour 9 × 12.
The Lifeboat.   Courtesy of Bourne Gallery

341. ROLAND VIVIAN PITCHFORTH   Water-colour 10 × 13.
A Heavy Roll.   Courtesy of Bourne Gallery

342. ARTHUR JOHN TREVOR BRISCOE   Water-colour $21\frac{1}{4} \times 14$.
On the Upper Topsail Yard. 1938.

343. JOHN SINGER SARGENT   Pencil   18 × 24.
Study for "Gassed" 1918.   Courtesy of Michael Parkin Fine Art Ltd.

344. PAUL LUCIEN MAZE   Pastel   16 × 21.   Courtesy of The Artist
The Trooping of the Colour.

345. SIR HERBERT JAMES GUNN Water-colour 9 × 13.
Thames View, Blackfriars Bridge. Courtesy of Andrew Leslie, Leva Art

346. FRANCIS JOHN MINTON Gouache 12 × 16.
Poplar after the Blitz. Courtesy of Michael Parkin Fine Art Ltd.

347. JAMES McBEY   Water-colour, pen and ink   17×26.
Jerusalem.   Courtesy of The Fine Art Society Ltd.

348. HENRY SIMPSON   Water-colour $9\frac{1}{2} \times 13\frac{1}{2}$.   Courtesy of Henry Towner
Native Fishermen.

349. HENRY A. PAYNE   Water-colour   7 × 9½. Courtesy of John Constable
The Norwegian Fiord. 1914.

350. CHARLES RENNIE MACKINTOSH   Water-colour   14½ × 16½.
Mount Alba.   Courtesy of The Fine Art Society Ltd.

351. JAMES ABBOTT McNEILL WHISTLER   Pastel $10\frac{1}{2} \times 6\frac{1}{2}$.
A Japanese Figure.   Courtesy of The Leger Galleries Ltd.

353. MARGERY L. LAWRENCE
Fruits Défendus.
Water-colour   14 × 10.
Courtesy of Harold Day

352. JOHN HASSALL   Water-colour   14 × 10.
Portrait of Lawrence of Arabia.   Courtesy of John Constable

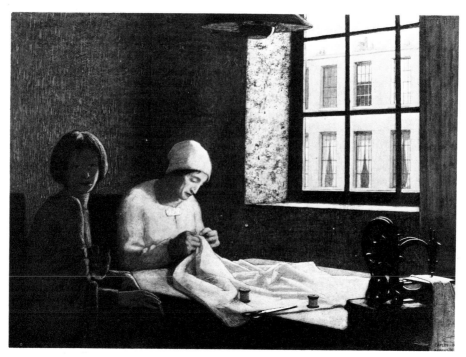

354. FREDERIC CAYLEY ROBINSON Tempera $13 \times 18\frac{1}{2}$.
The Old Nurse. 1926. Courtesy of The Fine Art Society Ltd.

355. HELEN ALLINGHAM Water-colour $8\frac{1}{4} \times 10\frac{3}{4}$.
The Old Place. Courtesy of The Leger Galleries Ltd.

356. CHARLES DIXON   Water-colour   6½ × 10.
Clipper Accompanied by Tugs. 1895.

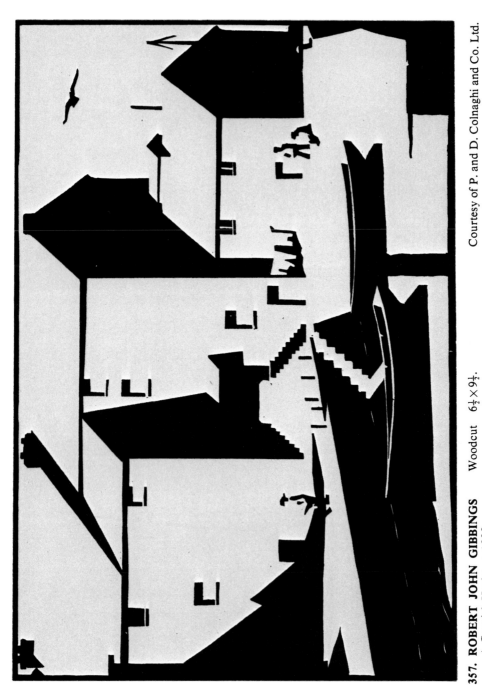

357. ROBERT JOHN GIBBINGS   Woodcut $6\frac{1}{4} \times 9\frac{1}{2}$.
A Cornish Harbour. 1920.

358. ETHELBERT WHITE Wood engraving $3\frac{1}{2} \times 4\frac{1}{2}$.
The Rick Yard. Courtesy of P. and D. Colnaghi and Co. Ltd.

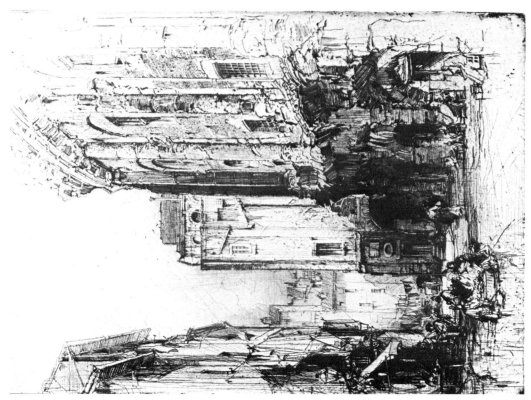

361. HEDLEY FITTON Etching 15¼ × 11. Private Collection
Italian Town Scene.

359. NELSON DAWSON Soft ground etching
The Ferry, Venice. 6½ × 8¼.
Courtesy of P. and D. Colnaghi and Co. Ltd

360. IAN STRANG Etching 6¼ × 7¼.
The Caravan. 1923.
Courtesy of P. and D. Colnaghi and Co. Ltd.

363. ENID LACEY   Wood engraving   5 × 4.
Three Gods of Sleep.   Courtesy of P. and D. Colnaghi and Co. Ltd.

362. EDWARD GORDON CRAIG   "Black Figure" print
Irving as Hamlet welcoming the Actors. 1927.   4½ × 4½.
Courtesy of P. And D. Colnaghi and Co. Ltd.

365. EDMUND BLAMPIED Etching $10\frac{1}{2} \times 10\frac{1}{2}$.
At the Fair. 1929. Courtesy of Harold Day

364. GERALD LESLIE BROCKHURST Etching $7\frac{1}{2} \times 6$.
Caspar. Courtesy of Alan Fortunoff

367. ETHEL LEONTINE GABAIN Lithograph 11½ × 6¼. Profile (nude). 1908. Courtesy of P. and D. Colnaghi and Co. Ltd.

366. ROBERT SARGENT AUSTIN Engraving 9 × 7. Evening. 1940. Courtesy of P. and D. Colnaghi and Co. Ltd.

368. HARRY BECKER   Lithograph   16 × 23.   Courtesy of Yoxford Gallery
Stone Pickers.

369. LEON UNDERWOOD   Lithograph   14½ × 19.
The Plaza Gardens.

                                        Courtesy of G. K. L. Ogilby

370. ARTHUR ERIC ROWTON GILL   Woodcut   20 × 20.
Spirit and Flesh. 1917.   Courtesy of P. and D. Colnaghi and Co. Ltd.

373. EDGAR LONGLEY LANDER
The Fancy Dress Party.

Coloured etching 13½ × 10.
Courtesy of Henry Towner

371. WILLIAM LIONEL WYLLIE
Herring Fishers, Fisherrow.
Courtesy of P. and D. Colnaghi and Co. Ltd.

Dry point 8 × 16.

372. ALFRED CHARLES STANLEY ANDERSON
Somerset House. 1910.
Courtesy of P. and D. Colnaghi and Co. Ltd.

Etching 8½ × 15.

375. SYBIL ANDREWS Linocut 7 × 11.
Steeplechasing. Courtesy of Michael Parkin Fine Art Ltd.

374. CYRIL POWER Colour linocut 12½ × 9½.
Whence and Whither.
Courtesy of P. and D. Colnaghi and Co. Ltd.

376. HENRY SPENCER MOORE   Bronze ht. 7.   Courtesy of Tate Gallery
Project for a Family Group. 1945.

377. DAME BARBARA HEPWORTH   Bronze ht. 35½.   Courtesy of Tate Gallery
Curved Form (Travalgan).

378. WILLIAM C. GRAVENEY   Oak carving ht. $9\frac{1}{4}$.   Courtesy of Tate Gallery
Cormorants.

379. SIR JACOB EPSTEIN   San Stefano stone ht. 23.   Courtesy of Anthony d'Offay
Sunflower. 1910.

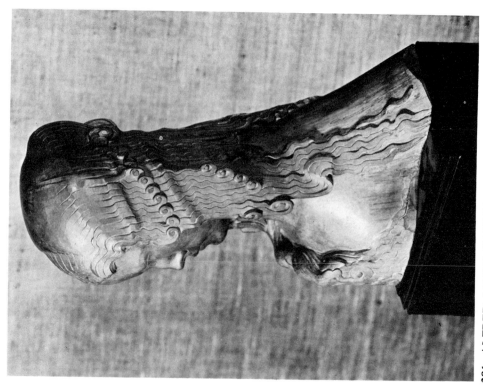

381. ALFRED JAMES OAKLEY Pearwood ht. 18¼.
Mamua. Courtesy of Tate Gallery

380. GERTRUDE ANNA BERTHA HERMES Bronze ht. 20.
Kathleen Raine. Courtesy of Tate Gallery

383. SIDNEY BOYES   Bronze ht. 12.
The Prince of Wales. 1920.
Courtesy of Harold Day

382. DAVID BERNARD McFALL   Bronze ht. 5.
Courtesy of The Fine Art Society Ltd.
Winston Churchill.

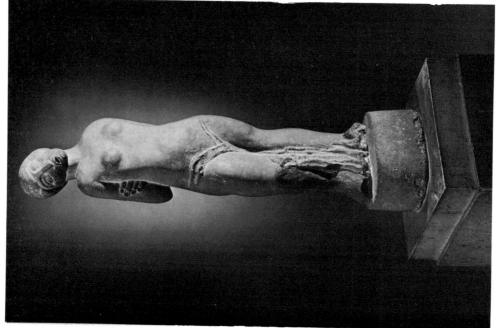

384. HENRI GAUDIER-BRZESKA   Derby stone
Singer. 1913.   ht. 33½.
Courtesy of Tate Gallery

385. SIR CHARLES THOMAS WHEELER   Bronze ht. 64.
Spring.   Courtesy of Tate Gallery

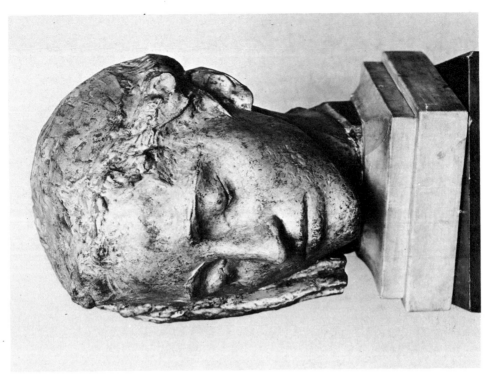

386. MAURICE LAMBERT Bronze ht. 13¾.
Head of a Woman. Courtesy of Tate Gallery

387. ANDREW O'CONNOR. Bronze ht. 14¾.
The Golden Head. Courtesy of Tate Gallery

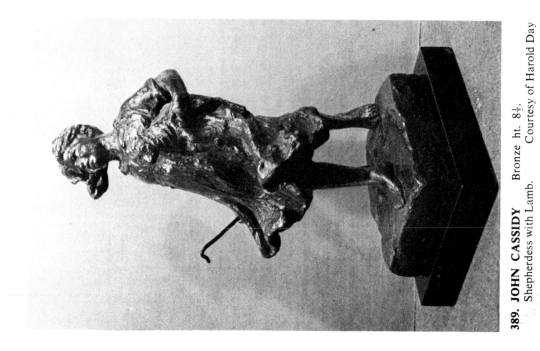

389. JOHN CASSIDY   Bronze ht. 8½.   Courtesy of Harold Day
Shepherdess with Lamb.

388. REGINALD FAIRFAX WELLS   Bronze ht. 15½.   Courtesy of The Fine Art Society Ltd.
Hedger.

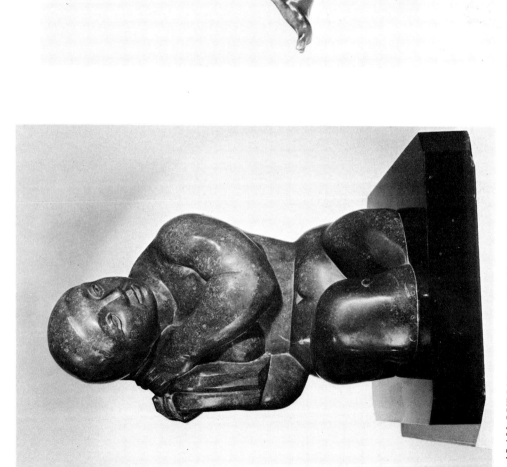

391. SIR WILLIAM REID DICK   Bronze ht. 11.
The Kelpie.   Courtesy of The Fine Art Society Ltd.

390. ALAN LYDIAT DURST   Marble ht. 16.
Girl Binding her Hair. 1929.   Courtesy of Tate Gallery

392. JULIAN PHELPS ALAN   Bronze ht. 14½.   Courtesy of Tate Gallery
Marjorie. 1928.

Photoset, printed and bound in Great Britain by
R. J. Acford Ltd., Industrial Estate, Chichester, Sussex